Educational Testing

To EAB and JF

Educational Testing

A Competence-Based Approach

Text for the British Psychological Society's
Certificate of Competence in Educational
Testing (Level A)

James Boyle and Stephen Fisher

The
British
Psychological
Society

BPS Blackwell

A BPS Blackwell book

BLACKWELL PUBLISHING
350 Main Street, Malden, MA 02148-5020, USA
9600 Garsington Road, Oxford OX4 2DQ, UK
550 Swanston Street, Carlton, Victoria 3053, Australia

First published 2007 by The British Psychological Society and Blackwell Publishing Ltd

1   2007

Library of Congress Cataloging-in-Publication Data

Boyle, James.
    Educational testing : a competence-based approach text for the British Psychological Society's certificate of competence in educational testing (Level A) / James Boyle & Stephen Fisher.
       p. cm.
    Includes bibliographical references and index.
    ISBN-13: 978-1-4051-4659-3 (1405146591 : alk. paper)
    1. Educational tests and measurements—Great Britain.   2. Teachers—Certification—Great Britain.   I. Fisher, Stephen.   II. British Psychological Society.   III. Title.
    LB3056.G7B69 2006
    371.20943—dc22

                                                                                        2006001705

A catalogue record for this title is available from the British Library.

Set in 10.5 on 12.5 pt Minion
by SNP Best-set Typesetter Ltd, Hong Kong

The publisher's policy is to use permanent paper from mills that operate a sustainable forestry policy, and which has been manufactured from pulp processed using acid-free and elementary chlorine-free practices. Furthermore, the publisher ensures that the text paper and cover board used have met acceptable environmental accreditation standards.

For further information on
BPS Blackwell, visit our website:
www.bpsblackwell.com

Contents

Preface

Professionals working in educational settings are required to administer, score and interpret tests. They also receive reports based upon test information from among others, educational and clinical psychologists. However, there are few opportunities to learn about the range of tests used, what they measure, and their technical adequacy, outside of professional training courses, usually in psychology.

This book is written for those who wish to remedy this by undertaking training for the British Psychological Society's Certificate of Competence in Educational Testing (CCET) (Level A) (BPS, 2004a), but will be of interest to anyone who is a stakeholder in good practice in the use of tests in education. This will include Special Needs Coordinators (SENCOs), those with a responsibility for test use in educational settings, careers guidance teachers, others involved in special needs assessments and in additional support planning, and educational administrators, as well as parents.

The book provides:

- An overview section for each of the Units of the CCET, explaining the relevance of each for test use, based upon the criteria laid down in the *Guidance for Assessors* document (BPS, 2004b) for short-term and cumulative evidence.
- A section providing model answers, worked examples, case studies and self-assessments, where appropriate, linked to assessments for each element of the Units.
- Appendices with the *Competences* and *Guidance for Assessors* documents in full, together with suggestions for further reading, useful

websites, and examples of tests that would be covered by the CCET (Level A).

As assessors will vary in how they will assess competence, it is not possible to give specific examples for each Unit of every form of assessment that might be employed in a training programme (14 methods of assessment are discussed in the *Guidance for Assessors* document, and there are more that could be employed), but we will discuss the range of means by which the core competences may be assessed by the assessor, based upon the BPS *Guidance for Assessors* document (BPS, 2004b).

Acknowledgements

We are grateful to the British Psychological Society for permission to reproduce the *Competences for Educational Testing (CCET) (Level A)*, the CCET Information Pack and the *Guidance for Assessors* documents. Thanks are also due to Jacqueline Döll, Lisa Woolfson, Dave Bartram and Pat Lindley for helpful comments on the text.

Introduction

Test use in education is of more recent vintage than the use of tests for occupational selection in China over 3,000 years ago. Educational testing has its origins in the eighteenth and nineteenth centuries with the use of tests for selection for academic as opposed to vocational or technical schooling, the identification of learning difficulties and needs for additional support, and monitoring standards in schools (Oakland, 2004).

The twentieth century saw a rapid rise in the development and use of educational and psychological tests. Oakland (2004) notes that there are 5,000 standardized instruments available, although not all are in general use. Oakland and Hu (1993) reported the findings of a survey of test use in educational settings in over 44 countries, and the results revealed that the tests most commonly used by professionals working with school students were instruments measuring intelligence, personality and achievement.

Educational tests of ability, attainment and aptitude are the most widely used in the UK and the Certificate of Competence in Educational Testing (CCET) has been developed by the British Psychological Society (BPS) to meet a need for standards for the use of tests in education in the UK by psychologists and non-psychologists alike. A *General Information Pack* (BPS, 2004a) with full details of the Certificate is available from the BPS Psychological Testing Centre, and is reproduced in Appendix 1, together with *Guidance for Assessors* (BPS, 2004b), shown in Appendix 2, and information about the BPS Psychological Testing Centre in Appendix 3. The *General Information Pack* also includes the BPS's *Code of Good Practice for Educational Testing* (see BPS, 2004a, p. 15).

In the United States, standards for test use in education were developed jointly in 1985 by the American Educational Research Association, the American Psychological Society, and the National Council on Measurement in Education and were updated in 1999 (American Educational Research Association, 1999). These standards provide not only guidance in test use across a wide range of practice settings but also technical standards for those who develop and publish tests. A number of other psychological associations and societies have followed suit, including the Canadian Psychological Association (1987), the Australian Psychological Society (1997), the New Zealand Psychological Society (2002), who subsume issues relating to test use in their Code of Ethics for psychologists, and the International Test Commission (2000). However, there has been nothing comparable for the broader range of educational test users in the UK until the introduction of the CCET.

The CCET was launched by the BPS in April, 2004 with the aim of providing test users in education in the UK with an objective means of supplying evidence of a high level of competence in the selection, administration, scoring and interpretation of results from tests of ability, attainment and aptitude, that is, 'psychological' tests used in educational settings. Based upon the earlier *Level A Competences in Occupational Psychology* (BPS, 1995), the educational testing standards consist of 71 core competences arranged in seven units, as shown in Appendix 1. The standards provide guidance for those who may wish to use tests, and in particular, criteria that may be used in the assessment of an individual's competence to use tests.

All of these competences must be demonstrated to achieve the Certificate, which indicates that the holder has acquired the basic knowledge and skills required to administer and use tests in educational settings to a quality standard.

Rationale of the CCET (Level A)

The CCET standards define those things which the BPS considers a test user should know and should be able to do in order to use tests fairly, properly and in a professional manner. They cover the minimum requirements for using most standardized group and individual tests of literacy, numeracy and curriculum subjects, together with group tests of reasoning ability and measures of aspects of social competence, and provide a framework for assessments of competence leading to the award of the CCET (Level A).

However, the CCET goes further than other standards or guidelines in two ways. First, the competences are linked to a qualification, the Certificate of Competence in Educational Testing, and second, a holder of the CCET is subject to a process of quality assurance in test use to ensure high levels of practice in the workplace.

Benefits of the CCET (Level A)

The CCET (Level A) provides test users in education with the following benefits:

- a clear specification of what he/she needs to know and be able to do to use tests properly;
- an understanding of testing as one strand of the wider process of assessment;
- an awareness of the relative merits of alternative forms of assessment;
- a clear understanding of the relationship between test use, the purpose of testing and the context in which the instruments will be used;
- a set of minimum standards for training in the use of educational tests;
- a set of specific objectives that test users on training courses can match against the content of their training course; and
- a nationally recognized transferable qualification in test use in education, which is not restricted to specific tests, publishers or trainers.

While the BPS encourages test publishers and suppliers to accept the CCET as a basis for their registration of test users, it should be noted that the CCET will not allow the holder to access certain psychological instruments, sometimes referred to as 'closed' tests, for example, measures of cognitive ability such as the Wechsler Intelligence Scale for Children Fourth UK Edition (WISC-IV^{UK}) (Wechsler, 2004) or the British Ability Scales Second Edition (BAS-II) (Elliott, 1997) or some tests of achievement, such as the Wechsler Objective Reading Dimensions (WORD) (Wechsler, 1993), the Wechsler Objective Numerical Dimensions (WOND) (Wechsler, 1996), or the Wechsler Individual Achievement Test – Second UK Edition (WIAT-II^{UK}) (Wechsler, 2005). Access to such tests is restricted to those with specialist qualifications, such as educational or clinical psychologists, as the interpretation of the results requires background knowledge of psychological theory which is not covered in the CCET.

However, there is a provision for teachers to use the WIAT-II^{UK} provided that a psychologist is satisfied with the teacher's competence to administer the test, it is ordered by the psychologist, and is used under the supervision of the psychologist in connection with the work of the psychologist in the teacher's school.

Test suppliers may require users to have specialist training in specific instruments or to hold an additional qualification in Special Needs to access some instruments. Appendix 4 provides links to the main UK educational test publishers' websites, and Appendix 5 lists examples of published tests available to users in educational settings in the domains of cognitive abilities, reading, diagnostic tests of reading, spelling, language, number, motor skills, self-esteem/coping/emotional literacy, Attention Deficit Hyperactivity Disorder (ADHD) and Autism/Asperger's Syndrome.

Short-term and Cumulative Evidence

A distinctive feature of the CCET is the requirement that assessees provide not only *short-term evidence* of competence, for example, of the kind that could be provided following initial training, but also *cumulative evidence*, which is based upon the assessee's actual test use in his/her workplace, to demonstrate that the knowledge and skills gained during training in regard to the selection and use of tests are evident and are being applied in the work setting. Accordingly, assessors require assessees to complete both short-term and cumulative assessments and to present a portfolio of evidence based upon these assessments that meets the required standard for the award of the CCET. Short-term assessments are required for all 71 competences, but cumulative assessments are only required for Units 4, 5, 6 and 7.

Obtaining the CCET

The process for obtaining the CCET is detailed in the BPS's (2004a) *General Information Pack: Certificate of Competence in Educational Testing (Level A)*. In summary, an *assessee* must undertake training and then have his or her competence affirmed by an *assessor*, a Chartered Psychologist whose assessment methods have been verified by the BPS. Assessors have the task of ensuring that candidates provide the necessary level of evidence to demonstrate their competence. The BPS requires assessors to have their assessments verified by trained 'Verifiers' to ensure that quality standards are met. Only Chartered Educational Psychologists with Current Certificate or Statement of Competence in Educational Testing who are also assessors can be appointed by the BPS as a Verifier, and all Verifiers receive special training to carry out their duties.

Many trainers will also be assessors, but they do not have to be. A list of assessors can be obtained from the BPS's Psychological Testing Centre website: www.psychtesting.org.uk. Before starting any training, check with the trainer that the course will lead to eligibility for the issue of the CCET, and that the assessor holds a current assessor's Certificate.

Once the assessor is satisfied that you have achieved the necessary standard of competence for all of the 71 elements, he/she will complete an *Affirmation of Competence in Educational Testing (Level A)* which should then be sent to the BPS together with a fee, £65 at the time of writing, which covers the costs of issuing the Certificate. The BPS has also established a *Register of Competence in Psychological Testing (Educational)*, to which holders of the CCET may be added for an additional annual fee, £20 at the time of writing.

Any person wishing to make use of tests in education is eligible for the CCET. But note that the Certificate is not a qualification in educational psychology, *but a qualification in the theoretical background and practical aspects of educational testing.*

A Note for Assessors

Any Chartered Psychologist holding a CCET or a Statement of Competence in Educational Testing (available on a time-limited basis to Chartered Educational Psychologists and/or members of the Association of Educational Psychologists) who wishes to become an assessor should contact the BPS Psychological Testing Centre (see Appendix 3 for details) to obtain copies of the *Assessor's Information Pack Educational Testing Level A* (BPS, 2004c) and *Guidance for Assessors: Certificate of Competence in Educational Testing (Level A)* (BPS, 2004b), which is reproduced in Appendix 2.

Organization of this Book

The book follows the order of CCET with the 71 core competences arranged in seven Units covering psychometrics, general theories of testing and psychological attributes, test administration, reporting and feedback:

- *Unit 1: Defining the Assessment Needs*: This Unit contains competences dealing with the purpose of testing, identifying assessment needs that can best be met by means of a test, describing the effects of environmental factors upon measures of ability and attainment, examples of corroborating information, the differences between tests of attainment, ability and aptitude, the differences between the formative and summative uses of tests, and between norm-referenced, criterion-referenced and curriculum-based measures.

- *Unit 2: The Basic Principles of Scaling and Standardization*: This Unit deals with the statistical concepts needed to use tests in educational settings.
- *Unit 3: The Importance of Reliability and Validity*: This Unit deals with the psychometric concepts needed to use tests.
- *Unit 4: Deciding when psychological tests should or should not be used as part of an assessment process*: This Unit deals with the selection of tests and issues relating to their appropriateness in specific situations. Note that the *Guidance for Assessors* (BPS, 2004b) refers to this Unit as 'Deciding whether a particular test should or should not be used as part of an assessment process'.
- *Unit 5: Administering tests to one or more students/pupils/learners and dealing with scoring procedures*: This is a skill-based Unit, which assesses the test user's competence in the administration and scoring of individual and group tests.
- *Unit 6: Making appropriate use of test results and providing accurate written and oral feedback to clients and candidates*: This Unit emphasizes the interpersonal skills required to provide oral and written feedback together with the skills required to score and interpret test results.
- *Unit 7: Maintaining security and confidentiality*: This Unit deals with issues of security and confidentiality in regard to access to, and storage of, tests and test results

The seven Units thus cover the following four areas of test use:

- *Underpinning knowledge* – the basic foundations of psychometric theory and statistics required to select an appropriate test and interpret the findings: Units 1, 2 and 3.
- *Practical task skills* – of planning and conducting a test session, administering the test, scoring the results, reporting the findings, and ensuring safe and secure storage of the test and record forms (if any) and also of the results: Units 5, 6 and 7.
- *Practical application of this knowledge* – with particular regard to issues concerning test selection, equity and fairness: Unit 4.

- *Decision making and intervention* – recognizing the relationship between test use and issues of how best to proceed on the basis of the findings: Units 1–7.

In what follows, note that:

- *'Assessee'* refers to the person whose competence is being assessed; and
- *'Client'* refers to the 'commissioning agent' – the person or organization for whom the test is carried out.

1

Unit 1: Defining the Assessment Needs

Unit 1 of the CCET (Level A) deals with a number of key issues in testing. Assessees are expected to be aware of the nature of the relationship between testing and assessment and be able to identify assessment needs that would best be dealt with by using a test (and conversely, those for which a test would not be appropriate). They are also expected to be able to justify the choice of a particular test with reference to the learner's development and the skills being assessed, and to show how the results from tests of ability and attainment can be affected by factors such as ethnicity, gender, social class and disability, as well as more direct factors in the testing environment, such as heat, noise, test anxiety and variables associated with test administration. Assessees should also be able to identify sources of information that can corroborate the information from a test, and be able to distinguish between different types of test. We shall consider each of these issues in turn.

The Relationship between Testing and Assessment

There will be few, if any, educational test users who are unfamiliar with the process of assessment, which is defined by Salvia and Ysseldyke (2004, p. 4) as: 'a process of collecting data for the purpose of making decisions about individuals and groups'.

This identifies three aspects of assessment:

- It involves a *process over time*, not just the observation of how a learner performs on one occasion.

- It is always carried out for a *reason*, for example to answer particular questions such as '*How do the learner's reading skills compare with those of other pupils of the same age?*' or '*What are the learner's strengths and weaknesses in regard to learning new phonic skills in reading?*'
- It should test one or more specific *hypotheses* about the learner's performance (for example, about possible factors that may precipitate or maintain a problem or explain why a problem may have occurred), which will both increase understanding and provide support for decisions as to how best to proceed.

Real-life problems are complex with many inter-related dimensions. For example, a difficulty in reading may result in problems with self-esteem and motivation, with resultant reluctance to complete classwork and homework, possible problems in peer relationships with classmates or behaviour difficulties in class, and tensions between home and school. The process of assessment has to reflect this complexity by gathering, structuring and analysing information to identify the key dimensions of the problem and understand how they interact, so that a clearer understanding both of the problem(s) and of what must be done to improve the situation can be generated.

To achieve this, information may be gathered by education professionals in collaboration with stakeholders, such as parents/carers, the students/pupils/learners themselves, and any others who may be involved, to develop a shared understanding of the nature of the problem and of the intervention required to assist decision making and achieve change. This information can be gathered in respect of an individual, or a group, for example, a class, and is a key component of the process of teaching and learning.

Such information is commonly collected in respect of concerns about academic performance, generally on account of concern about progress in the curriculum or some aspect of basic skills in language, literacy or numeracy; problems in behaviour, such as disruption, difficulties in social relationships, or withdrawn, shy behaviour; or the effects of known physical problems, for example, with vision, hearing, motor skills or mobility, or traumatic head injury.

But as Salvia and Ysseldyke (2004, pp. 23–38) and Urbina (2004, pp. 23–6) note, it is important to ensure that we gather information *from a range of sources*, (using both available information and cumulative information, such as portfolios of evidence of the learner's work) and *in different contexts* (to make the process as representative as possible) about:

- The *teaching and learning environment*, for example, whether the learner's teaching arrangements and the teaching techniques and curriculum employed are appropriate for his/her needs in regard to interest and relevance, level of difficulty, progression, presentation, and the nature of the response required; the social context of the setting and relationships with other learners; and the organization of the settings in which the learner's teaching and learning takes place.

- Factors outside the immediate educational setting, from *home and family, school and community*, which affect the learner's performance, for example, the experience he/she brings to school from home; the effects of whole-school factors, such as ethos, policies, legislation, guidelines and school development plans; and community influences upon attitudes towards learning and achievement).

- The *learner*, for example, his/her levels of confidence and independence as a learner; motivation; knowledge and use of strategies; levels of existing skills, knowledge and understanding in regard to a task or activity; learning styles; the extent to which he/she can generalize from what has been learned by reflecting upon the activity and seeing its relevance and connections to existing knowledge; and effects and influences of gender, ethnicity and social class.

There are a number of ways in which we can do this, including:

- *Direct observation* of the student/pupil/learner's performance or behaviour, perhaps by means of a systematic approach such as an observation schedule to investigate specific pre-defined behaviours, such as time spent 'on task', or a less systematic approach, such as a 'running record' of everything the learner does during a specified period of time. However, as well as requiring a considerable amount of time, observations can be subject to bias resulting from subjective judgements on the basis of labels (for example, such as 'gifted' or 'dyslexic'), physical attributes, other characteristics of the learner, or from *expectancy effects* (Salvia and Ysseldyke, 2004, pp. 27–8), where our beliefs colour what we observe, and 'we see what we expect to'. Thus, a teacher carrying out an evaluation of a behaviour management programme in his/her class may be more likely to observe negative behaviours if they have no confidence in the programme, and in contrast, more likely to observe positives if they believe that the programme has been successful.

- *Existing information*, such as portfolios of the learner's work, which can be compared with those of others in the class, can also be used, although interpretation will be restricted to what information is available and to the circumstances in which it was gathered.

- *Interviews* with those who know the learner well, such as former teachers or parents, also provide useful information.

- *Professional judgements* of those who have worked with the learner in the past or are currently working with the learner in the here and now. However, sources of bias include the possibility that key information may be forgotten, that the informant may not recognize the importance of particular information, or that informants may be selective with the information they provide.
- Finally, *a test* may be used.

Test use is a sub-set of the assessment process (Salvia and Ysseldyke, 2004, p. 6). But what do we mean by a 'test'? One of the leading experts in test use, Lee J. Cronbach (1984, p. 26), noted that 'There is no fully satisfactory definition for *test*'. With this caveat, let us consider some attempts at a definition:

> A test is a predetermined set of questions or tasks for which predetermined types of behavioral responses are sought. Tests are particularly useful because they permit tasks and questions to be presented in exactly the same way to each person tested. (Salvia and Ysseldyke, 2004, p. 29)

> A psychological test is a measurement instrument that has three defining characteristics:
>
> - A psychological test is a sample of behaviour.
> - The sample is obtained under standardised conditions.
> - There are established rules for scoring, or for obtaining quantitative (numeric) information from the behaviour sample. (Murphy and Davidshofer, 1994, p. 3)

> A psychological test is a systematic procedure for obtaining samples of behaviour relevant to cognitive or affective functioning and for scoring and evaluating these samples according to standards. (Urbina, 2004, p. 1)

From these definitions, we can see that a test is a form of systematic assessment, with standardized procedures, from which numerical scores are taken. But as Urbina (2004, p. 25) notes, use of a test differs from other assessment approaches in the following ways:

- Testing is quicker and simpler than a more general assessment approach involving a range of processes, such as interviewing or observation.
- In testing, the individual test taker is the principal source of data, whereas there are other sources of information, for example, teachers, family, peers routinely involved in a more general assessment approach.

- Testing tends to compare the test taker(s) with others, whereas assessment may also consider the uniqueness of the individual or group or the context.
- Testing is highly structured, with objective procedures, whereas assessment may be less structured and more subjective, relying more on professional judgements.

But it is worth recalling that tests not only provide quantitative data, that is, the actual scores obtained, but also qualitative data in the form of observations about the test taker's performance or how the performance was achieved. As we shall see in Unit 8, such qualitative data can be important in the interpretation of the results from a test.

There are many different types of test. Rust and Golombok (2000, pp. 38–47), for example, identify the following:

- *Norm-referenced* tests (where an individual's scores are compared with those for a representative sample from a population) versus *criterion-referenced tests* (where scores are related to an external criterion, usually the completion of a task to a predefined standard).
- *Knowledge-based* tests (measuring ability, attainment, achievement and aptitude) versus *person-based* tests (measuring attributes such as personality, attitudes, moods, self-esteem, and social competence using rating scales or other self-report measures). Knowledge-based tests are tests of *maximum performance*, where the score is determined by the test taker's success in completing a well-defined task, that is, a measure of what the test taker can do in the test situation. Most standardized tests used in education, such as measures of ability, attainment or achievement, are of this kind. Person-based tests are tests of *typical performance*, where there is no 'right' or 'wrong' answer.
- *Objective* tests (with pre-specified scoring criteria) versus *open-ended* tests, such as essays or projective tests, where ambiguous pictures are presented and the test taker asked to describe what they see.

Salvia and Ysseldyke (2004, p. 29) identify two related dimensions that we need to take account of in making sense of test scores: *performance standards* and *informational context*. Performance standards provide the basis for comparisons between the learner and other students/pupils (a comparative standard) or between the learner's scores from two administrations of the same test (an absolute standard). But the learner's performance must also be contextualized and related to other information gathered. Good assessment – and test use – in this way utilizes *multiple sources of information* in the interpretation of results to assist the decision-making process.

So when should a test be used? When you want to compare the results with those from other students/pupil/learners. As we have noted, it is important to factor in contextual and wider environmental variables, such as teaching approaches or the curriculum, or the learner's interests or views, when carrying out an assessment. But this can be a drawback if you want to draw comparisons across teachers or schools. Tests are designed to be presented in a standardized way and to elicit performances that can be scored in a consistent and comparable fashion, irrespective of the individual who administers the instrument, provided that he/she is trained and competent to do so, and adheres strictly to the procedures for administration and scoring.

Identifying Assessment Needs Which Would Best be Dealt With by Using a Test (and Conversely, Those For which A Test Would not be Appropriate)

The key to effective assessment is to match the strategy for gathering information to the questions being asked. For example, a teacher who has concerns about a pupil's progress in mathematics and asks a SENCO colleague for ideas to help tailor instruction to the pupil's areas of difficulty will be under-whelmed by assessment findings which merely confirm that the pupil has problems in mathematics.

Good practice consists of two steps: first, clarifying the purpose of assessment and then second, selecting the most appropriate, reliable and valid means of gathering information (which we will consider in more detail in Unit 3). Test use can be highly informative, but users need to be aware of the 'pros' and 'cons' of different approaches to assessment so that they can select the most appropriate means of answering questions.

The CCET (Level A) requires test users in education to be familiar with the following four approaches to assessment:

1 *Norm-referenced* assessment: where we compare the learner's performance with that of the other individuals in the normative sample of the test on whom the test norms are based, using *developmental scores* (for example, age-equivalent scores, such as 'Reading Ages' or 'Spelling Ages') or *derived scores* (for example, standard scores, or percentiles). Use a norm-referenced test when you wish to compare the pupil's knowledge base with norms (i.e. normative standards for his/her age).

2   *Criterion-referenced* assessment: where we compare the learner's performance against a specific, objective, pre-defined standard, or *criterion* on measures of single skills (for example, 'Can Jacqui correctly add 3 + 4'?) or on measures of more complex multiple skills (for example, 'Can Nicky read aloud pages 3 to 6 of his reading book with 90 per cent accuracy?'). Use criterion-referenced tests when you wish to assess the content of a pupil's knowledge base within a specific domain (i.e., when you want to measure mastery of information or skills: what the pupil can or can't do in terms of absolute standards).

3   *Curriculum-based* assessment: a derivative of the above, where we compare the learner's performance with the content of his/her existing curriculum. Use a curriculum-based test when you wish to assess the pupil's instructional needs based upon his/her on-going performance on the existing content of curriculum.

4   *Dynamic* assessment: an approach which holds that a learner's performance will improve with appropriate support and follows a 'test – teach – re-test' sequence, providing training in the form of guidance using cues and graded prompts. This approach highlights the importance of assistance (referred to as *mediation, facilitation* or *scaffolding*) and of the learner's responsivity towards tasks. Use this approach when you wish to find out more about the opproprinteness of the strategies used by the student/pupil/learner, how they react to suggestions made by a teacher, and identify barriers to learning. Proponents of dynamic assessment view norm-referenced, criterion-referenced and curriculum-based approaches as 'static', focusing upon outcomes in achievement with little attention paid to the processes which underpin learning. There are published dynamic assessment 'tests' (see Tzuriel, 1990; 2000), with an emphasis upon mediation.

But as Rust and Golombok (2000, p. 42) point out, the items of all tests have to be related to some criteria, which are determined by the purpose of the test. Consequently, all tests, even those which are norm-referenced may be regarded as being criterion referenced.

Assessment needs in education are of four main types:

1   Those related to *entitlement* or *eligibility* for additional support:
    • Does a pupil have a significantly more marked, learning difficulty than the majority of learners of his/her age which makes him/her eligible for additional support (for example, specialist teaching or special examination arrangements on account of dyslexia)? This may involve individual assessment or perhaps screening a class to identify learners with additional support needs.

- Should a learner be referred to a specialist agency?
- Documenting the nature and range of a learner's additional support needs.

2 Those related to *accountability*:
- Evaluating progress of a support plan or programme;
- Evaluating outcomes from special initiatives;
- Determining 'value added'; and
- Monitoring standards of attainment in literacy and numeracy in a class.

3 Those related to *instruction*:
- Identifying what pupils have learned to inform the planning of what they should be taught;
- Identifying strategies to improve pupils' attainments;
- Deciding how to group pupils; and
- Testing hypotheses about the nature of a pupil's additional support needs to help in the formulation of a programme.

4 Those related to *gathering information over time from a range of specific contexts*:
- Determining the nature and extent of a pupil's behavioural difficulties (which are often context-specific) by classroom observation;
- Monitoring 'on-task' behaviour in class; and
- Evaluating the effectiveness of intervention for pupils with social, emotional or behavioural difficulties.

Assessment need	Possible assessment method
Determining entitlement or eligibility for additional support	Norm-referenced, standardized tests
Establishing accountability	Norm-referenced, standardized tests
Gathering information about instructional needs	Criterion-referenced, curriculum-based or dynamic assessment approaches
Gathering information about situated, or context-specific problems, such as social, emotional or behavioural difficulties	Interviews and observations in different settings over a period of time

As the table above shows, there is a degree of overlap between assessment approaches and assessment needs. However, norm-referenced (*psychometric*), standardized tests are particularly informative in addressing assessment needs related to entitlement/eligibility and accountability issues, but somewhat less so in regard to issues regarding instruction or the details of intervention, although the scores and associated qualitative data could yield relevant information. But in general, criterion-referenced, curriculum-based or dynamic assessment approaches would be more appropriate in regard to addressing assessment needs relating to instruction. As Lidz (1991, pp. 121–2) puts it:

> If we wish to determine how far the child's knowledge base deviates from the norm, we will continue to administer a psychometric measure. If we wish to determine the content of a child's knowledge base within a specific domain, we will administer a curriculum-based test. If we wish to derive hypotheses about how the child learns, how responsive the child is to attempts to intervene, and what seems to be interfering with the child's ability to profit from existing attempts at instruction, we will use dynamic assessment.

However, there are other assessment needs, for example, associated with situated, or context-specific problems, such as social, emotional or behavioural difficulties, where test use would be less helpful. With such problems, interviews gathering information about the history and nature of the concerns, and observations in different settings over a period of time would yield information about the difficulties themselves and their history, as well as the characteristics of the individual and relevant factors in the contexts in which the problems are presented and would be helpful in suggesting how best to proceed.

Justifying the Choice of a Particular Test with Reference to Knowledge of the Learner's Level of Development and the Skills being Assessed

One possible pitfall in test use is to fall into the habit of using the same test or tests over and over again without adequate consideration of the purpose of carrying out the assessment in the first place. One rule of thumb to help guard against this is to ask the question: 'What will I do differently once I have the test results?' If you do not have an answer to this, then the chances are that you are not clear about why you are using the test.

Competent test users should be familiar with any test that they are anticipating using. They need to know the details of the materials and must be practised in administration. But equally, they should be able to provide a rationale and justification for the selection of a particular test taking into the account not only the purpose of assessment, as discussed above, but also the learner's level of development and the skills being assessed.

Learner's level of development

In the case of the learner's level of development, this means taking factors such as the following into account:

- The *appropriacy of the norms* (for example, the representativeness and size of the norm group, the age-range covered, and whether the norms are up-to-date, in the case of standardized tests). The learner's scores on a standardized test will be compared with the scores of the participants in the norm group. Accordingly, the test user must ensure: (i) that the norms of any test used are based upon participants who are representative of the test takers; (ii) that they are based upon an adequate number of participants (see Unit 2 for discussion); (iii) that the age-range of the test is appropriate for the test taker; and (iv) that the date of standardization is no more than 10 years from the date of administration for achievement tests and no more than 15 years for ability tests (see Salvia and Ysseldyke, 2004, pp. 114–15 for a discussion).
- The *appropriacy of the level of the items*. If the test norms are to be used to score the test taker's performance, the test user must ensure that the learner is not administered items which are outside of the age-range for his/her age. If out-of-age level items are used in this way, the test taker is not being compared with same-age participants and the score would be invalid. But in cases where the learner has marked difficulties, the test user should also consider whether the materials are appropriate for the test taker's age and developmental level, even if the items have been standardized on an appropriate age-group.
- The *interest level of the test items*. Care must be taken to ensure that the test taker does not consider the materials to be too difficult or too 'easy'. This may be a particular consideration in the case of a younger learner who may lack self-confidence and whose interest is not engaged, or in the case of an older test taker with learning difficulties, who may consider that the materials are more appropriate for a younger learner.

The skills being assessed

In the case of the skills being assessed, this means taking into account factors that relate to the accessibility of content of materials:

- *The accessibility of the test materials*. The test medium (for example, the format of the test, the mode of administration and the mode of presentation, basal and ceiling levels) and the language of the test items (for example, the vocabulary used, any literacy demands that might be made and any cultural referents) are important considerations when selecting a test. If a test taker cannot understand what he/she is required to do, then that measure is clearly invalid as a test of the particular skill or ability which it is intended to assess. This may even contravene equal opportunity and/or disability legislation. For example, tests presented orally to test takers with severe hearing impairments unable to understand the instructions and task demands would be unfair. Such instruments could also be problematic for those with severe language and communication problems or for those for whom English is an additional language if not presented in the test taker's primary language. Similarly, test items with instructions presented in print form would be unfair not only for test takers with marked visual impairment, but also for those with problems in reading, who are unable to access the meaning of what they are required to do. With regard to cultural relevance and referents, the test materials should not give an unfair advantage to test takers from a particular religion, ethnic group or social class, nor offence to others. The choice of selecting an individually administered or a group-administered test may also have an effect upon the test taker's performance. For example, group-administration of a test may have significant sources of distraction, which could disadvantage a learner with poor concentration or attention problems. It may also be harder to ensure that all of the test takers are clear about what they are required to do. Finally, a test should have clear instructions for establishing a *basal level*, the level below which it is assumed that the test taker will get all of the items correct, and a *ceiling level*, the point at which it is assumed that the test taker will fail all items and testing is discontinued.

• *The appropriacy of the response to the test material.* The test format will determine how the test taker is required to respond to the test items. This may be: (i) verbally; (ii) in writing, as in the case of a multiple-choice test or rating scale; or (iii) perhaps by means of a motor response, as in some non-verbal performance tests which may involve the manipulation of blocks or other objects. But if a test taker's sensory or physical difficulties were to constrain his/her ability to respond, then the test results would be invalid, and perhaps also illegal. Thus a learner with a severe speech and language delay or disorder may have difficulty in providing a clear verbal response, and a learner with a physical disability or motor difficulty, such as developmental coordination disorder/dyspraxia, may have problems responding in writing or via the manipulation of objects, particularly if the test has time limits. Again, the selection of a group-administered rather than an individually administered test would also be a consideration as it is likely that there would be more reliance upon writing skills, and possibly reading skills in the case of a group-administered test.

• *The learner's exposure to the material being tested.* A test taker who has not had experience of the material being tested, or perhaps not as much exposure to the curriculum being assessed as his/her peers, will be at a relative disadvantage to a test taker who has. Thus, a learner with poor school attendance, or a test taker recently re-located from a different country or culture would be at a disadvantage in regard to a test of a curricular area if he/she missed the opportunities for instruction afforded to good attenders. In such cases, the results from the test might reflect more the lack of opportunity to learn than problems in the skill or ability being tested and would raise concerns about the fairness of the test use.

The Effects of Factors such as Ethnicity, Gender, Social Class and Disability, as well as More Direct Factors in the Testing Environment, such as Heat, Noise, Test Anxiety and Variables Associated with Test Administration upon the Results from Tests

Effective test use depends not only upon careful selection of the instrument and practice in administration and scoring on the part of the test user, but also in ensuring that possible sources of bias and distraction in the testing environment are removed or at least minimized. This is particularly important where test takers are children, indeed children with additional support needs. Known environmental variables that have a direct and adverse effect upon the test taker's concentration and ability to attend and hence his/her performance include heat, poor lighting, noise and over-crowding. The test user should thus ensure:

• that the session is *free from interruptions* (a 'Do not disturb' sign outside the test room may be helpful); and
• that the room used for testing is *adequately ventilated*, with an appropriate background temperature; *well-lit*, *free from extraneous noises* and where possible free from other possible distracters (such as food or drink, or third parties who might influence the test taker's response); and has *appropriate seating and space* for test takers (for example, a desk and chair of the correct height, and well-spaced out desks or tables for administration of a group test to minimize copying of answers).

In addition, there are cognitive and emotional variables that are important. Tiredness and lack of motivation, for example, can adversely affect the child's performance, as can *test anxiety*, where the experience of being evaluated, fear of failure, the context in which testing takes place or even the specific type of test used (for example, a timed test or perhaps a test of mathematics) causes the test taker to feel anxious. While a degree of such anxiety may increase the test taker's physiological levels of arousal and actually improve their performance, an excess can have a catastrophic effect.

Variables associated with the *test administration* can also have an effect upon the results. If the test user does not provide clear instructions, is unfamiliar with the test materials or procedures for administration, and does not encourage the test taker, then the results will not be an accurate reflection of the learner's level of ability or skill. That it is why it is important for the test user to establish *rapport* with the test taker, to help the test taker to relax and to ensure that he/she is clear about the purpose of the test administration. Success on the practice items on a test can also be a good way of helping to reduce test anxiety and boosting confidence and motivation, together with encouragement from the test user to try hard and avoid careless mistakes. It goes without saying that the test user should be sufficiently practised in the administration of the test so that he/she can be attentive to the test taker's performance, and also that failure to adhere to the standardized instructions and scoring procedures will render the test results invalid.

It is also worth noting that a test taker's experience of tests can also have an effect upon his/her performance. In general, the more experience the test taker has of a particular test, the better their performance is likely to be, because of the effects of practice, reduced uncertainty (and hence anxiety) and increased confidence. This is why many publishers have guidelines for minimum intervals between re-administrations of tests. It can be useful to ask a test taker about their experience with a particular test before administering it.

Factors such as *gender, ethnicity, social class* and *disability* can also have an impact upon test results over and above the effects of the appropriacy of the format of the test, the medium of the test and the language used by the test which we considered in the last section. It is possible that test items may have a specific bias to the advantage or disadvantage of demographic groups. As Urbina (2004, p. 249) puts it:

> An item is considered to be biased only if individuals from different groups who have the same standing on a trait differ in the probability of responding to the item in a specified manner. In tests of ability, for instance, bias

may be inferred when persons who possess equal levels of ability, but belong to different demographic groups, have different probabilities of success in an item.

This is known to test developers as *Differential Item Functioning* (DIF) and can result in systematic differences in average scores across different gender, social or ethnic groups, or between those with disabilities and those without, raising serious legal and ethical issues. This can arise from differences in the test takers' experiences of the content, as a result of *acculturation*, learning opportunities and experiences in both formal and informal settings.

It is important, therefore, to ensure that the developers of any instrument that is being considered for use have made the items in a test as fair as possible, without any content which may be offensive, inappropriate or even advantageous to a particular demographic group. Test materials should represent people from different ethnic, gender and social groups, disabled and non-disabled alike, in non-stereotypic as well as traditional roles and situations. Items that generate pronounced differences between demographic groups should be revised or deleted by the test developers. In this way, tests can take into account different acculturation and diversity in experiences to minimize any consistent underlying biases.

Identifying Sources of Information which can Corroborate the Information from a Test

The use of *multiple sources of information* in the interpretation of results to assist the decision-making process has already been highlighted as a characteristic of good practice in the use of tests. It is important that test results should be cross-validated with other evidence as a check on their validity, particularly if they will be used to support important placement or resource allocation decisions. The test manual or a review of the test will provide useful information in this regard and should be consulted by the test user. Test data may also be corroborated by means of:

- *existing school records*, which may include the results of other recently administered standardized tests or class-based assessments, or SATs;
- *examples of pupils' current coursework* including portfolios of classwork;
- *direct observation* of the learner's performance in class or other relevant setting (for example, the playground, as in the case of behaviour difficulties, or concerns about social relationships or bullying);

- *teachers' reports* on the learner's performance or behaviour; and
- reports from *assessments carried out by other professionals, such as speech and language therapists, educational psychologists, clinical psychologists* and *career guidance teachers* available as part of multi-disciplinary or inter-agency work.

Distinguishing between Different Types of Test: Tests of Attainment, Tests of Ability and Tests of Aptitude

The CCET (Level A) distinguishes between tests of *attainment*, tests of *ability* and tests of *aptitude*. Tests of attainment (or achievement) are the most frequently used tests in education. They have the following attributes:

- are designed to evaluate knowledge and understanding in curricular areas (for example, reading, spelling, number);
- may be individual or group-administered;
- may be used for screening or to determine progress or to evaluate the effectiveness of the curriculum;
- may include diagnostic tests;
- are generally norm-referenced, but may be criterion-referenced or curriculum-based; and
- are not designed primarily to be predictive.

Examples of tests of attainment may be found in Appendix 5 with details of publishers, and include such instruments as the Neale Analysis of Reading Ability – Second Revised British Edition (NARA II), the Wide Range Achievement Test – Expanded Edition (WRAT-Expanded), and the Numeracy Progress Tests Numeracy Baseline/Tests 1–6.
    Tests of ability, on the other hand, are:

- designed to measure underlying general cognitive ability ('intelligence') or specific cognitive ability (for example, short-term memory, or verbal ability, or numerical ability) using tests of general knowledge, reasoning, problem-solving and memory rather than measures of what a test taker has learnt from his/her curricular experience; and
- in many cases, are designed to be predictive, to provide an indication of a learner's future academic performance.

Examples again are shown in Appendix 5, and include the Cognitive Abilities Test: Third Edition (CAT3), the Working Memory Test

Battery for Children (WMTB-C), and the Nonverbal Abilities Tests 6–13.

Finally, tests of aptitude are not widely used in education but are:

• tests of aptitude for practical tasks, such as musical aptitude, mechanical aptitude and spatial relations; and
• designed to be predictive.

Examples of tests of aptitude include the Primary Measures of Music Audiation (K–Grade 3) (Gordon, 1979) and Intermediate Measures of Music Audiation (Grade 1–6) (Gordon, 1982), both published by GIA Publications: Chicago.

Distinguishing between Different Types of Test: Formative and Summative Uses of Tests

A further distinction is made between *formative* and *summative* uses of tests. As William (2000) notes, formative test use is prospective in character, and may be regarded as *assessment for learning*. It is designed to provide:

• a source of effective feedback to the test taker about a gap between present performance and a desired longer-term goal;
• a means of actively involving the test taker in his/her own learning by gaining an understanding of his/her strengths and weaknesses; and
• information from the results of the test to help those teaching or supporting the test taker to identify ways of making teaching and learning more effective.

In contrast, summative test use is retrospective in character, and may be regarded as *assessment of learning*. It is designed to provide:

• a summary overview of what the individual knows, understands or can do at the time of testing; and
• a means of guiding formative test use.

Formative and summative test use are not different kinds of assessment but, rather, are different ways to which information arising from the assessment can be put. The outcome of the same assessment might serve more than one function and thus a given test can serve either a formative or a summative use depending upon the purpose of the assessment or the assessment question. As William (2000) further points out, a key distinction is the extent to which test use utilizes information about *process* to provide suggestions for future action to help close the gap between present and desired levels of performance, or focuses upon the *outcome*. Thus a test of attainment in spelling could be used in a summative way if the purpose of assessment is to provide a standard score to summarize the test taker's performance relative to the norm group. But the same information could be used in a formative way if: (i) the data are used diagnostically to identify problems with particular spelling 'rules'; (ii) feedback is provided to the test taker regarding these difficulties; and (iii) teaching is modified to help him/her to learn these rules. See Black and William (1998, pp. 3–5) for a review of the evidence for the effectiveness of formative assessment use.

Distinguishing between Different Types of Test: Norm-Referenced, Criterion-Referenced and Curriculum-Based Measures

We considered the relationship between norm-referenced, criterion-referenced and curriculum-based measures and assessment needs in an earlier section. The CCET (Level A) requires test users to be able to distinguish between these three different types of measures:

- *Norm-referenced* measures interpret the learner's performance relative to that of the other individuals in a specific population, the normative sample of the test on whom the test norms are based in terms of *developmental scores* (for example, age-equivalent scores, such as 'Reading Ages' or 'Spelling Ages') or *derived scores* (for example, standard scores, or percentiles).
- *Criterion-referenced* measures interpret the learner's score in terms of an empirical, statistical relationship between the test score and an external specific, objective, pre-defined standard, or *criterion* (for example, pass/fail, right/wrong, number correct, percentage correct, or number of correct responses per minute).
- *Curriculum-based* measures interpret test scores in terms of specific aspects of the content of the learner's existing curriculum usually in terms of specific instructional objectives.

By way of caveat, it should be noted that the quality of norm-referenced tests is dependent upon the adequacy and representative of their standardization, and on their reliability and validity (which we will discuss in more detail in Unit 2). The quality of criterion-referenced and, by extension, curriculum-based tests, is dependent upon what constitutes an acceptable level of performance for the attribute being measured. Should the criterion be 100 per cent or 80 per cent correct, for example? And should this criterion change as a function of the test taker's cognitive abilities, gender, social class or ethnicity?

Completing the Unit 1 Competency Assessments

We shall now see how this fits in with the BPS competences and the answers required by the assessment that you will be required to undertake. Only short-term assessments are required for Unit 1, but two pieces of evidence are required for each element. The examples provided utilize short note answers, together with opportunities for self-assessment using multiple choice questions, and simulation exercises from a test publisher's catalogue. But your assessor may provide you with case studies or scenarios and ask you to provide a commentary. Note that '1.1' below refers to the assessment for Unit 1 Element 1 and '1.2' to Unit 1 Element 2 and so on. The competences are shown in full in Appendix 1, and the *Guidance for Assessors* material is reproduced in full in Appendix 2.

Examples of How the BPS Competences might be Assessed and Answered

1.1   Which of the following assessment needs would you consider a test to be 'highly appropriate' in addressing?

Assessment need	Indicate 'Yes" or 'No
To compare the learner's knowledge base with the norm for his/her age	Yes/No
To assess the content of a learner's knowledge base within a specific domain	Yes/No
To generate hypotheses about how the test taker learns	Yes/No
To investigate how responsive the learner is to attempts to intervene	Yes/No
To assess what may be interfering with the learner's ability to benefit from existing levels of instruction	Yes/No
To determine the amount of time a learner spends 'off-task' in class	Yes/No

(Check your response with the answer shown in Appendix 6.)

1.1   What is the relationship between assessment and testing?

Assessment is a process of collecting data for the purpose of making decisions about individuals and groups by means of:

- *Direct observation* of the student/pupil/learner's performance or behaviour.
- *Existing information*, such as portfolios of the learner's work.
- *Interviews* with those who know the learner well, such as former teachers or parents also provide useful information.
- *Professional judgements* of those who have worked with the learner in the past or are currently working with the learner in the here and now.
- A *test* may be used.

Testing is thus a sub-set of assessment.

1.2   Which assessment needs might best be addressed by the use of a test procedure?

In general, assessment needs relating to entitlement or eligibility for additional support or accountability might best be addressed by means of a test. Examples would include:

- How effective is the cued spelling programme in the KS2 class?
- Should a student receive special arrangements in statutory examinations?
- How many pupils in the Year 1 intake have poor levels of phonological awareness?
- Does a pupil require additional learning support to address literacy problems?

In contrast, assessment needs relating to instruction or where use of a test would be problematic because of an inappropriate norm group, disability, or cultural bias, might be more appropriately addressed by means of an alternative assessment approach, such as observation, criterion-referenced measures, curriculum-based assessment or dynamic assessment. Examples would include:

- Has a pupil mastered addition and subtraction number 'facts' to 20?
- How can a pupil most effectively learn to spell correctly words misspelled in an essay?
- Can a pupil read a given text with 90 per cent accuracy?

- Does a pupil for whom English is an additional language and who is newly arrived in the UK have a problem in receptive vocabulary?

1.2 Complete the following table to match assessment approach to assessment need

Indicate which assessment needs would best be addressed by the use of a test procedure and those which might be more appropriately addressed by means of an alternative approach.

Assessment approach	Assessment need[a]		
	Entitlement/ eligibility	Accountability	Instruction
Norm-referenced			
Criterion-referenced			
Curriculum-based			
Dynamic assessment			

[a] '√√' denotes highly appropriate, '√' appropriate and 'X' not particularly appropriate

(Check your response with the answer provided in Appendix 6.)

1.3 Select a specimen test or a test from a catalogue. Use your knowledge of: (a) child development; and (b) the skills being assessed, to support its use

The Neale Analysis of Reading Ability – Second Revised British Edition (NARA II) is an individually administered, norm-referenced timed test of oral reading. It consists of two parallel forms designed to assess the rate, accuracy and comprehension of reading of children aged between 6 and 12 years, together with supplementary diagnostic tests of phonemic awareness, memory for regular and irregular word patterns and auditory discrimination.

The manual provides detailed instructions for the administration and scoring of the test together with background information about its development. There is also a demonstration cassette with examples of prompting and of recording errors and a commentary highlighting good practice and possible problems that the test user may encounter. The test was standardized in 1996, so the norms are less than 10 years old and are based upon 1,928 children for Form 1 and 1,546 for Form 2 from across the UK.

The norms are also weighted for gender and for social class, using free school meals.

The test consists of graded passages, or narratives, presented in book form. Each narrative is a self-contained story and is accompanied by a picture, which sets the scene but does not provide details of the story. Accuracy is assessed by recording the number of errors and rate of reading by calculating the number of words correctly read per minute. Comprehension is assessed by questions about the main idea of the narrative, the sequence of events, recall of details and questions that also require the test taker to draw inferences about the material read. Separate norms for accuracy of reading, rate of reading and comprehension are provided.

The level of difficulty and interest levels of the narratives and questions are appropriate for the 6–12 year age-range. The format of the test, instructions and materials are also appropriate for a test of oral reading and there are no problematic cultural references. Pupils respond orally by reading a passage aloud and then answering standard comprehension questions asked by the test administrator. This is appropriate for a test of oral reading. Provision is made in the instructions for helping test takers deal with words in the narratives that they may be unfamiliar with. The test user is allowed to correct errors or to supply words which the pupil does not know.

A practice passage is provided to ensure that the test takers know what is expected of them, and there are clear instructions for establishing a basal level, the level below which it is assumed that the test taker will get all of the items correct (here, no more than two errors), and a ceiling level, the point at which it is assumed that the test taker will fail all items and testing is discontinued (here, no more than 16 errors are made on passages 1–5 or no more than 20 errors on passage 6). Administration of the test should thus take no more than 20 minutes, which is appropriate for pupils in the target age-range. There is also an extension passage for use with older pupils or more able readers within the age-range, with more demanding vocabulary and concepts.

In conclusion, this is an attractively produced test of reading which is well-suited to the purpose of assessing the reading skills of pupils in the 6–12 year age-group.

1.4   Describe how measures of ability and attainment of students/pupils/learners are influenced by environmental factors and give specific examples

Factors such as temperature, poor lighting and noise can affect the test taker's concentration and ability to attend and hence his/her performance on measures of ability and attainment. Overcrowding may also make it difficult for the test taker to hear instructions and can also provide sources of distraction, and an increased likelihood of copying answers or cheating.

The test user should ensure that the room used for testing is adequately ventilated, with an appropriate background temperature, and is well-lit, free from extraneous noises and from other possible distracters (such as food or drink, or third parties who might influence the test taker's response), with appropriate seating and adequate space for test takers (for example, a desk and chair of the correct height, and well-spaced-out desks or tables for administration of a group test to minimize copying of answers). The session should also be free from interruptions.

Tiredness and lack of motivation, for example, can adversely affect the test taker's performance, as well as test anxiety. Test anxiety is a fear of being evaluated, or fear of failure, or anxiety about the context in which testing takes place or perhaps even about the specific type of test used (for example, a timed test or perhaps a test of mathematics). If severe, test anxiety can have an adverse effect upon the test taker's performance on tests of ability or attainment.

Variables associated with the test administrator can also affect the results obtained. If the test user does not establish rapport with the test taker to relax him/her and ensure that they are clear about the purpose of the test session, does not administer the test properly following the standardized instructions, does not provide encouragement to the test taker, and does not score the results accurately and in accordance with the guidance in the test manual, then the results would be invalid.

Finally, factors such as *gender*, *ethnicity*, *social class* and *disability* can also have an impact upon measures of ability and attainment at two levels. First, they can have an effect at the level of the appropriacy of the norms for specific demographic groups defined in terms of gender, ethnicity, social class and disability, the appropriacy of the level of the items (both in terms of the developmental stage of the test taker and interest level), the accessibility of the test in terms of its format, the appropriacy of the modes of presentation and of responding, the language used by the test, and also the learner's exposure to the content being tested. Second, it is possible that test items may have a specific bias to the advantage or disadvantage of certain demographic groups.

To illustrate this, tests presented orally to test takers unable to understand the instructions and task demands (for example, those with severe hearing impairments, or with severe language and communication problems, or those for whom English is an additional language) would be unfair. A learner with a severe speech and language delay or disorder may have difficulty in providing a clear verbal response, and a learner with a physical disability or motor difficulty, such as dyspraxia, may have problems responding in writing or via the manipulation of objects, particularly if the test has time limits. Similarly, tests that assume that the test takers are able to read items and instructions independently and to record their responses in writing could be unfair for those with marked visual impairment, and for those with literacy or motor skill problems. A learner with a poor record of school attendance, or perhaps a test taker recently relocated from a different country or culture would be at a disadvantage in regard to a test of a curricular area if he/she had missed the opportunities for instruction afforded to regular attenders at school. Test results in such cases might be held to reflect the effects of opportunities to learn rather than the skill or ability being tested.

In addition, the test materials should neither give offence (for example, text or pictures of pigs in the case of some cultural and religious groups) or an unfair advantage or disadvantage to test takers from a particular gender, religion, ethnic group, social class or disability in the form of systematic differences in average scores across such demographic groups. This can arise from differences in the test takers' experiences of the content, as a result of *acculturation*, their learning opportunities and experiences in both formal and informal settings. Test materials should represent people from different ethnic, gender and social groups, disabled and non-disabled alike, in non-stereotypic as well as traditional roles and situations. Items which generate pronounced differences between demographic groups should be revised or deleted so that tests can take into account different acculturation and diversity in experiences to minimize any consistent underlying biases.

1.5   Give examples of the kinds of information which may be used to corroborate the information elicited by a test or other assessment technique

Test data may be corroborated by means of:

- *existing school records*, which may include the results of other recently administered standardized tests or class-based assessments, or SATs;
- *examples of pupils' current coursework* including portfolios of classwork;
- *direct observation* of the learner's performance in class or other relevant setting (for example, the playground, as in the case of behaviour difficulties, or concerns about social relationships or bullying);
- *teachers' reports* on the learner's performance or behaviour; and

- reports from *assessments carried out by other professionals, such as speech and language therapists, educational psychologists, career guidance teachers* available as part of multi-disciplinary or inter-agency work.

1.6 Explain the differences between tests of attainment, tests of ability and tests of aptitude

Tests of attainment (or achievement) are the most frequently used tests in education and:

- are designed to evaluate knowledge and understanding in curricular areas (for example, reading, spelling, number);
- may be individual or group-administered;
- may be used for screening or to determine progress or to evaluate the effectiveness of the curriculum;
- may include diagnostic tests;
- are generally norm-referenced, but may be criterion-referenced or curriculum-based; and
- are not designed primarily to be predictive.

Examples of tests of attainment include such instruments as the Neale Analysis of Reading Ability – Second Revised British Edition (NARA II), the Wide Range Achievement Test – Expanded Edition (WRAT-Expanded), and the Numeracy Progress Tests Numeracy Baseline/Tests 1–6.

Tests of ability, on the other hand, are:

- designed to measure underlying general cognitive ability ('intelligence') or specific cognitive ability (for example, short-term memory, or verbal ability, or numerical/quantitative ability) using tests of general knowledge, reasoning, problem-solving and memory rather than measures of what a test taker has learnt from his/her curricular experience; and are
- in many cases, designed to be predictive, to provide an indication of a learner's future academic performance.

Examples of tests of ability include the Cognitive Abilities Test: Third Edition (CAT3), the Working Memory Test Battery for Children (WMTB-C), and the Nonverbal Abilities Tests 6–13.

Finally, tests of aptitude are not widely used in education but are:

- tests of aptitude for practical tasks, such as musical aptitude, mechanical aptitude and spatial relations; and
- designed to be predictive.

Examples include the Primary Measures of Music Audiation (K–Grade 3) (Gordon, 1979) and Intermediate Measures of Music Audiation (Grade 1–6) (Gordon, 1982), both published by GIA Publications: Chicago.

1.6   Consult the publishers' catalogues and indicate which of the following are tests of attainment, which tests of ability and which tests of aptitude

Test:	Test of attainment	Test of ability	Test of aptitude
Naglieri Nonverbal Ability Test – Individual Administration (NNAT) (http://www.harcourt-uk.com)			
Wechsler Individual Achievement Test – Second UK Edition (WIAT-II) (http://www.harcourt-uk.com)			
SPAR (Spelling & Reading) Tests A & B (http://www.hoddertests.co.uk)			
Verbal Abilities Tests 6–10 (http://www.hoddertests.co.uk)			
Music Aptitude Profile (Grades 5–12) (http://www.giamusic.com)			
Raven's Progressive Matrices & Vocabulary Scales (http://www.nfer-nelson.co.uk)			
Primary Reading Test (Levels 1 & 2) (http://www.nfer-nelson.co.uk)			
Modern Language Aptitude Test – Elementary (http://www.2lti.com/mlate.htm)			

(Check your response with the answer provided in Appendix 6.)

1.7   Explain the difference between formative and summative uses of tests, giving examples of each type

Formative test use is prospective in character, and may be regarded as *assessment for learning*. It is designed to provide:

- a source of effective feedback to the test taker about a gap between present performance and a desired longer-term goal;

- a means of actively involving the test taker in his/her own learning by gaining an understanding of his/her strengths and weaknesses; and
- information from the results of the test to help those teaching or supporting the test taker to identify ways of making teaching and learning more effective.

Summative test use is retrospective in character, and may be regarded as *assessment of learning*. It is designed to provide:

- a summary overview of what the individual knows, understands or can do at the time of testing; and
- a means of guiding formative test use.

Formative and summative test are not different kinds of assessment, but rather different ways to which information arising from the assessment can be put. The outcome of the same assessment might serve more than one function and thus a given test can serve either a formative or a summative use depending upon the purpose of the assessment or the assessment question.

A test of attainment in reading or spelling would be used in a summative way if the purpose of assessment was to provide a standard score to summarize the test taker's performance relative to the norm group.

A test would be used in a formative way if the data were used diagnostically to identify problems, feedback provided to the test taker regarding these difficulties, and teaching modified to help him/her to learn these rules.

1.8   Differentiate between norm-referenced, criterion-referenced and curriculum-based measures

- *Norm-referenced* measures interpret the learner's performance relative to that of the other individuals in a specific population, that is, the normative sample of the test on whom the test norms are based, in terms of *developmental scores* (for example, age-equivalent scores, such as 'Reading Ages' or 'Spelling Ages') or *derived scores* (for example, standard scores, or percentiles).
- *Criterion-referenced* measures interpret the learner's score in terms of an empirical, statistical relationship between the test score and an external specific, objective, pre-defined standard, or *criterion* (for example, pass/fail, right/wrong, number correct, percentage correct,

or number of correct responses per minute). A criterion-referenced measure is used to measure mastery of information or skills, what the learner can or can't do in terms of absolute standards.

- *Curriculum-based* measures interpret test scores in terms of specific aspects of the content of the learner's existing curriculum usually in terms of specific instructional objectives.

2

Unit 2: The Basic Principles of Scaling and Standardization

In this unit we will examine ways to make sense of the scores that we get from our tests. The unit begins with an examination of how we can get a feel for our data by using some descriptive statistical methods.

We will look at the ways we can describe a group of scores using statistics such as the *mean*, *median* and *mode* as well as the *spread* or *distribution* of scores we have. Methods of graphically presenting data in the form of *histograms* and *frequency polygons* will also be described.

The concept of confidence levels will be introduced with an application related to a calculation called the Standard Error of the Mean, which tells us how sure we can be that the mean of a small group of people's scores or Sample, represents a large group or the Population mean.

The topic of score distributions will be developed with a discussion of the nature and use of the normal distribution. The chapter will conclude with an examination of the various standard scales such as the z Scale, Percentiles, Stens, Stanines, T Scores and 'deviation' IQs that are used to portray scores.

Descriptive Statistics

Measures of central tendency

The mean
The first step in examining the data that have been generated from a testing session with a number of people is to look at the scores. Probably the first thing we'll want to do is to work out the average score for our group by adding all the scores together to give a total and dividing that by the number of scores.

Technically this number is called the arithmetic mean or as it is usually abbreviated, the *mean*. Here's a very simple example:

$$24$$
$$30$$
$$8$$
$$12$$
$$14$$
$$Total = 88$$
$$88 \div 5 = 17.6$$
$$Mean = 17.6$$

As you can see it is all the numbers added up, which we call their sum, divided by how many numbers there are; five in this example. The mean is the first of three numbers we will use to measure what is called *central tendency*. The other two are the *median* and the *mode*.

It is because there are three *measures of central tendency* that we tend not to use the word average, as there could be confusion between the three.

The median

So what are the median and mode? The median is the number that divides a list of scores that have been put in numerical order into a lower and upper half. For example, in the list below 8 is the median as there are three scores below it and three above.

$$1$$
$$3$$
$$4$$
$$\mathbf{8}$$
$$10$$
$$23$$
$$35$$

This works fine when the list is made up of an odd number of scores but what happens when there is an even number? In this case, we look at the two scores that divide the list into a bottom half and a top half and take the mean of the two and use that as the median, like this:

$$1$$
$$3$$
$$\mathbf{4}$$
$$\mathbf{10}$$
$$23$$
$$35$$

$$4 + 10 = 14; \text{ then } 14 \div 2 = 7$$

So the median in this case would be **7**.

The median is especially useful when we have a small number of very low or high scores that would distort the mean.

The mode

Sometimes we are interested in finding out what the most commonly occurring score is and this is where the *mode* comes in.

We use the mode mainly when we only have data that are measured in a form that would make working out the mean or median meaningless, for example where we have a frequency count of 'things' rather than scores. For example, the mode of 48 chairs, 12 tables and 10 cushions is 48. That is the category with the most in it. It doesn't make sense to have an arithmetic mean or median of furnishings.

The normal distribution

Up to now we have been looking at numbers based on looking at a simple list of scores. It is worth mentioning at this point that the scores we obtain from marking a test are called *raw scores*. The next step is to look at a 'picture' of these raw scores that orders them from low to high or what is called the *distribution of scores*.

The usual way to do this is to draw a graph that plots scores against the number of times that scores occur in a list. There are a number of ways that we can do this.

In an ideal world our scores form a symmetrical or 'bell-shaped' pattern with most scores being around the mean with equal 'tails' tapering on either side. This is the *normal distribution*. It looks like this.

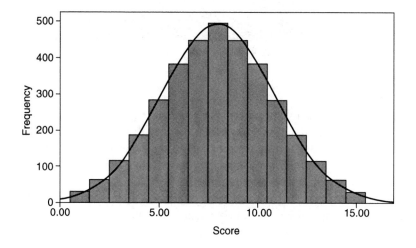

You can see that not many people score very low scores and not many score very high ones. Most are grouped either side of the middle, which is of course the mean score.

Populations and Samples

This distribution represents the scores we would obtain from a very large *population*, for example everyone in the British Isles. In practice we do not have available all these scores and have to be content with a smaller *sample*. Sample distributions are drawn from a population, for example if 20 youngsters are tested we will not have anything like this perfectly symmetrical shape. So in practice we never get a perfect normal distribution and our sample distributions might end up looking like this or even worse!

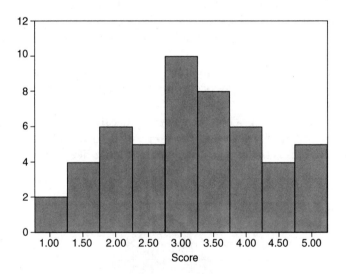

The smaller the sample of scores that you have the less likely it is to represent the large population from which they are drawn. This is important as in our day-to-day testing we are nearly always concerned with samples of populations from which we may try to estimate how well individuals are doing compared to a large population.

There are some other reasons why we are also concerned with looking at how many high or low scores we might have and whether we have more high than low or more low than high.

There are a number of practical issues here, if we find that most people have scored highly on our test we suspect it has been too easy for most people and we say there is a *ceiling effect*, in other words, the test is not showing peoples' full potential as if some harder questions were asked some people would have scored higher still. The test would then be said to have produced 'better discrimination'.

Here's a chart of a distribution of scores that suffer from a ceiling effect:

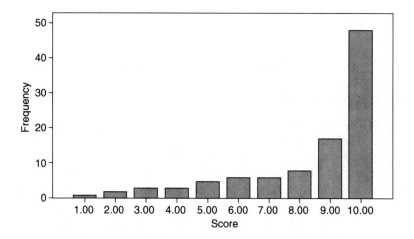

Of course if the opposite happens and most people scored low we would conclude that the test was too difficult.

There is a technical term for scores that are not normally distributed around a mean and that is *skewness*. If scores are seem to have a 'tail' which lies to the right of the main group of scores the distribution is said to be positively skewed and it is an indication that our test is perhaps too hard for the people we have used it on. If the 'tail' lies to the left of the main group of scores they are said to be negatively skewed, an indication that the test is too easy. The above bar chart shows an example of a negatively skewed distribution.

In any event, whether a test is too difficult or too easy, the fault lies with the selection of the test in the first place. By looking at the distribution of scores we can tell whether we have chosen the wrong test for our group.

Another reason for looking at the distribution of scores is that if our distribution looks normal we can find out a lot about how extreme an individual's score is.

Because of the mathematical properties of the normal distribution we can determine what the proportion of scores will be above and below any given point on the distribution.

The simplest illustration is that of the mean score, which we know will have 50 per cent of scores below it and 50 per cent above if the scores are distributed normally.

When we come on to converting our raw scores in to *z scores* that we shall do later in this chapter we will see how we can use statistical tables to see how extreme any of our raw scores are.

Drawing Frequency Distributions

Ungrouped method

One of the exercises you will be asked to do as part of your CCET (Level A) assessment portfolio will be to draw graphs showing the way in which a set of test scores are distributed and to check, among other things, whether they are spread over the tests scale in a roughly normal way. There are two possible ways of drawing a frequency distribution of scores. The first is an *ungrouped frequency polygon*. To construct one of these the first step is to find the highest and lowest numbers and to draw up a table of scores in between. We then count up the number times that each score occurs. It is traditional to use the 'five-bar gate' method of counting. A sample of data may look like this:

Score	Count	Frequency
12	|	(1)
13		(0)
14	||	(2)
15	|||	(3)
16	⌗ |||	(8)
17	||||	(4)
18	||	(2)
19	|	(1)
20	|	(1)

We then simply total up the number of scores which are then called *fre-quencies* (shown above in brackets) and use them to draw a graph where the vertical line, known technically as the *Y axis*, represents these numbers and the horizontal line or *X axis* the scores. A dot or *point* is drawn where an imaginary horizontal line drawn from the Y axis crosses an imaginary vertical line drawn from the X axis, this being done for the frequencies of all score values.

This is how it looks:

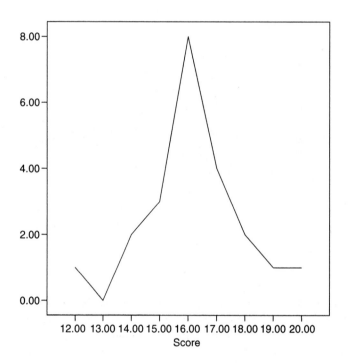

Alternatively, you can draw your distribution in the form of a *histogram*. Here numbers of scores are represented as a series of bars rather than points on a graph:

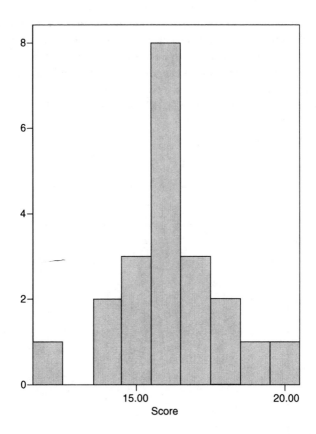

Grouped method

As an alternative to an ungrouped frequency polygon or histogram we can decide on convenient boundaries into which we can group the scores and draw a *grouped frequency histogram or polygon*. This is particularly useful where the difference between the highest and lowest score – the *range* – is large. The main difference between the two approaches is that rather than counting the frequencies of individual scores we count the frequencies of groups of scores. These groups of scores are called *classes*. One of the first questions that arise is how many classes or groups of scores should we have? The answer is usually somewhere between 10 and 20.

So if for example we have a lot of scores between 16 and 63 we may look at the range, 63 − 16 that is 47, and if we want around 10 classes of numbers we need class intervals of 5 (i.e. roughly 47 ÷ 10).

Class interval	Count	Frequency
14–18	|	(1)
19–23	|	(1)
24–28	||||| ||	(7)
29–33	||||| ||||| |||	(13)
34–38	||||| ||||| ||||| ||||	(19)
39–43	||||| ||||| ||||	(14)
44–48	||||| ||||	(9)
49–53	||||| ||	(7)
54–58	|||||		(6)
59–63	|	(1)

This time we use the 'five-bar gate' method to count up the number of times a score falls within a class boundary and use them to draw a graph where the Y axis represents the frequencies and the X axis class intervals.

Here's what our grouped frequency data looks like when charted:

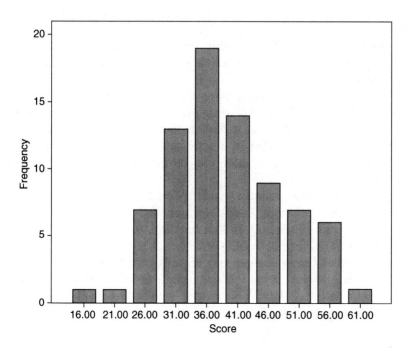

A computer can also be used to draw a variety of frequency charts. Microsoft Excel ©, Lotus 1-2-3 © and other programs allow you to do this. The charts and graphs drawn in Units 2 and 3 of this book use SPSS© (2003) a comprehensive and widely used statistical package.

The Standard Deviation

Just looking at a distribution of scores is very informative but in some cases it's not enough and we need some reliable numbers to summarize what we may (or possibly may not) see from visual inspection. Often these numbers are required in the calculation of another number that will help us interpret test scores better. One of these numbers that is intimately linked to the normal distribution is the *standard deviation*, often abbreviated to *SD*. This gives us an indication of how spread out or dispersed our scores are. More importantly, it gives us a basis for judging how extreme an individual person's score is compared to those it is a part of. It is used in the calculation of many other statistics that we will introduce later.

There are two formulae for the standard deviation, one used on populations, and one that is used to calculate the sample SD.

There are several ways of calculating a standard deviation. The easiest and most commonly used these days is to use a calculator or computer.

Many 'scientific calculators' have a built-in function that will work out a standard deviation for you. All you have to do is to key in your raw scores and press a further button for the answer to be displayed. Calculators differ in exactly how they do this, so make sure the one you get has the function and read the manual to see how you obtain it.

The second way of getting a standard deviation is to use a spreadsheet program such as Microsoft Excel © or Lotus 1–2-3 © which has the standard deviation formula built in as a function. In Microsoft Excel © the function is STDEVP(a:b) or STDEV(a:b).

The third and most onerous way of getting the standard deviation of your scores is to work it out by hand using a formula although you will still need a basic calculator. This method is to be avoided if possible as it can take a long time and is prone to mistakes.

Here's the formula for a population SD:

$$SD = \sqrt{\sum \frac{(X - \overline{X})^2}{N}}$$

Let's take it to bits so we can see what we have to do to work it out.

First of all when we complete all the calculations to the right of the equals sign it will give us the standard deviation or SD as we will abbreviate it.

$SD =$

Thinking of the letters in a formula as abbreviations is a helpful way of looking at things for some.

Then there is the square root sign

$\sqrt{}$

This tells us to work out the square root of the result of all the calculations we do underneath this sign. It is the last thing we do in our calculation. Although you can look this figure up in mathematical tables even the most basic calculator is likely to have a key for this.

$\underline{X}$ is an abbreviation for an individual raw score.
$\overline{X}$ represents the mean of the scores. The bar '$\overline{}$' as it is known, over the X is shorthand for the arithmetic mean. In this case the mean of all the X or raw scores.

Then there is the Greek letter sigma

Σ.

This tells us to add up or *sum* all the numbers to its immediate right, in this case all the raw scores minus their mean score.

Finally,

N

is the total number of scores that you have.

Let's put the formula back together and work out an example.

X	$X - \overline{X}$	$(X - \overline{X})^2$
23	−12.93	167.18
43	7.07	49.98
54	18.07	326.52
43	7.07	49.98
62	26.07	679.64
22	−13.93	194.04
43	7.07	49.98
24	−11.93	142.32
44	8.07	65.12
19	−16.93	286.62
18	−17.93	321.48
44	8.07	65.12
28	−7.93	62.88
37	1.07	1.14
35	−0.93	0.86

$N = 15$ $\text{Variance} = \sum \dfrac{(X - \overline{X})^2}{N} = 164.19$ $\sum (X - \overline{X})^2 = 2462.86$

$\text{Mean} = 35.93$ $SD = \sqrt{\sum \dfrac{(X - \overline{X})^2}{N}} = 12.81$

In the calculations detailed above you will see an intermediate stage where the *variance* is computed. Variance is also a measure of spread of scores around the mean. You can see from the above calculations that it is the mean of the sum of the squared differences between the raw scores and the mean of the raw scores. Variance will be referred to in a later chapter.

You will recall the distinction we made between a population and sample when dealing with the normal distribution. The formula we have used here calculates the SD of our population scores, if we want to estimate the SD of the population, however, we would simply substitute the N in the formula with N − 1. In Microsoft Excel © the function **STDEV (a:b)** rather than **STDEVP(a:b)** can be used.

Sample Statistics

The standard error of the mean

When we test a group of people we may want to know how that group compares with some larger group. As we have said, our smaller group of test scores is technically known as a sample and the larger group we want to compare it to is known as a population. For example we may want to know whether the mean of our sample is close to the population mean or whether we have a group of people whose scores do not represent the population. There is a calculation we can make that allows us to get an idea of how likely it is that our sample mean is near to the population mean. It looks like this:

$$SE_{mean} = \frac{SD}{\sqrt{N}}$$

SD is the standard deviation of the population and $\sqrt{N}$ the square root of the number in the sample.

The *standard error of the mean* (SE_{mean}) gives us a number that we both add and subtract from our sample mean. This gives us the range within which the population mean will be allowing for error in our measurements. It gives an estimation of what our theoretical 'error free mean' is likely to be. If we take this number we can be sure that 68 per cent of the time our population mean will lie within those ± bounds. As error in extreme cases could be theoretically infinite we can never be 100 per cent sure that we have the bounds wide enough to account for all eventualities. That is why we have what are called *Confidence Limits*. The confidence level is 68 per cent if you use just one SE_{mean} it means our range will contain our 'error free mean' 68 times in every 100 times we do the calculation or, looking at it another way, 32 per cent of the time our 'error free mean' will fall outside this range. Sometimes we will want to be surer than that and want to be 95 per cent certain. All we have to do to achieve this level of confidence is to multiply our SE_{mean} by 1.96.

For example, if our sample mean was 30 and we worked out the SE_{mean} to be 2 we could say that our 'error free mean' would be between 28 and 32, 68 per cent of the time or for a 95 per cent confidence level between 26.08 and 33.92.

Transformations

We mentioned earlier that the numbers we get after scoring a test are known as raw scores because as yet they do not tell us anything about how well a person has performed. To make sense of these scores we must look at both the mean and standard deviation of our group and use these to change or *transform* these raw scores into numbers that have a meaning, these we call *standard scores*. It is most important to note that all of the methods we will discuss assume that what we are measuring is distributed normally as they make use of the mathematical properties of the normal distribution to tell us how good, bad or indifferent our obtained or raw scores are. We are thus able to say how an individual test taker has performed compared with a group of people with whom we wish to compare them.

In later units we will introduce *norm tables* that are the way in practice you will convert raw scores to standard scores. The test constructor will usually have done all the hard work for you, reducing the process to a simple table look-up operation. However there are occasions when you might like to use a different standard scale to that used by the test author, the rest of this unit shows you how to do this.

z Scores

The most basic standard score is the *z Score*, it has a mean of 0 and a standard deviation of 1. Thus about 68 per cent of a population falls between −1 and +1. The formula for converting raw scores to z scores is:

$$z = \frac{X - \overline{X}}{SD}$$

Where is X is a raw score, $\overline{X}$ the mean of the group and SD its standard deviation.

In practice z scores are inconvenient to use, as they need to be calculated to two or three decimal places to represent a score and range between both positive and negative numbers. However the z scale is the basic building block of other important and more convenient ways of expressing scores.

By knowing a raw score's associated z score equivalent we can convert or *transform* that score to any convenient scale with any mean and standard deviation that we choose.

The formula used is:

$$t_s = (z_s \times SD) + \overline{X}_s$$

Where t_s = the transformed score and SD the standard deviation of the scale that we want and $\overline{X}_s$ the mean of the scale we want.

In practice we don't often use our own combinations of SD and Mean but rather use one of the conventional standard scales used by many other people to interpret test scores. These are the *Sten Scale* short for standard ten, the *Stanine Scale* short for standard nine and the *T Scale* – the 'T' here is the initial of the early testing pioneer Thorndike – and finally '*Deviation IQs*'. Unlike the percentile that will be discussed later you can carry out the usual arithmetic calculations on these Standard Scores.

Stens

The Sten Scale divides the normal distribution into 10 equal divisions with whole numbers ranging from 1 to 10. There is no whole number mean Sten score but rather Stens 5 and 6 straddle the mean that is 5.5. The Sten Scale has a standard deviation of 2.

You can see if we substitute 2 and 5.5 into our transformation formula given above we can see how we can change z scores into Sten scores.

$$Sten = (z_s \times 2) + 5.5$$

Raw to Sten score conversions are usually rounded to the nearest whole number rather than being expressed with decimal places. Means and standard deviations of groups of Sten scores are calculated with decimal places however. The usual arithmetic operations including the calculation of the mean and standard deviation can be used on these Standard Scores.

Stanines

The Stanine Scale, as its name implies, divides the normal distribution into 9 equal divisions with whole numbers ranging from 1 to 9. There is a whole number mean Stanine score that is 5, one reason why some people prefer the Stanine over the Sten. The downside is that the Stanine gives slightly wider intervals (9 rather than 10) with a possible loss in measurement accuracy. The standard deviation of the Stanine Scale is also 2.

The formula given below is for transforming a z score into a Sten score. The SD of the Stanine scale is 2 like the Sten scale but the mean is 5.0.

$$Stanine = (z_s \times 2) + 5$$

Again you can carry out the usual arithmetic calculations on Stanine scores.

Once again Raw to Stanine conversions scores are usually rounded to the nearest whole number rather than being expressed with decimal places and as with the Sten scale means and standard deviations of groups of scores are calculated with decimal places.

T Scores

The T scale is a very useful way of interpreting test scores that is again based on a transformation of raw scores converted into z scores. It has a mean of 50 and a standard deviation of 10. From our knowledge of the normal distribution we know, therefore, that scores below 40 are seen as below average and scores above 60 above average. Once again we can convert any raw score by calculating its z score and putting it into the linear transformation formula below with 50 and 10 substituted.

$$T = (z_s \times 10) + 50$$

Usual arithmetic calculations are permitted on T scores.

'Deviation IQ'

The 'Deviation IQ' Scale has a mean of 100 and a standard deviation of 15 (in very rare cases you may find some authors quoting an SD of 16 or 24 but this is unusual). It is most important that the IQ scale should only be used with tests that measure intelligence as considerable confusion could be caused if, say, scores from a mechanical ability test were presented in this way.

Unlike the other scales we can only transform raw scores drawn from a general population to produce meaningful deviation IQs as the convention is that the mean of general population IQ is 100. The method of conversion remains the same however. A raw score is transformed into a z score and inserted into the linear transformation formula with 100 and 15 used for mean and SD. The formula is:

$$IQ = (z_s \times 15) + 100$$

Reversing transformations

Sometimes given a standard score such as a T Score we want to convert this back to a z score. We may want to do this so that we can then go on and derive another standard score, for example, a Sten. To do this we use the following formula:

$$z_s = \frac{t_s - \overline{X}_s}{SD}$$

Where t_s is the standard score (T, Sten, Stanine etc.) that we want to convert into a z score.

So if we have a T score (t_s) of 60 and knowing that a T Scale has a Mean ($\overline{X}_s$) of 50 and an *SD* of 10 we can derive the z score thus:

$$z_s = \frac{60-50}{10}$$

$z_s = 1$

To convert from Sten or Stanine scales simply substitute the relevant mean and SD.

Percentiles

Percentiles are a very useful way of getting over to a test taker how well they have done. They simply tell you where your score would be placed when compared with 100 others. So if you had a percentile of 80 you would expect 79 people in 100 to have done worse than you. A percentile of 10 would mean 9 people in 100 would have scored worse.

It is important to note that unlike the other methods of making a raw test score meaningful that have been discussed you cannot carry out some of the basic arithmetic operations on percentile scores. As the percentile scale does not have equal intervals between scores (the difference between 1st and 2nd percentile is not the same as 50th and 51st for example) you cannot have a mean or standard deviation of a group of percentile scores.

Unlike the standard scales, percentiles are arrived at using tables of the proportion of area under the normal distribution. Below is a very small section of such a table. The dashes in the table represent intermediate values of z that can range from 0.00 to beyond 4.00.

z	Area between mean and z	Area beyond z
0.00	0.0	.50
–	–	–
1.00	.34	.16
–	–	–
2.00	.48	.02

Let us see how we can derive percentiles from a table such as this. Starting with the simplest example a z score of 1.00, if we look at the table we see that for a z score of 1.0 given in the first column, the second column 'Area between mean and z' gives us the proportion of .34. What is not included in this is the proportion of the area below the mean. We know that in a normal distribution .50 or 50 per cent of our distribution is below the mean so we need to add that to the .34 to obtain the total percentage of scores falling below our z score in this case a proportion of 0.84. To convert this to a percentage and hence percentile score we simply multiple by 100, i.e., 84 per cent. We can, therefore, state that this score is at the 84 percentile. (Note this is sometimes abbreviated to %ile.)

If we have a z score of 0 we know that this is the mean of the z scale so 50% of our normal distribution will fall above this point. If we look at the table we see that the second column 'Area between mean and z' gives us the proportion of .0. We know that .50 or 50 per cent of our distribution is below the mean so we add that to the 0 to obtain the proportion of .50. To convert this to a percentage and hence percentile score we again simply multiple by 100, i.e. 50 per cent.

Things become a little more complicated when we have a negative z score. Take the example of a z score of −2.00. Our table gives only positive z scores. However knowing that any negative z score indicates a score below the mean we can use the third column in the table 'Area beyond z' to tell us what proportion of the scores are below our z score. This is really the size of the 'tail' of the more extreme scores and as a normal distribution is symmetrical, that is the half above the mean is the same shape as the half below the mean. We can use the number in the third column to give us the proportion of cases below our score − in this case .02 or 2 per cent.

Completing the Unit 2 Competency Assessments

Let us now look at how all this fits in with the BPS competencies and the answers that you may have to come up with in the assessment that you will be required to do.

2.1   Depict graphically how a sample of test scores accumulates at different points throughout the range of ability covered by the test

Using the following data construct a histogram or frequency polygon of the scores.

Verbal reasoning raw scores from 33 test takers

38
42
21
38
39
38
37
41
46
36
21
27
27
38
31
47
43
33
40
34
42
18
32
36
30
41
33
33
35
36
36
28
29

It should end up looking something like this if you draw a histogram with data grouped in fives.

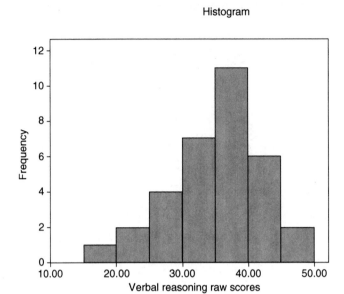

This is an example of *positive* skew.

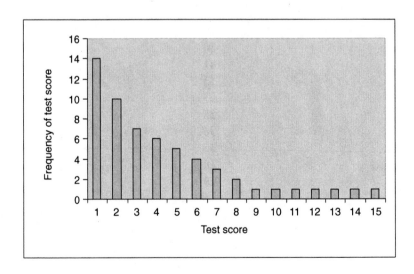

This is an example of *negative* skew.

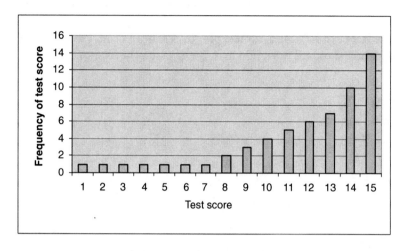

2.2 Undertake calculations to convey how much variation there is amongst a set of test scores

Work out the standard deviation of the above scores.

SD = 6.93

2.3 Describe how alternative ways of expressing the average of a set of test scores (mean, median or mode) are affected by their distribution throughout the range of scores

There are three ways of expressing the average or central tendency of a set of scores, the *mean*, *median* and *mode*.

Using the same data calculate the *mean*, *median* and *mode* and *standard deviation* of these scores.

Mean = 34.73
Median = 36
Mode = 36 and 38
SD = 6.93

2.4 Describe the relationship between the standard error of the mean of a sample of scores and the size of the sample

As the size of the sample increases the standard error of the mean decreases. In other words as the sample size gets closer to the population size, the more confident we can be that our sample mean is a good approximation of our population mean.

The Standard Error of the Mean is a statistic that allows us to calculate how confident we can be that a given sample mean represents the population mean.

We test 6 students and our test produces a mean of 10. We estimate our population standard deviation as 4. So by using the formula:

$$SE_{mean} = \frac{SD}{\sqrt{N}}$$

$$SE_{mean} = \frac{4}{\sqrt{6}}$$

$$SE_{mean} = \frac{4}{2.45}$$

$$SE_{mean} = 1.63$$

2.5   Explain how variation among a standardization sample of test scores and their mean can be used to determine the level of confidence that we can have in people's scores on that test

Variation among a standardization sample of test scores and their mean can be used to calculate the levels of confidence that we can have in people's scores on a test, for example, the 68 per cent and 96 per cent confidence limits.

If we look back at the previous calculation of the SE_{mean} i.e. 1.63. we add and subtract this number from our mean, which is 10, we get the 68 per cent confidence limits which are 8.37–11.63.

If we then multiple our SE_{mean} by 1.96 we get 3.19 and we can use that to calculate the 95 per cent confidence limits, which are 6.81–13.19.

2.6   Demonstrate an understanding of the properties of the Normal Distribution and their relevance to measurement in general

If the frequencies of scores on a test are plotted they should ideally produce a normal or bell-shaped distribution. There will be a few people scoring very low scores, a few people scoring very high scores, with most people scoring in between. Because of the mathematical properties of the normal distribution we can determine what proportion of scores will be above and below any given point on the distribution. For example, we know that if our scores are normally distributed 68.26 per cent will fall within the range of ±1 standard deviation either side of the mean.

2.7   Use statistical tables to establish the percentage of cases likely to fall below a particular test score

Using the table below write down the percentage of cases that will fall below z scores of 1, 0, −1 − 1.5.

z	Area between mean and z	Area beyond z
0.00	0.000	0.500
0.25	0.099	0.401
0.50	0.192	0.308
0.75	0.273	0.227
1.00	0.341	0.159
1.25	0.394	0.106
1.50	0.433	0.067
1.75	0.46	0.04
2.00	0.477	0.023
2.25	0.488	0.012
2.50	0.494	0.006
2.75	0.497	0.003
3.00	0.499	0.001

Answers are: 84.1 per cent, 50 per cent, 15.9 per cent and 6.7 per cent.

2.8   Demonstrate how raw test scores can be converted into any of the scales frequently used to measure test performance (for example, percentile scores, z-scores, T-scores etc.)

Using the linear transformation formula complete the following conversions. (Answers in brackets)

Convert a z score of 2.00 to a T score.   (70)

$$T = (2 \times 10) + 50$$

Convert a T score of 20 to a z score.   (−3.00)

$$z_s = \frac{20 - 50}{10}$$

Convert a z score of 1.25 to a Sten score.   (8)

$Sten = (1.25 \times 2) + 5.5$

Convert a Sten score of 7 to a z score.   (0.75)

$$z_s = \frac{7 - 5.5}{2}$$

Convert a z score of −0.50 to a Stanine score.   (4)

$Stanine = (-0.5_s \times 2) + 5$

Convert a Stanine score of 7 to a z score.   (1)

$$z_s = \frac{7 - 5}{2}$$

Rather than the transformation formula a simple table look-up method is sometimes used. This is a lot easier but also a lot less accurate.

z Score	T Score	Sten Score	Stanine Score	Percentile
−2.00	30	1.5	1	2.3
−1.50	35	2.5	2	6.7
−1.00	40	3.5	3	15.9
−0.50	45	4.5	4	30.9
0.00	50	5.5	5	50
0.50	55	6.5	6	69.1
1.00	60	7.5	7	84.1
1.50	65	8.5	8	93.3
2.00	70	9.5	9	97.7

Using the table above complete the following conversions. (Answers in brackets)

Convert a Percentile of 50 to a z score   (0.00)
Convert a z score of 1.50 to a Percentile.   (93.3)
Convert a z score of −1.00 to a T score.   (40)
Convert a T score of 65 to a z score.   (1.5)
Convert a z score of 1.00 to a Sten score   (7.5)
Convert a z score of −1.50 to a Stanine score.   (2)

3

Unit 3: The Importance of Reliability and Validity

This unit looks at how we can objectively judge that a test is good, bad or indifferent. It discusses the important subjects of *Reliability* and *Validity*. Reliability is the extent to which test questions are measuring the same thing and whether a test's measurements are consistent over time. Validity is how well our test measures what it says it measures.

To understand these concepts we must look at a method for measuring the relationship between two sets of numbers – a process called *Correlation*.

Correlation

In everyday life we often observe relationships between things, for example, by and large as peoples' height increases so does their weight. A correlation is the measure of this relationship and the *correlation coefficient* is the statistic that gives a number to it. Correlations have to be worked out on pairs of measures, in our case, scores from the same person. Correlation is also about prediction, predicting one value from another. For example if we know that muscle strength is correlated with sporting success we can predict the level of sporting success of an individual if we know their muscle strength.

Pairs of values taken from the same set of individuals can increase in proportion to each other, in other words, as one value increases so does the other, this is called a *positive correlation* or equally usefully for prediction, as one value increases the other value decreases – a *negative correlation*.

So what type of numbers can we correlate? For our purposes they need to be pairs of measurements taken from the same person. In a wider context, correlations can be calculated between many different pairs of variables, but we are concerned only with data derived from people. The next consideration concerns the accuracy of our measurements. Technically speaking, the data have to be measured on at least an *interval* scale, which means that the divisions between numbers have to be equal. Temperature is an example here as the difference between 0°C and 1°C is the same as between 20°C and 21°C, that is 1°. In addition the numbers need to be roughly normally distributed (see Unit 2). If we are using data from psychological tests then the data are likely to be good enough to use a statistic known as 'Pearson's Product Moment Correlation', named after its inventor Karl Pearson. Lower case 'r' refers to this most commonly encountered correlation coefficient.

You may come across other correlation coefficients from time to time, for example, those that can be used with ranked or what is technically called *ordinal* data. But these need not concern us here, and *Pearson's r* is the only one we will need for the CCET (Level A) certificate.

When confronted with a correlation coefficient what do we look for to understand what it means? First of all we will be interested in the size of the correlation. Correlation coefficients can only range between +1, a perfect positive correlation, and −1, a perfect negative correlation, with 0 indicating no correlation or relationship whatsoever. Using data derived from human beings we never get 1 or −1 correlations but often get them approaching 0! The larger the coefficient (in either a negative or a positive direction) the greater relationship is implied between the pairs of numbers.

There is a further complication, which concerns the likelihood that, due to there being errors in measurement, the correlation we have obtained is not really there or rather could be 0. To check that we have not just been lucky in getting the result we have obtained we need to do one further thing and that is to look up in a table, found in the back of statistics texts, to see if the correlation we have is actually present. We call this 'finding the significance of the correlation'. For this we need to know the number of pairs of numbers we used to calculate the coefficient as well as the size of the coefficient itself. The significance levels given in tables are decimals that express the number of chances as a proportion of 1 that our correlation, accounting for the error in our measurement, overlaps 0. A significance level of 0.05 means that there are 0.05 chances in 1 that our correlation is 0 or to put it another way 5 chances in 100. Conventionally this value is regarded as 'significant', that is, good enough to say that a correlation exists.

It is worthwhile at this point to revisit our discussion of populations and samples found in Unit 2. When we correlate two variables we are usually correlating samples of a population. It follows that the bigger the size of the sample the more representative of the population it is likely to be. A small sample may yield a correlation that is not significant, but in turn this small sample might not be representative of its population in which a significant correlation could exist. To summarize, the larger your sample the more likely it is to represent the population and, therefore, the more likely you can place confidence in your correlation coefficient.

As mentioned above, correlations can be both positive and negative. If a correlation turns out to be negative a minus sign is put in front of the value of the coefficient, for example, −0.45. If the correlation is positive it is not conventional to use a plus sign, for example, 0.76.

Correlation coefficients are statistics that are calculated using formulas. You don't need to do these calculations for the CCET (Level A) certificate: you just need to be able to understand what they mean and their implications for testing.

One way of looking for correlations without actually calculating them is to draw a special type of graph called a scattergram. There are two reasons for doing this, the first is to estimate the correlation between our two measures and the second and perhaps more useful is to visually inspect our data for problems such as extreme scores, or 'outliers' as they are technically known, which could affect a calculated correlation coefficient and perhaps give an impression of a relationship which is not there. Here are some examples of scattergrams that reflect some values of correlation coefficients.

Perfect positive correlation r = 1.0

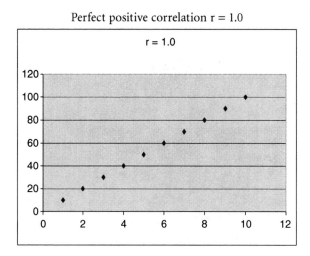

Perfect negative correlation r = −1.0

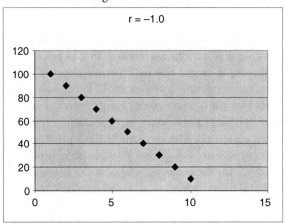

No correlation r = 0.0

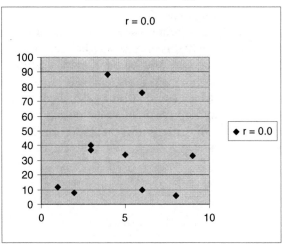

Correlation r = 0.7

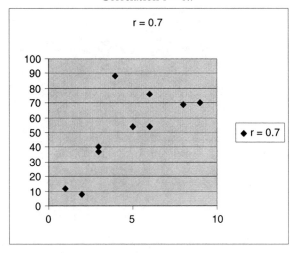

Here is what can happen if you have some extreme numbers or outliers in your data:

Effects of an outlier

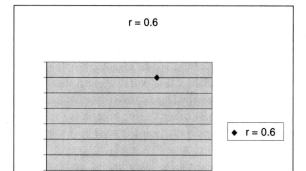

Although it is fairly clear that there is no relationship between the two sets of numbers the extreme score produces a calculated correlation coefficient of 0.6!

Although quite often we are not concerned with making a prediction there is a convention when drawing scattergrams to use the vertical line, technically known as the *Y Axis*, for the quantity that you are going to predict and the horizontal line, known as the *X Axis*, as the measure from which you want to predict it.

An important reason for understanding what correlation and correlation coefficients are all about is to be able to interpret the next two topics to be discussed – reliability and validity, both of which are measured by the correlation coefficient.

Reliability is related to the correlation between the scores of individuals on two halves of a test, or on the scores of individuals who have taken a test twice. Validity is the correlation between test scores and a measure of the quality you are trying to assess.

Reliability

For a test to yield a useful score it must have two qualities, it must be *reliable* and *valid*. Here we will introduce the concept of what it is for a test to be reliable. *Reliability* is concerned with how accurate a test score is. In making physical measurements we can usually rely on our measuring instrument to measure the same time and time again. Things are not quite as simple when it comes to psychological tests however, these give less perfect measurements. A test score, sometimes called an *obtained score*, is seen as having an *error* component. How large this error is is reflected in the reliability of the test and is indicated by its *Reliability Coefficient*. Reliability coefficients should be treated like correlations, with high reliability reflected in a high reliability coefficient approaching +1. In general, reliability of 0.7 or above is usually considered acceptable. It is worth noting that although psychological tests are acknowledged by their constructors to have error, this error is likely to be much less than other testing methods such as conventional examinations. Another important point is that as a reliability coefficient can be calculated and the amount of error can be estimated and allowed for, with conventional measures this is an unknown quantity.

There is more than one type of reliability. The first mentioned in this element is *inter-rater reliability* and is encountered when two or more judges measure the same quality. As you might expect judges disagree, so if you correlate one judge's measurements with another's you will find the degree to which they are in agreement and that is the *inter-rater reliability*.

The second type of reliability mentioned in the competencies is *internal consistency* and this is probably the most often quoted reliability. It is a measure of whether each question in a test measures the same thing. There are various ways of calculating this figure but the one you are most likely to encounter is *Cronbach's alpha*. Other, older, possible measures such as Kuder-Richardson KR20 and KR21 and Rulon may also be quoted.

All of these statistics do the same job; they effectively split up the test in various ways and correlate combinations of questions together, for example, odd with even, first half of the test with second half. Because there is a splitting of the test items this type of reliability is sometimes referred to as *split-half reliability*. Internal consistency is a useful measure of reliability that is relatively easy for a constructor to produce as it requires only one sitting of the test, however it does not tell us anything about its reliability over time, an important quality that will now be discussed.

A ruler measuring a centimetre one day will measure the same centimetre the next day. Even in the case of a physical measurement, however, this is not strictly true. If we measure the centimetre on a hot day and then on a cold day the ruler will have contracted on the cold day and we will get a very slightly different reading. This effect in a test is more marked. Due to a variety of reasons tests do not give the same readings from day to day even though they may be trying to measure a quality that is unchanging.

Things are further complicated by the fact that in education qualities often do change over a relatively short period so it is not possible to say if the error is due to test error or an accurate reflection of real change.

If we expect what we are trying to measure is a stable quantity then there is another form of reliability that will interest us. *Test-retest reliability* tells us how stable our measurement is over time, assuming that what we are measuring hasn't changed. This type of reliability requires a group of test takers to sit the same test twice. The two attempts are then correlated and this gives us the *Test-retest reliability coefficient*, an indication of how consistent our measure is over time. The period between the test and re-test is variable and determined by the nature of the test and may range between days and months. There is a potential problem with this type of reliability and it is particularly acute if the test and re-test are close together. Here there is a danger of responses from the first test being remembered and reproduced in the re-test leading to an artificially high result. To avoid this some test constructors produce what are variously called *alternate*, *equivalent* or *parallel forms* of the same test. These are two tests measuring the same quality that have been demonstrated to be the same in what they measure and look like, the only difference being is that they use different questions. Remembering your answers from the first test does not help you when doing the second form. Correlating the performance on these two tests produces *alternate*, *equivalent* or *parallel form* reliability. This is useful if we want to know how stable our measurement is over shorter periods of time.

Validity

It is possible, but unlikely, to have a near perfectly reliable test that doesn't measure anything useful. Reliability is only part of the story of what constitutes a good test, we must also establish that the test measures what we want it to measure, and this is *validity*. As with reliability there are several types of validity and we need to know about four of them – *face*, *content*, *construct domain* and *criterion-related*.

- *Face validity* is essentially 'does the test look as if it measures what it says it measures?' We should rightly conclude that this is not a sound basis for judging the value of a test. However there are circumstances where the *acceptability* of a test to a test taker is compromised because it doesn't look as though it measures anything sensible. There is a danger that in such cases the test is not taken seriously.

- *Content validity* is concerned with the degree to which the test questions fairly represent what the test is intended to measure. For example a test of arithmetic that misses out questions on division would not be content valid.
- *Construct validity* is the degree to which a test measures the underlying concept it sets out to measure. It is often arrived at by correlating the scores of people on a test for which construct validity is being sought with those of a test that is taken as a 'benchmark'.
- *Criterion-related validity* is of two types, *concurrent* and *predictive*. In each case we are trying to establish a relationship between a *criterion* which is a less convenient assessment of the thing we are trying to measure or predict with our test. *Concurrent validity* is when we measure the criterion at the same time as the test is taken. *Predictive validity* is when we correlate our test with a criterion that is taken at a later date. As the name suggests predictive validity is when we are trying to predict something in the future.

Completing the Unit 3 Competency Assessments

3.1   Explain the notion of correlation as a measure of the degree of relationship between two measures. What types of data can be correlated? Why is it important in psychological testing?

Correlation is the statistical way of demonstrating a relationship between pairs of measurements. The Pearson's Product Moment Correlation is the name given to the correlation coefficient most usually calculated; it is denoted by the lower case r. The data used to calculate a correlation must be in pairs and derived from the same person, the measurements must be on an interval scale and be roughly normally distributed.

It is important in psychological testing as it forms the basis for the measurement of reliability and validity of tests.

3.2   Define the conditions under which correlation is maximized (both positively and negatively) and minimized

If a score increases on one measure as it increases on another a positive correlation is indicated. If one measure increases as the other decreases then there is a negative correlation. The correlation coefficient is the statistic that is calculated to give the strength of the relationship and is a number that can range from +1, indicating a perfectly positive relationship to −1, a perfectly negative relationship, through 0, no relationship at all.

3.3   Provide reasonable rough estimates of the correlation
coefficients represented by the following examples of
various bivariate scattergrams

Scattergram 1 estimate r = 0.8

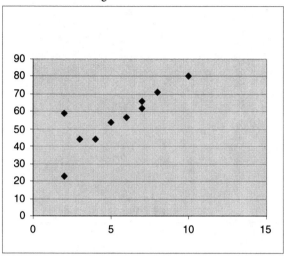

Scattergram 2 estimate r = −0.05

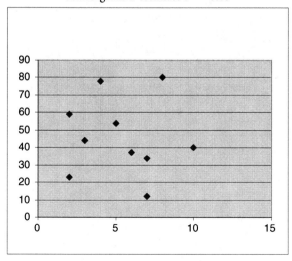

Scattergram 3 estimate r = 0.3

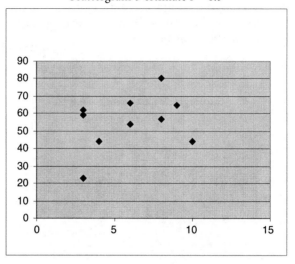

Scattergram 4 estimate r = −0.8

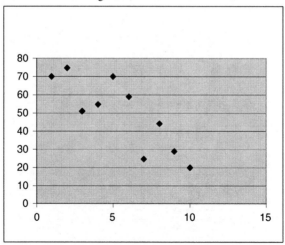

Scattergram 5 estimate r = 0.5

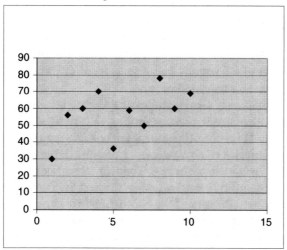

Scattergram 6 estimate r = 0.4

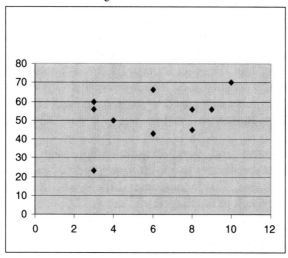

3.4 Explain in outline the methods of estimating reliability (inter-rater reliability, internal consistency, test-retest, same or alternate form) and describe their relative pros and cons

Inter-rater reliability refers to the degree of agreement between judges. It is needed when two or more people are rating something like a person's behaviour and you want reassurance that they are making the same judgements. It is not usually an issue when psychological tests are used as a standardized test should minimize this element of judgement.

Internal consistency is a measure of whether each question in a test is measuring the same thing. It is usually expressed as the statistic Cronbach's alpha which is interpreted like a correlation coefficient with values in excess of 0.7 usually being considered as indicating acceptable levels of agreement between questions.

Test-retest reliability demonstrates the degree to which a test yields stable measurements over time, assuming that what is being measured does not change. It involves the same set of test takers sitting the same test twice with an interval of days, weeks or months in between the sittings, depending on the nature of the test. The two sets of scores are correlated. This is a useful indication of whether the test is likely to suffer from changes over time. However, if the two sittings are close together there is a danger that an artificially high reliability will be obtained because people will be able to remember their responses from the first test and simply reproduce them at the second sitting.

Parallel, equivalent or alternate form reliability also tells us something about a test's stability over time. It uses two versions of the same test which are demonstrated to be psychometrically equivalent except the questions are different, that is, they measure the same thing in the same way using different questions. Test takers sit one version or form of the test one day and the other form of the test at another time and the two sets of scores are correlated. This type of reliability has the advantage that shorter periods can be used to separate test and retest and remembering your responses on the first test will not help you fill in the second one.

Both test-retest and parallel/equivalent/alternate form reliability require the test constructer to get the same group of people together for two testing sessions. This is sometimes difficult and in consequence the one sitting approach of internal consistency has become more favoured.

3.5 Describe and illustrate the distinctions between face, content, construct domain and criterion-related validity

Face validity refers to whether the test looks as though it measures what it says it measures or a reliance on a reassurance from a test constructor not backed up by statistical evidence. Face validity should not be used as a justification for using a test but sometimes tests that lack face validity have problems of acceptability when it comes to the test taker. Lack of motivation could occur if a test appears to measure nothing related to the purpose of testing.

Content validity is an indication of whether a test covers all the aspects of what it purports to measure. For example a test of Asian geography which only asked questions about India would not fairly represent the domain of Asian geography and would not be content valid.

Construct validity. A construct is the underlying concept that the test is trying to measure. It is often arrived at by correlating the scores of people on a test for which construct validity is being sought, with those of a test that is taken as an authoritative and accepted measure.

Criterion-related validity. There are two types of criterion-related validity, concurrent and predictive. Concurrent validity is where we correlate a test scores with criterion scores measured at the same time. Predictive validity is where we want to show that a test score can predict something in the future, for example, academic success.

4

Unit 4: Deciding when Psychological Tests Should or Should Not be Used as Part of an Assessment Process

Unit 4 of the CCET (Level A) builds upon the three preceding units and requires assessees to be aware of issues relating to test selection and equal opportunities and fairness in testing. Assessees are required to be able to demonstrate that they are able to select appropriately tests of attainment, ability and personal/social development, taking into account the effects of age, gender, cultural or ethnicity, ability range, attainment level, special educational needs, and any possible practice effects resulting from repeated test administration, together with the requirements of Equal Opportunities, Race Relations, Sex Discrimination and Disability Discrimination legislation. We shall examine each of these issues in turn.

Test Selection

This Unit follows on from Unit 1 and assumes that you have already identified the assessment need and that test use is appropriate. So, what factors need to be considered when selecting a test to use?

First, what you do want the test to measure:

- General, or specific ability (for example, to develop a profile of the learner's cognitive strengths and areas of relative difficulties)?
- Attainment or achievement in a specific domain, such as reading, spelling or number?

- The pupil's learning style, social competence, self-concept or self-esteem, motivation (for example, to gain an understanding of emotional factors that may be contributing to a learning difficulty or to social, emotional or behavioural problems)?

Next, what type of test will answer your assessment question(s):

- A norm-referenced test?
- A criterion-referenced test or diagnostic test?
- A curriculum-based test? or
- A dynamic assessment test?

If a norm-referenced test is to be used, consider the following:

- *Date of publication*: Test takers' performances in standardized tests show upward trends from generation to generation which have been attributed to factors such as education, better nutrition and to other cultural and societal influences. This is referred to as the 'Flynn Effect', after a 1987 study by Flynn, which revealed substantial increases in IQ scores of the order of 5 to 25 points across 14 countries over a 30 to 40 year period. In consequence, the more recently standardized a test is, the more likely it is to be representative of the present population, as older norms may over-estimate the test taker's level of performance. This is why it is important that test norms should be updated from time to time, and why the accompanying documentation should include information about the details of the standardization sample[1] and the dates when the standardization was carried out. Unfortunately, there is no hard and fast criterion for determining when a given test should be re-standardized. But as a rule of thumb, it seems to us that test norms should be no more than 10 years old for a test of attainment and no more than 15 years for a test of ability, although other writers, such as Salvia and Ysseldyke (2004, p. 115) argue for 7 years as the maximum life of achievement tests.
- *Norms*: What type of scale of measurement does the test use (for example, ordinal, or rank-ordered, or equal interval, which is the most commonly used in educational tests)? How many participants are in the norm group? How was the norm group selected and how representative are they of the population from which they were sampled in regard to gender, ethnicity and disabilities? Are any systematic differences between demographic groups reported (for example, females scoring higher than males, or vice versa) and how have these been dealt with?

For all types of test, consider the following:

- *Administration time*: The longer the administration time, the greater the likelihood that the test taker may become tired or bored and lose concentration. Conversely, if the test is too short, it may be less reliable, as in general, the more items in a test, the higher its reliability.
- *Design of the test*: Is the format and design of the test attractive to test takers, relevant and appropriate for the purpose of the assessment and for the characteristics of the test taker(s) in regard to age, developmental level, gender, ethnicity? Are there any practice items to help the test taker understand what is required of him/her and to help them deal with test anxiety? If the test requires the presentation of materials, are these convenient for the test user to handle and to store safely (for example, in any provided test case)? Could they be dangerous to a young test taker (for example, are they small enough to swallow)? Can they be cleaned if mouthed by a test taker? Are the test forms for recording the test taker's responses well-designed and easy to use?
- Are the *items*: (a) appropriately graded (for example, if items are too coarsely graded, then the score for one item would account for a large increase in a derived score such as a standard score and one slip on the part of the test taker could make a marked difference to their final overall score); and (b) attractive for the test taker?
- *Rationale for item selection*: Was the selection of the items used in the test informed by any underlying theory or by a task analysis? Although some specialized personality tests, such as the Eysenck Personality Questionnaire (Eysenck and Eysenck, 1975) and the Myers-Briggs Type Indicator (Myers and McCauley, 1985), and some ability tests, such as the Cognitive Assessment System (Naglieri, 1999), are based upon an underlying psychological theory, many tests are based upon a task analysis of the component skills that underpin the behaviours of interest. Thus, for example, the Cognitive Abilities Test (Lohman *et al.*, 2003) is based upon verbal, quantitative and nonverbal tasks known to be predictive of subsequent school achievement, and the Neale Analysis of Reading Ability – Revised (Neale, 1997) is based upon a task analysis of reading ability that identifies three component processes of reading accuracy, reading comprehension and rate of reading.
- *Adequacy of directions/training required to administer and score the test*: Is the layout of the test administrator's manual clear? Are the instructions clear (for example, in regard to establishing basal and ceiling levels, and in how to score ambiguous responses), and is any specialized training required?
- *Reliability* (for example, inter-rater; internal consistency; split-half; test-retest; alternate, equivalent or parallel form): How reliable is the

test? This will depend upon how the test results will be used. But in general, tests used for screening and for measuring learning style, social competence, self-concept or self-esteem or motivation should have a reliability coefficient of at least 0.70, and preferably 0.80, and tests of attainment and ability a reliability coefficient of at least 0.80, and preferably 0.90, based upon sample sizes of at least 30 in all cases. Some test authors utilize a *delayed, alternate form* design whereby two alternate forms of a test are administered with a time interval in between and a different form used for each administration. This provides a single reliability coefficient, which estimates both time sampling and content sampling sources of error (see Urbina, 2004, p. 134).

- *Validity* (for example, face; content; construct; criterion-related): What evidence is provided in the test manual for the validity of the test? Content validity is clearly important in the case of attainment tests, but the accompanying documentation for ability tests may also provide information about construct validity, as well as criterion-related validity, either in the form of concurrent validity or as predictive validity.
- Is any advice provided in the manual regarding the impact of possible *practice effects* arising from the test being re-administered? Is there a recommended minimum period which should elapse before the test is re-administered? Are alternate or parallel forms of the test available to minimize practice effects?
- *Comments regarding fairness*: Are there any restrictions on areas of use? Are any modifications of test items or procedures for administrations suggested in the manual to meet the needs of test takers with disabilities or from different ethnic or cultural groups?
- Is an *individual* or *group-administered* test the most appropriate means of gathering data to answer the assessment question(s)?

Note that a combination of test approaches may be required to address assessment needs fully. For example, a norm-referenced test would provide confirmation of a problem and an indication of its severity, and a diagnostic test used as a follow-up would provide information about strengths and weaknesses, which could inform the instruction provided to the learner.

Equal Opportunities

Tests are designed to differentiate, but at the end of the day, no instrument can be 100 per cent valid and 100 per cent reliable in all circumstances. Even if we select appropriate tests to answer our assessment questions, it is possible that we may use the tests or results incorrectly to the disadvantage of the test taker. Issues of possible bias, fairness and equal opportunity are, therefore, central to good practice in the use of tests and in the interpretation of test results.

It is useful to draw a distinction between *bias* and *fairness* in regard to test use. We discussed the problems of bias in Unit 1, in regard to whether items or other psychometric properties of a test may have a specific bias to the advantage or disadvantage of demographic groups. As we have seen, demographic groups do score differently on certain tests, although some of these differences are specific to particular test instruments and can be reduced by means of training. But a test can be used fairly or unfairly, and even an unbiased test could be used unfairly to support decision making about a test taker. For example, if a test user decided to extrapolate the findings from a reading test to draw conclusions about the general cognitive abilities of the test takers, then this would disadvantage able students with literacy problems, such as those with dyslexia. Issues of fairness in test use thus centre around test selection and the nature of the decisions made on the basis of test scores.

The BPS *Code of Good Practice for Educational Testing*[2] (BPS, 2004d) advises test users to ensure that they 'give due consideration to factors such as gender, ethnicity, age, disability and special needs, educational background and level of ability in using and interpreting the results of tests'. The CCET (Level A) operationalizes this by requiring test users to comply with relevant national legislation in this area, which in England, Scotland and Wales[3] currently includes:

- The Race Relations Act 1976 and the Race Relations Amendment Act 2000;
- The Sex Discrimination Act 1975 and the Sex Discrimination Amendment Act 1986;
- The Disability Discrimination Act 1995; and
- The Special Educational Needs and Disability Act 2001.

These Acts make it unlawful to discriminate, or treat a person less favourably, on the grounds of race, gender or disability in regard to employment, training and education and in the provision of services. Test use, and assessment more generally, both fall within the legislation.[4] Two forms of discrimination are identified in regard to race and gender:

- *Direct discrimination*, when someone is subject to unfair treatment because of their race or sex, even if this unintentional and is not motivated by prejudice; and

• *Indirect discrimination*, when conditions which cannot be justified, and which appear to apply to everyone, in fact discriminate against individuals on grounds of race or sex.

In the case of those for whom English is an additional language, any test administered in English is not only a test of the ability or skill under consideration, but also a test of either oral or written language due to the demands of accessing and understanding the test instructions and making an appropriate response. Even those who are bilingual may have differences in their facility with English and their other language(s), perhaps processing English more slowly, or 'code-switching' (Hoff, 2001) – mixing vocabulary from the two different languages, which could affect performance in timed tasks. Further, test takers from other cultures may respond differently to the social demands of test situations, for example, not elaborating upon their responses, even when asked to do so. While it may be appropriate in some circumstances to translate items into the test taker's first language, this will not produce a version of the instrument which is equivalent to the original in terms of content, reliability or validity. But a test user who can use the test taker's first language or who can access the services of an interpreter may be better placed to ensure that any test instructions are explained clearly, and to prompt and elicit responses. Some tests also have separate norms for use with pupils for whom English is an additional language (see Whetton (1997) for supplementary norms for The British Picture Vocabulary Scale (Second Edition) (Dunn *et al.*, 1997)).

The UK Disability Discrimination Act 1995 defines disability as 'a physical or mental impairment, which has a substantial and long term adverse affect on a person's ability to carry out normal day-to-day activities'. Conditions such as epilepsy, AIDS, asthma, diabetes and muscular dystrophy are covered by the Act, together with motor impairments, visual and hearing impairments, learning difficulties (including specific learning difficulties such as dyslexia), and clinically recognized mental health conditions. The Disability Discrimination Act 1995 was primarily intended to address discrimination against disabled people in employment but has been amended more recently by the Special Educational Needs and Disability Act 2001 which is designed to prevent discrimination by ensuring that both disabled and non-disabled persons have equal opportunities in regard to their access to education. Assessment, and by extension, test use, are specifically covered by this Act, which identifies two duties for those working in educational settings:

1   Not to treat disabled pupils and students less favourably for a reason related to their disability, unless it can be shown that this has been

done for a 'material and substantial' reason which is significant enough to justify discrimination; and

2   To take 'reasonable steps' to avoid putting disabled pupils and students at a substantial disadvantage relative to their non-disabled peers.

Further details of the implications of the above Act may be found in the Code of Practice produced by the Disability Rights Commission (2002).

There are a number of sources of additional information relating to test use with those who are disabled. The SHL Group (2000) and ASE (2000) have both produced helpful sets of downloadable guidelines for testing people with disabilities which, while geared towards occupational testing, also contain advice that is relevant for test use in educational settings. The BPS (2003, p. 12) also provides the following advice for test takers in regard to disability:

> If you or your dependant has a disability and feel that you may need special conditions, it is important that this is brought to the notice of the person responsible for the testing as soon as the testing session has been arranged. This will give maximum time for the assessor to check what special requirements can be provided and what arrangements can be made.

It is important to ensure that any decisions about adaptations and accommodations to meet disability needs are made by those who know the test taker after consulting any relevant policy guidelines that are available. Details of any adaptations and the reasons for making them should also be clearly documented.

There are a number of ways in which tests developed for use with the general population may be adapted to make them accessible for individuals with disabilities:

- We can modify the medium in which the test instructions and questions are presented. Thus, large print, Braille, tape-recorded instructions, or having written instructions read aloud may be helpful to an individual with a visual impairment. Similarly, in the case of someone with a hearing impairment (particularly a pre-lingual hearing impairment), an interpreter who can sign the instructions and test items can help to make a test more accessible.
- We can modify the method used by the test taker to record his/her response. A tape recorder, typewriter or word processor, Braille writer,

or the use of a scribe could make a test accessible to individuals with a broad range of physical, motor and sensory impairments.

- Additional time could be made available, with extended time limits determined empirically.
- Test content could be modified to reduce sources of bias (for example, in the case of an individual with a visual impairment, items utilizing pictorial content could be left out).
- We can ensure wheelchair access, comfortable seating and tables of the correct size and height and adequate lighting.

On a practical level, many of these modifications will preclude group administration of tests. More importantly, they will affect the reliability and validity of the scores obtained, and test takers will not be able to rely upon the values stated in the manual based upon a general population using standardized procedures. Changes in medium and mode of response may also alter what is being measured by the test in terms of underlying constructs and cognitive processes, hence the importance of validation studies of test use with individuals with disabilities.

Section 2.3 of The International Test Commission's *International Guidelines for Test Use* (2000, pp. 19–20) (downloadable from www. intestcom.org or from the BPS Psychological Testing Centre www. psychtesting.org.uk, and reproduced in Appendix 8) details the steps that test users should take to ensure that tests are used fairly: (a) with individuals differing in terms of gender, cultural background, education, ethnic origin or age; (b) when testing in more than one language (which may also include sign language); and (c) when using tests with people with disabilities.

The ITC Guidelines highlight the importance of selecting tests that are unbiased and appropriate for groups being assessed, and which minimize any effects of group differences not relevant to the main purpose of assessment. They also stress the importance of seeking advice from relevant experts regarding the potential effects of disabilities upon test performance; of consulting the test takers themselves and giving consideration to their needs, views and wishes; of making adequate arrangements for administering tests to those with disabilities or for non-native English speakers; of considering alternative assessment procedures (including more suitable tests) where possible, rather than modifying tests; of tailoring any necessary modifications to the nature of the disability while minimizing effects upon the validity of the scores; and of reporting the nature of any modifications to those who interpret or will make decisions based upon the test scores.

In conclusion, it is worth reiterating that tests form only a part of an assessment procedure and that the legislation discussed above relates to the whole process of assessment. Avoiding the use of tests *per se* is not a way of avoiding problems of fairness, indeed, as we have seen, in some circumstances, the use of tests may be the most appropriate, and hence defensible, assessment approach. But if a test is to be used, it is important to ensure that:

- there is a clear rationale for choosing a specific test for a specific purpose;
- the manual and the materials are carefully examined before use for possible sources of bias and to see whether the test authors recommend any linguistic modifications for test takers whose first language is not English or modifications or accommodations for test takers with a disability; and
- use of tests is carefully monitored.

The BPS also produces a series of Educational Test reviews which are available online from the Psychological Testing Centre (http://www/ psychtesting.org.uk/cfm/). These provide useful information, which can inform a decision as to whether to use a particular test.

Completing the Unit 4 Competency Assessments

We shall now see how this fits in with the BPS competences and the answers for the assessments that you will be required to undertake for the CCET (Level A). Both short-term and cumulative assessments are required for Unit 4. Short-term assessments will be discussed in this unit, and the requirements for the cumulative assessment will be discussed in Unit 8. The examples provided utilize short note answers, together with simulation exercises from a test publisher's catalogue. However, your assessor may provide you with case studies or scenarios and ask you to provide a commentary. Assessors may require evidence of mastery across a range of attainment, ability and tests of personal/social development, but the principles are the same as in the examples that follow, which focus on attainment tests. Note that '4.1' below refers to the assessment for Unit 4 Element 1 and '4.2' to Unit 4 Element 2 and so on. Recall that the competences are shown in full in Appendix 1, and *Guidance for Assessors* may be found in Appendix 2.

Examples of How the BPS Competences Might be Assessed and Answered

4.1   With regard to the case study scenario provided, use test publishers' catalogues, specimen sets or other reference materials to identify one or more instruments potentially suitable for answering the assessment questions raised in the case study

Example of the type of case scenario that might be provided by an assessor: John is aged 10 years 8 months and is a Year 6 pupil in a large urban primary school, within a socially disadvantaged area. He is the second of three children, all of whom live with their mother, who is separated from the father. John is keeping up with his number work in class, but he is struggling to cope with reading and written language work at a Year 3 level, although he contributes reasonably well to classroom discussion when the topic is of interest to him. There is concern about how John is likely to cope with the transition to secondary school in 8 months time.

Assessment questions which arise from the above case scenario and for which the use of a test would be appropriate include[5]:

1   How do John's attainments in reading compare with those of pupils of the same age?
2   Does John have difficulties in both reading accuracy and reading comprehension or in only one of these subskill areas?
3   How do John's phonemic decoding skills compare with his sight word reading?

Suitable instruments for addressing the above questions with a pupil of John's age would include the Neale Analysis of Reading Ability (NARA II) (Second Revised British Edition) (M.D. Neale, 1997) (further details from http://www.nfer-nelson.co.uk) and the Test of Word Reading Efficiency (TOWRE) (J.K. Torgesen, R. Wagner & C. Rashotte, 1999) (further details from http://www.harcourt-uk.com).

4.2   Identify, for each of the instruments, information in the test manual which relates to the test's rationale, development, reliability, validity, its norms and any specific restrictions or limitations on its areas of use

The NARA II
Rationale: The NARA II is an individually administered oral reading test providing measures of reading rate, accuracy and comprehension for the

6 years to 12 years 11 months age range based upon short, graded passages of text presented in a naturalistic book form, with accompanying illustrations. There are two alternate forms of the test. Additional supplementary diagnostic tests and miscue analysis forms are also provided. Reading rate is assessed by calculating the number of words read by the child per minute, and accuracy is measured by counting the number of errors made in reading aloud. These errors, or 'miscues', can be classified into one of six categories, which are linked to possible strategies used by the child to read unfamiliar words and also to teaching strategies which may be used by the teacher. Comprehension is assessed by means of questions designed to test the young person's understanding of the narrative, sequence of events and ability to recall details and draw inferences. The format of the test, whereby the child reads aloud to an adult, mirrors instructional practice in the classroom and also the experience of many children in their reading at home. It is consistent with Neale's view of reading as a part of the language system which interacts with and serves the developmental and adaptive needs of the child. The NARA II is explicitly based upon a 'trusting relationship' between the test taker and a 'sympathetic' test user. The test user is able to correct the child's oral reading errors as he/she reads (up to a limit specified in the manual) to help maintain comprehension and also the reader's confidence.

Development: The NARA was first published in 1958, revised in 1988 and re-standardized, as the NARA II, in 1996. The original NARA was one of the first reading tests to move away from the use of graded lists of context-free words or single sentences to the use of narrative texts.

Reliability: Measures of alternate form and internal consistency reliability are provided. These are based upon some 360 pupils (an average of 90 at each of the following four age-points: 6:00–7:11; 8:00–9:11; 10:00–11:11; 12:00–12:11) in the case of alternate forms, and upon 1,832 pupils for accuracy for Form 1 (an average of 458 at each of the four age-points) and 1,847 pupils for comprehension for Form 1 (an average of 462 at each of the four age-points). Similar numbers of pupils were involved in determining the internal consistency of Form 2 for accuracy and reliability.

Alternate form reliability was calculated for accuracy (with coefficients ranging from 0.84 to 0.92 across the four age points, with an average of 0.89), comprehension (with coefficients ranging from 0.65 to 0.87, with an average of 0.82) and rate (with coefficients ranging from 0.50 to 0.83, with an average of 0.66).

Internal consistency reliability (Cronbach's coefficient alpha) was calculated for accuracy (with coefficients ranging from 0.82 to 0.88, with an average of 0.86, in the case of Form 1) and comprehension (with coefficients ranging from 0.93 to 0.95, with an average of 0.93, again in the case of Form 1). Similar values are reported for Form 2.

Validity: Evidence of content, criterion-related and construct validity are reported. In regard to content validity, the test requires oral reading and answering comprehension questions and hence may be regard as a valid test of these skills. However, the manual notes that no claims are made for the validity of the instrument as a test of silent reading.

In the case of criterion-related validity, a range of evidence for both concurrent and predictive validity is presented. In the case of concurrent validity, correlations between scores on the revised Australian 1988 revision of the NARA and the Schonell Graded Word Reading Test (Schonell and Goodacre, 1974) and verbal sub-tests of the Wechsler Intelligence Scale for Children – Revised (WISC-R) (Wechsler, 1974) are reported. Correlations of 0.95, 0.88 and 0.76 between the Schonell and the NARA Form 1 scores for accuracy, comprehension and rate of reading respectively are provided in the manual, based upon data from 545 children in Australia. Similar findings are reported for Form 2 scores, based upon 901 children. Correlations between the WISC-R Vocabulary and Similarities verbal sub-test scores and the Revised Australian NARA Form 1 scores ranged from 0.62 and 0.60 in the case of the NARA comprehension scores, from 0.58 and 0.56 in the case of the NARA accuracy scores, and from 0.46 and 0.41 in the case of the NARA rate scores. Slightly higher correlations between these measures were reported in the case of the Form 2 scores, which again were based upon 901 children. Evidence for concurrent validity from a UK population comes from a cited study carried out by Gregory and Gregory (1994), which reported correlations of 0.94 and 0.83 between scores on the 1979 British Ability Scales (Elliott *et al.*, 1979) Word Reading Test and the NARA 1989 revision (Neale *et al.*, 1989) accuracy and comprehension scores respectively. The NARA II was re-standardized with the Phonological Assessment Battery (PhAB) (Frederickson *et al.*, 1997) (see Appendix 5) and also with six scales from the British Ability Scales Second Edition (BAS II) (Elliott, 1997), which provides additional evidence for concurrent validity. The results reveal statistically significant positive correlations between NARA II scores and the BAS II sub-test and composite scores (particularly the General Conceptual Ability score and those involving verbal ability as opposed to spatial ability) and PhAB sub-test scores (particularly the non-word reading and spoonerisms sub-tests).

In the case of predictive validity, data are reported from an unpublished study carried out in Australia by Neale and McKay (1985) using Form 2 of the 1988 revision of the NARA, which examined the correlations between test-retest scores after a one-year interval, from the end of Year

1 until the end of Year 2. The results revealed correlations of 0.73, 0.83 and 0.78 for rate, accuracy and comprehension respectively.

Finally, in regard to construct-related validity, two strands of evidence are presented. First, *age differentiation*, that is, the consistent increases in score with age, which, however, show signs of a ceiling effect between 11 and 12 years, where the passages and questions are not of sufficient difficulty to measure differences in reading between higher achieving older children. The relationship between levels in reading for the National Curriculum for England and Wales and NARA II scores also shows a trend of progressive increase in scores, which levels off at Curriculum Levels 5 and 6 in the case of accuracy and after Level 4 in the case of comprehension, again reflecting a ceiling effect due to a lack of sufficiently challenging items to differentiate older, better readers. Second, the manual provides a summary of findings from a range of studies that demonstrate *group differentiation*, that is, showing that versions of the NARA can accurately distinguish children with reading problems from those whose reading is typical for their age (see Neale, 1997, pp. 65–6).

Norms: The NARA II was standardized in the UK in the last school term of 1996. The target sample for standardization was 4,400 pupils (2,200 for Form 1 and 2,200 for Form 2) from the Year 1 to Year 7 age range from a representative sample of 1,558 schools from across England, Scotland, Wales and Northern Ireland. A total of 3,474 pupils from 610 schools from across England, Scotland, Wales and Northern Ireland took part in the standardization. 1,928 pupils (88 per cent of the target) participated in the standardization of Form 1 and 1,546 (70 per cent of the target) in the standardization of Form 2. The sample was weighted for calculation of the norms to ensure that they were representative of the population in terms of free school meals and GCSE results (in the case of secondary schools). On average, there were 275 pupils at each Year point in the case of Form 1, and 221 in the case of Form 2, with broadly equal numbers of boys and girls. Norms are available for the 6 years to 12 years 11 months age-range. Derived scores for accuracy, comprehension and rate of reading provided comprise: reading age (with 68 per cent confidence band), standardized score (with mean of 100 and standard deviation of 15, together with 68 per cent confidence band), national percentile rank (based upon the pupils in the standardization sample of the same age), and stanines (which report scores in terms of nine bands of values, with each band equal to one-half of a standard deviation, and the mean of the scores being the mid-point of the fifth stanine).

Specific restrictions/limitations on areas of use: The manual (Neale, 1997, p. 3) notes restrictions on use of the NARA II on test takers outside of the age-range 6–12 years, although it does note that the test can be used diagnostically with older pupils and some adults with reading difficulties. It further recommends that the Supplementary Diagnostic Test 3: Graded Spelling should only be used with children above the age of 7 years. There are no additional specific restrictions or limitations on areas of use, although as a test of oral reading, it is assumed that the test taker is able to see the pages of text and associated illustrations and read aloud clearly, which may be a problem for some pupils with a marked visual, speech and language or severe hearing impairment.

The manual identifies five ways in which test results may be used: for planning teaching for an individual child; giving parents information on progress; identifying children with below average performance; identifying teaching and learning issues; and individual diagnosis (for example, examining discrepancies between actual scores on the PhAB and predicted PhAB scores from the NARA II). The manual further recommends that the passages from the Diagnostic Tutor Form can be used to compare a test taker's oral and silent reading comprehension and listening comprehension.

The TOWRE

Rationale: The TOWRE is designed for use across the 6 years to 24 years age range and comprises two sub-tests, *Sight Word Efficiency* (*SWE*), a measure of the test taker's ability to read familiar words provided out of context accurately and fluently (that is, without sounding the letters out), and *Phonemic Decoding Efficiency* (*PDE*), a measure of the test taker's ability to decode pronounceable non-words using knowledge of grapheme–phoneme correspondence. The test is based upon research evidence that emphasizes the importance of accurate word recognition and of good phonemic skills for efficient reading. With this in mind, items are presented with no supporting context to provide a more direct measure of word identification and the scores reflect both the accuracy and the speed with which the test taker can process the items. The authors view the test as a diagnostic assessment which can be used to help identify those who are experiencing difficulties and falling behind in their word reading. The scores from the SWE and PDE sub-tests can be combined into a composite *Total Word Efficiency* (*TWE*) score. There are two alternate forms of the test and advice in the manual of how to alternate these when re-testing.

Development: The test was developed in the US in the late 1990s, with the support of grants from the National Institute of Child Health and Human Development.

Reliability: The manual provides details of alternate-form reliability coefficients (which average 0.93 for the SWE, 0.94 for the PDE and 0.96 for the TWE across the 6–24 years age-range for 1,507 participants), test-retest reliability coefficients (with a range of 0.82 to 0.97 over a two-week period for 72 participants and some variability in the magnitude of the coefficients as a function of the age of the participants), and inter-scorer reliability (0.99, based on two raters scoring 30 completed test forms). Information is also provided regarding the equivalence of the two alternate forms. The average correlations between Forms A and B are 0.93 for SWE and 0.94 for PDE, confirming a high level of equivalence between the two forms of the test.

Validity: The manual provides details of content validity, criterion validity and construct validity. In regard to content validity, the TOWRE provides measures of word reading and of decoding non-words, with the items consisting of words of high frequency of use in English at the beginning of the test and decreasing frequency of use as the test progresses, and non-words which reflect a range of grapheme–phoneme correspondences and which become progressively harder to pronounce. An analysis of differential item functioning in respect of gender and ethnicity reveals relatively low levels of bias, with evidence that group membership (for example, male versus female, African American versus other test takers) accounted for score differences in only a few items (for example, 11 out of a total of 334, in the case of African American versus other test takers).

Turning to criterion validity, in the case of concurrent validity, correlations ranging from 0.92 to 0.94 between the scores on the SWE and the Woodcock Reading Mastery Tests – Revised (Woodcock, 1987) are reported for 125 participants from Grades 1–3 who were at risk of reading failure. The equivalent correlations for the PDE ranged from 0.89 to 0.91. Similar correlations (of 0.89 for SWE and 0.85 for PDE) were reported between the scores on the TOWRE and the Word Attack sub-test scores of the Woodcock tests for 145 participants at the end of Grade 1.

Evidence for predictive validity is presented in the form of correlations between the TOWRE and other measures of reading, with the manual (Torgeson *et al.*, 1999, p. 74) stating that: 'the longitudinal stability of word level reading skills is well known'. The results from a sample of pupils in the US with reading problems revealed stronger correlations between SWE scores and measures of reading rate, accuracy and comprehension (ranging from 0.80 to 0.87) than between PDE scores and the reading measures (which ranged from 0.47 to 0.66). Somewhat lower correlations were observed in the case of 201 randomly selected Grade 5 participants, who did not have particular problems in reading. However, these findings are more akin to concurrent validity than to predictive validity as they do not provide information about the extent to which the TOWRE scores predict performance on measures of reading at a later time.

Evidence for construct validity is presented in the form of age differentiation and group differentiation, with scores on the TOWRE sub-test showing increases over age-intervals and test takers with learning difficulties achieving significantly lower scores than the others in the normative sample. A confirmatory factor analysis also confirmed that SWE and PDE are correlated but nonetheless identifiably separate constructs, which supports the validity of the underlying model of the TOWRE.

Norms: The TOWRE was standardized in the US, with the norms based upon test data gathered between late 1997 and early 1998 on a sample of 1,507 individuals aged between 6 years and 24 years from 30 states. 1,395 participants (701 males and 694 females) were from the 6 years to 17 years school population, but over half of the overall sample consisted of primary school-aged children. 112 adult participants aged from 18 years to 24 years were also included. The sample is highly representative of the general US population in terms of gender, race and ethnicity, disability, residence (urban versus rural), family income and educational attainment of parents. Norms are available for the 6 years to 24 years 11 months age-range. Derived scores for SWE, PDE and TWE comprise standardized scores (mean of 100 and standard deviation of 15, with 68 per cent confidence band), percentile scores, age-equivalent scores and grade equivalent scores. The manual expresses concern about the use of age and grade equivalent scores because they are less accurate than standard scores as a result of the statistical processes used to derive them, and also because of problems in their interpretation.

Specific restrictions/limitations on areas of use: The manual restricts the use of the test to those between the ages of 6 years and 24 years 11 months who can understand the test instructions, produce a response and pass the practice items.

The manual indicates four areas of use for the TOWRE: to monitor growth and development of the efficiency of phonemic decoding and sight word reading skills in young primary school-aged pupils; identifying pupils with problems who require additional instruction in word-reading skills; contributing to the diagnosis of specific reading difficulties in older pupils and in adults; and research into reading. The manual also notes that the alternate use of the parallel forms for retesting will minimize the cumulative effects of practice upon the results. However, the use of both forms is recommended for assessments carried out to determine eligibility for specialized services, to maximize the reliability of the scores obtained.

The manual highlights the problems of successfully using the results from the TOWRE to provide instruction or intervention for pupils with deficits in their phonological processes and problems with attention who do not have high levels of support from home.

4.3   Identify relevant practical considerations, for example:
(a) ease of administration; (b) time required; and
(c) special equipment needed

NARA II

(a)   Administration of the NARA II involves establishing rapport with
      the test taker; explaining what is expected in the assessment; using
      the standardized instructions to introduce the test and to administer
      the Practice Passage; establishing a starting point; administering the
      test passages from the reader provided for the pupil to read aloud
      until a ceiling point is reached; providing prompts where necessary
      according to the instructions in the manual; asking comprehension
      questions at the end of each passage administered; and recording
      the pupil's responses and the time taken to read each passage. The
      instructions in the manual are clear and an accompanying cassette,
      A Guide to Successful Testing, provides further information and
      support for administration and scoring. The materials are also well
      designed and easy to handle and use.

(b)   The test takes around 20 minutes to administer, and around 10
      minutes to score.

(c)   In addition to the manual, reader and an individual record form
      for the test results and a pen, a stopwatch is required for timing.
      The manual also recommends the use of a tape recorder to tape the
      session so that timings and miscues/errors can be checked after
      the test session.

TOWRE

(a)   Administration of the TOWRE involves establishing rapport with the
      test taker; explaining what is expected in the assessment; using the
      standardized instructions to introduce the test and to administer
      the practice list; prompting accordingly if the test taker skips items
      on the practice list or hesitates; administering the test list(s) from the
      card provided for the pupil to read aloud for 45 seconds; providing
      prompts where necessary according to the instructions in the manual;
      scoring the number of items correctly read within 45 seconds. The
      materials are well designed, and the instructions in the manual are
      detailed and clear in regard to administration and scoring.

(b)   The test takes around 5 minutes to administer if only one form is
      used, and some 8 minutes if both forms are administered.

(c)   In addition to the manual, SWE and PDE reading cards, an indi-
      vidual record booklet for the test results, a pencil and a stopwatch
      are required.

4.4   Compare information presented about the test's validity with relevant aspects of the requirements of the assessment and make an appropriate judgement about their fit

The assessment requirements entail valid measures of oral reading rate, accuracy and comprehension and also of phonemic decoding and sight word reading. The NARA II and TOWRE both meet these requirements in terms of content validity. Estimates of concurrent validity are provided in the form of correlations between scores on earlier versions of the NARA with scores on the Schonell Graded Word Reading Test (correlations of 0.95, 0.88 and 0.76 for accuracy, comprehension and rate) and with the BAS Word Reading Test (correlations of 0.94 and 0.83 for accuracy and comprehension respectively). In the case of the TOWRE, correlations with the Woodcock Reading Mastery Tests – Revised ranged from 0.92 to 0.94 in the case of the SWE and from 0.89 to 0.91 in the case of the PDE.

In the case of predictive validity, scores from the 1988 Australian revision of the NARA for rate, accuracy and comprehension show significant levels of correlation with retest scores after a one-year test-retest interval (correlation coefficients of 0.73, 0.83 and 0.78 respectively). The data presented for the TOWRE in regard to predictive validity show the extent to which TOWRE scores are correlated with scores from other reading measures and hence are predictive of them. But it would appear that the scores were all collected at the same time and hence there is no information about how predictive the TOWRE is of performance on these reading measures over a period of time.

Finally, there is evidence of construct-related validity in the form of age differentiation and group differentiation for both the NARA II and the TOWRE and a confirmatory factor analysis which confirms the underlying model of the TOWRE.

In summary, the data presented in the test manuals confirm that the two instruments are valid measures and fit the assessment requirements. However, more up-to-date data regarding concurrent validity for the NARA II rather than earlier versions and data on the predictive validity of the TOWRE over an extended time period would be helpful.

4.5   Examine the norms and make a suitable judgement about their appropriateness in terms of representativeness and sample size

The NARA II and the TOWRE were both standardized on large numbers of participants (3,474 and 1,507 respectively). The NARA has a UK standardization, with weighting to ensure that the norms are representative of the population in terms of social disadvantage and GCSE results. The TOWRE has a US standardization and the sample is highly representative of the US population in regard to gender, race and ethnicity, disability, urban versus rural residence, family income and parents' educational attainment.

The norms for both instruments are based upon adequate numbers of participants at each age-point and are technically appropriate for the purpose of test use here, with the caveat that we do not know the extent to which the derived scores from the TOWRE based upon a US sample are generalizable to test takers in the UK. But note that the assessment question that the TOWRE has been selected to address is concerned with a relative comparison of performance on the SWE and the PDE rather than on the actual standing of the scores in terms of the standardization sample.

4.6   With regard to a specific test: Indicate what restrictions there are on areas of use (for example, age, gender, cultural or ethnic limitations; ability range; attainment level; special educational needs)

The NARA II has restrictions on use in regard to age. The test is designed for use within the specified age-range covered by the norms unless the instrument is being used diagnostically. However, there are no specific limitations cited in the test manual in regard to gender, cultural or ethnic factors, ability range, attainment level or special educational needs, although it may be assumed that the test taker's ability to access the materials, to understand the instructions, produce a response, and pass the practice items are restrictions to use.

However, there are some cultural assumptions within the NARA II passages which may challenge some pupils from different ethnic or cultural backgrounds, and there is also evidence of ceiling effects between 11 and 12 years due to a lack of items that are sufficiently difficult to differentiate between higher achieving older children.

Pupils for whom English is an additional language may also be at a disadvantage for the reasons noted above. Test takers with a visual impairment may also be at a disadvantage in regard to having to read items in a fairly small font and those with a hearing impairment or language disorder may be at a disadvantage in terms of understanding the orally presented instructions and/or in providing a clear verbal response.

Indicate how these restrictions would influence your judgement
as to whether or not to use the test with a test taker
Given the above, the NARA II would not be used with a pupil outside of the specified age-range unless prior information from the pupil, school or parents suggested that it would provide useful diagnostic information, for

example, the use of the supplementary tests or the diagnostic tutor form in the case of an older pupil with reading difficulties. In cases where English is not a first language and/or where the test taker has a disability, consideration would be given to the issue of whether alternative assessment procedures would be more appropriate, following the ITC Guidelines (2000), or to modifications of the test medium, materials or administration.

How might possible practice effects influence the frequency of use of a test to measure progress?
Practice effects are the result of using the same test or alternate forms of a test repeatedly with the same participant. In such circumstances, second scores are generally higher than the first due to the practice provided by the first administration which also reduces uncertainty and anxiety on the part of the test taker. Practice effects are more pronounced when the time interval between the administrations is short, and/or where the test taker learns strategies which he/she is likely to remember and to use again.

In the case of the NARA II, the manual (Neale, 1997, p. 57) provides information about possible practice effects based on retest data from 428 pupils. Around half received Form 1 administered by the school, followed by Form 2 administered by an external assessor, with the other half receiving Form 2 from the school, followed by Form 1 from the external assessor. The results revealed an administration effect, with teachers giving slightly higher scores for accuracy (of around one tenth of a standard deviation), but also an order effect, with the second administration giving slightly lower scores, which runs counter to the expectation that practice improves scores. This would tend to suggest that use of alternate forms of the NARA II minimizes possible practice effects. But no information is provided in the manual about the length of the test/retest interval used and there are no guidelines as to the recommended intervals between re-administrations. However, it is clear that re-administering the test within a short time period will result in increases in scores due to practice effects rather than true progress. There is a need, therefore, to ensure that appropriate time passes between the first and second administration and that parallel forms are used alternately to minimize practice effects.

4.7 Identify to what extent use of the above specimen test meets the requirements of Equal Opportunities, Race Relations, Sex Discrimination and Disability Discrimination legislation

The standardization of the NARA II utilized stratified sampling to ensure broadly equal numbers of males and females. The balance of male and female characters in the narrative passages used in the test was altered in the re-standardization of the NARA II to minimize any perceived sex role stereotyping, although the manual (Neale, 1997, p. 66) notes that there is still a 'very slight male bias in the content'. Girls achieve higher scores than boys for rate and accuracy up until 8:11, although the difference tails off thereafter. The standardization sample was also weighted to ensure that it was representative of low income groups pro rata to their proportion in the population as a whole. However, there is no discussion of issues relating to race, ethnicity or disability in the manual. In contrast, the TOWRE provides norms which are representative of racial, ethnic and disabled groups in the US population as well as gender, and also provides details of alternate form reliability coefficients and an analysis of differential item functioning for gender, racial and ethnic groups. The NARA II attempts to fulfil the requirements of the legislation in force at the time of its development, but future revisions should aim to ensure representativeness in regard to race/ethnicity and disability and to provide information about differential item functioning and any other sub-group differences in relation to gender, low income, race, ethnicity and disability.

Notes

1   'Standardization sample' is the term used for the individuals on whom the test is standardized in terms of the procedures for administration and scoring and the development of the norms. Details of the standardization sample can generally be found in the manual for a test.
2   The *Code of Good Practice* may be found on page 15 of the *General Information Pack: Certificate of Competence in Educational Testing (Level A)*, which is reproduced in full in Appendix 1.
3   These Acts do not currently apply in Northern Ireland, although at the time of writing, disability discrimination legislation similar to that elsewhere in the UK is planned. Those using tests in education in the Province are recommended to check the Northern Ireland Department of Education website (http://www.deni.gov.uk/index.htm) for any updates.
4   Note that the Welsh Language Act 1993 requires schools and education authorities in Wales to treat the Welsh and English languages on an equal footing. As a result, Welsh language versions of a number of popular UK tests have been produced (see Appendix 5 for examples).
5   Other appropriate questions might include whether John has specific reading difficulties of a dyslexic kind, which would entail the use of more specialized diagnostic instruments (see Appendix 5 for further details) and possibly an ability test (see Appendix 5), or whether literacy difficulties have adversely affected his personal and social development, for example self-esteem, for which an appropriate inventory could be administered (again, see Appendix 5 for further details).

5

Unit 5: Administering Tests to One or More Students/Pupils/ Learners and Dealing with Scoring Procedures

This unit deals with the planning of a test session, establishing rapport and the administration of the test(s), and the scoring of the results. It requires test users to demonstrate their competence in the use of individual and group tests. Both forms of tests are widely used in educational settings, and it is important to ensure that those using tests in education are equally competent in the administration, scoring and interpretation of findings from both types of instruments.

As Urbina (2004, pp. 121–2) notes, there are three sources of error in psychological tests:

- the *context* in which testing takes place;
- the *test taker*; and
- the *test* itself.

In performance terms, this unit requires assessees to demonstrate competence in actual educational settings or in a simulated setting, using role play. While the test user has a responsibility to select an appropriate measure, the reliability and validity of an instrument lie within the province of the test author(s). But error arising from a test taker's approach and from the administration of the test and scoring of the results can be minimized by:

- *Preparation* both on the part of the test user, and of the test taker, for the administration of an individual or group test;

- *Organization* of the test setting and the materials used, checking and taking account of any special considerations that might affect the test taker's performance (for example, disability, English as an additional language, cultural and religious factors);
- *Administration* of the test according to the instructions laid down in the manual or record sheet; and
- *Scoring* the test responses accurately using any guidance in the test manual to score ambiguous responses, transferring the raw scores to record sheets and computing any standard or age-equivalent scores according to the instructions in the test manual.

We consider each of these four areas in turn, together with issues relating to the individual and group tests, before moving on to consider how the elements in this unit might be assessed.

Preparation

Prior to the administration of a test, the test user should ensure that he/she is familiar with the purpose of the assessment, and with the instructions, materials and scoring of the test. In addition to careful reading of the test manual, practice under the supervision of an experienced user of the test is a particularly helpful way of achieving this, and will help the test user to deal with any questions that a test taker may ask, and also to cope with any emergencies that may arise. This is also a means of finding out about the kinds of modifications and accommodations that may be appropriate for test takers with disabilities or for whom English is an additional language. Test users should ensure that they seek relevant professional advice before making any modification to test administration instructions. It also goes without saying that the test user must also ensure that he/she has obtained informed consent from the parents or guardians of the test takers, and from the test takers themselves, where they are able to give this on their own behalf, prior to the administration of a test. Test takers should be given adequate notice of where and when the test will be administered.

It is important for the test user to prepare the test taker by establishing a good rapport from the onset, to provide encouragement and maintain the participant's interest and cooperation. This is crucial if the test score is to be reliable and valid.

On a practical note, it is essential to check the test materials to ensure that there are no marks or other clues as to how previous test takers have responded, which might influence responses.

Organization

Good organization of the setting in which testing is carried out is an integral part of reducing distraction. It is good practice to administer a test in a quiet location, which minimizes extraneous sources of noise, and also to ensure that there are no other distracters, such as food, drink, or sweets present. In addition, ambient heating, lighting and ventilation should be appropriate, and there should be suitable seating and space. There should also be an adequate supply of pens or pencils, test record forms, and any other equipment or materials necessary for administration of the test and for the recording of the test user's responses. Ideally, there should be no other person present in the room when an individually administered test is presented, apart from a parent, in the case of a very young child, or an interpreter or parent, in the case of a test taker with a communication difficulty or disability.

Administration

It is essential that test users adhere strictly to the standardized instructions with regard to the administration of tests. In the case of a norm-referenced test, these are the actual instructions and procedures that were used in the standardization of the test. The norms are of known reliability and validity only if the instructions are used verbatim and the procedure carried out according to the manual. It is good testing practice also to record any verbal responses that the test taker makes in their entirety, so that the scoring of items can be checked, and any additional information about strategies used gleaned. Test users also have to ensure that they are familiar and practised in the pacing of the presentation of the materials, with any timing of responses that may be required, and with any rules for starting and discontinuation points. At the end of the test session, all materials must be collected and checked to ensure that everything has been returned, and then the test materials must be stored securely so that test takers do not have the opportunity to gain any advantage from seeing the materials prior to administration.

Finally, it is important to ensure that details of any changes or modifications to the standardized procedures that may be necessary, for example, in the case of test takers for whom English is an additional language or disabled test takers, are provided in any report or other record of the test session.

Scoring

Careful preparation, organization and administration of tests can be for naught if the responses are not scored accurately. Research studies reveal that errors in scoring are all too common (for example, Simons *et al.*, 2002) and it is important to ensure that standardized instructions for scoring are followed, and that great care is taken in entering the test taker's correct date of birth, calculating their chronological age at the time of testing, recording their responses, recording and adding up raw scores, and looking up the correct tables to determine derived scores, such as percentiles and standard scores.

Individual versus Group Tests

Unit 5 requires test users to demonstrate their competence in the use of both individually administered and group-administered tests. In general, individual tests are more sensitive than group-administered tests, with higher reliability and validity coefficients. This can be demonstrated by selecting a domain, such as literacy, numeracy, social competence, and comparing the reliability and validity coefficients for one or two individually administered tests with those for one or two group-administered tests.

The reasons for this are not hard to see. It is usually easier to establish rapport when working with an individual, although notable exceptions might include a very shy person, or someone with Autistic Spectrum Disorder. This helps to ensure that the individual will be relaxed, less anxious, and more engaged in the process of testing. Individual administration also provides more opportunities to ensure that the test taker understands what they are required to do, and also to prompt clarification of any ambiguous responses. It also means that any time-limits can be sensitively applied to maximize the motivation of the test taker and also make the administration more efficient, which may help to increase the cooperation and interest of the test taker and make less demands upon his/her concentration.

On the other hand, the group administration of tests is a more efficient way of gathering information. But there is a downside. First, it is harder to establish rapport and to ensure that everyone understands what they have to do. Some test takers may be reluctant to put their hand up in front of the others to ask questions or show that they do not understand what they have to do. Second, there may be group pressure not to take the test seriously. Third, there will be scope for possible distractions, at the very least, from an awareness of the others in the testing room and of any responses they make (for example, comments, dropped pencils).

There are also the additional demands of organizing a group adminis-tration of a test. Are there sufficient seats/desks? Are they far enough apart so that test users cannot see other's responses? Should test forms be handed out at the beginning of the session, or left on the desks before the start of the session? How will time-limits be handled? Some test takers will be finished earlier than others, how can this be managed so that it does not disrupt or even discourage those who are need longer to complete the test? These are issues that the test user must anticipate and address in the plan-ning, organization and administration of a group test.

Completing the Unit 5 Competency Assessments

As before, we shall now see how this fits in with the BPS competences and the assessments that you will be required to undertake. Both short-term and cumulative assessments are required for Unit 5, and as before, short-term assessments will be discussed in this chapter, with requirements for the cumulative assessment considered in Unit 8.

How Might Performance on this Unit be Assessed?

This unit requires direct observation by the assessor (or by a delegated assessor) of the actual practice of the assessee. The assessee is required to demonstrate competence in the administration of both individual and group tests, so performance will be assessed by means of observation of actual test use in an educational workplace setting, or observation of simulated practice, using role play. Many assessors will use an observation checklist based upon the CCET (Level A) items. The example shown below has reorganized the elements into the following phases of test use for both individual and group tests:

- before the session begins;
- during the session; and
- at the end of the session.

Here the assessor would indicate whether the assessee has demonstrated competence in regard to each of the elements (i.e. 'Yes', 'No' or non-applicable, 'N/A').

Certificate of Competence in Educational Testing (Level A)
Test Administration Observation Checklist

Assessee's name:
Assessor's name:
Date of observation:

Unit no.	Competence	Outcome	Comments
Before the sessions begins			
5.1	Did the assessee ensure that any necessary equipment was operating correctly and that sufficient materials were available for the test taker(s)?	Yes No N/A	
5.2	Did the assessee ensure, where re-usable materials were used, that they were carefully checked for marks or notes which may have been made by previous test takers?	Yes No N/A	
5.3	Did the assessee arrange a suitable quiet location for carrying out the testing?	Yes No N/A	
5.4	Did the assessee inform test takers(s) of the time and place well in advance and ensure that they were adequately prepared?	Yes No N/A	
In the case of group tests:			
5.21	Did the assessee plan test sessions with due regard to the maximum numbers of test takers who can be assessed in one session and the maximum duration of each session?	Yes No N/A	
In the case of individual tests:			
5.24	Did the assessee establish a satisfactory rapport with the test taker prior to the commencement of testing and maintain this throughout the session?	Yes No N/A	
At the start of the session			
5.5	Did the assessee record the test taker's personal details together with relevant details of the test instruments used, etc?	Yes No N/A	

Unit no.	Competence	Outcome	Comments
5.6	Did the assessee use standard test instruction and present them clearly and intelligibly to the test takers?	Yes No N/A	
5.7	Did the assessee provide the test takers with sufficient time to work through any example test items?	Yes No N/A	
5.10	Did the assessee explain any time limits?	Yes No N/A	
In the case of group tests:			
5.22	Did the assessee arrange seating and desk space to maximize comfort and to minimize possibilities for cheating?	Yes No N/A	
During the session			
5.8	Did the assessee make careful checks to ensure proper use of answer sheets and response procedures?	Yes No N/A	
5.9	Did the assessee deal appropriately with any questions that arose without compromising the purpose of the test?	Yes No N/A	
5.11	Did the assessee adhere strictly to test-specific instructions regarding pacing and timing?	Yes No N/A	
In the case of group tests:			
5.23	Did the assessee ensure that during the test test takers did not distract each other and, where appropriate, maintained silence?	Yes No N/A	
In the case of individual tests:			
5.25	Did the assessee prompt the test taker where appropriate in accordance with the test instructions and without invalidating the test item?	Yes No N/A	
5.26	Did the assessee use appropriately discreet scoring procedures so that the test taker did not become unduly conscious of failure?	Yes No N/A	

cont'd

Unit no.	Competence	Outcome	Comments
5.27	Did the assessee follow discontinuation procedures in line with the guidelines in the test manual while ensuring that the test taker did not become disheartened through obvious failure?	Yes No N/A	
At the end of the session			
5.12	Did the assessee collect all materials when each test was completed?	Yes No N/A	
5.13	Did the assessee carry out a careful check against the inventory of materials to ensure that everything has been returned?	Yes No N/A	
5.14	Did the assessee keep all materials in a secure place with due regard to confidentiality?	Yes No N/A	
5.15	Did the assessee thank test takers for their participation at the conclusion of the test session and explain the next stage in testing (if any) to them?	Yes No N/A	
5.16	Did the assessee make notes on factors that might have affected the test taker's performance (for example, any particular problems that arose during the session; the test taker's motivation, perseverance, or level of anxiety etc)?	Yes No N/A	
5.17	Did the assessee visually check answer sheets for ambiguous responses which could cause problems in scoring?	Yes No N/A	
5.18	Did the assessee demonstrate the use of a range of different scoring keys and/or 'self-scoring' forms?	Yes No N/A	
5.19	Did the assessee accurately score, compute responses and transfer raw score marks to record sheets?	Yes No N/A	
5.20	Did the assessee use norm tables to find relevant percentile and/or standard scores and transfer these to the test takers' record sheets?	Yes No N/A	

Concluding Comments

However your assessor chooses to gather information about how you set about a test administration setting, ensure that you:

- plan beforehand how you will set up the session;
- are seen to be complying with the appropriate equal opportunity legislation to ensure that the test taker's rights will be observed in regard to any modifications or accommodations;
- know how to administer and score the tests you are using, observing any time-limits, ensuring that you know any discontinuation instructions, that you have the correct form of the test, the necessary test record forms and equipment (don't find out midway through the session that a previous test user has mislaid some of the materials so that you can't present all of the items), a stop watch, if needed, and last but not least, a pencil for the test taker; and
- at the end of the session, collect all of the materials and check test booklets and equipment for marks and damage, removing those that cannot be restored. Store all materials and equipment securely. These steps will ensure that anyone else using the test after you will have everything they require and that other test users will not have prior access which would allow them to practise or provide the opportunity to look up answers in the manual, both of which would invalidate the use of norms.

6

Unit 6: Making Appropriate Use of Test Results and Providing Accurate Written and Oral Feedback to Clients and Candidates

This unit deals with the ability to score correctly, interpret and feedback test results about an individual. It requires assessees to apply their understanding of test reliability and validity, and to show their awareness of the importance of the *Standard Error of Measurement*, a measure of the variability in test scores that we might expect from measurement error which can be used to set up *confidence intervals* which in turn show how accurate the test scores really are. Assessees also have to demonstrate that they can integrate test results with other information about the test taker, such as other test and assessment results, or his or her performance or behaviour in different educational settings. Finally, assessees are required to demonstrate that they can provide appropriate feedback of the test results, both verbally and in writing, to test takers, as well as to other stakeholders, such as parents, carers, teachers or other professionals. This will also entail the assessee showing his or her awareness of test takers' and carers' rights of access to all data (including test data) kept on file.

Appropriate Use of Norm Tables

When using a norm-referenced test, it is important to ensure that the norms are used appropriately. In practice, this entails the following steps:

1   Recording accurately the date of testing and the test taker's date of birth.
2   Calculating and then recording accurately the test taker's chronological age (CA) at the time of the administration of the test, usually in years and completed months.
3   Checking that the raw score has been correctly added up and has been written accurately on the Record Form.
4   Using the appropriate conversion table for standardized scores for the test taker's CA and writing the standardized score accurately on the Record Form.
5   If provided, using a conversion table to look up the percentile rank for the standardized score and recording this accurately on the Record Form.
6   Using appropriate tables if available to calculate confidence intervals for the standardized score and recording the values in the boxes provided on the Record Form.
7   Looking up the percentile rank for the upper and lower bound scores of the confidence intervals and again recording the values in the boxes provided on the Record Form.
8   If desired, looking up the appropriate table to convert raw scores to age equivalent scores with their associated 68 per cent confidence intervals.

An error at any one of these 8 steps will adversely affect the correct interpretation of the test findings and great care is required to ensure that no mistakes are made.

Basal and Ceiling Effects

Where tests cover a broad age-range and/or level of difficulty, test takers are not always required to attempt every item. As we saw in Unit 1, test authors and designers commonly make use of *basal* and *ceiling* items or sets of items to help the administrator present only those items that are appropriate for the test taker. Consider the BPVS II (Dunn *et al.*, 1997). This consists of 168 items, covering a particularly wide age-range, from 3 years to 15 years 8 months. The use of basal and ceiling items reduces the possibility that on the one hand, a young test taker, or a test taker with difficulties, may be given items that would be too hard and give rise to frustration, and on the other hand, that an older, or more able test taker, is not given items that are too easy and would lead to boredom. The basal item/set of items is the point in the test below which it is taken for granted that the test taker will get all items correct. In contrast, the ceiling set is the point in the test above which it is assumed that the test taker will fail all items. It is important that assessees follow instructions in the test manual regarding establishing basal and ceiling points to ensure that the test is scored correctly.

But there is another sense in which test developers use the terms 'basal' and 'ceiling'. This refers to the fact that tests do not discriminate between different levels of performance at the limits of the age range or range of ability for which they are test is intended. Consider by way of example the Neale Analysis of Reading Ability – Revised (NARA II) (Neale, 1997), which is standardized on the age-range 6 years to 12 years 11 months and provides measures of reading accuracy, comprehension and rate. In the case of a child aged between 6 years 0 months and 6 years 2 months, a raw score of 0 for accuracy yields a standard score of 71, a raw score of 1 a standard score of 75, and a raw score of 2 a standard score of 78. In the case of comprehension scores, a raw score of 1 yields a standard score of 83, and a raw score of 2 a standard score of 89.

Rathvon (2004, p. 49) suggests that a test such as the NARA II should be capable of discriminating the lowest 2 per cent of test takers, that is, those who score more than 2 standard deviations below the mean. With a mean standard score of 100 and a standard deviation of 15, a raw score of 1 should ideally yield a standard score of 69 or less. But as we have seen, a raw score of 1 actually equates to a standard score of 75 in the case of accuracy and to a standard score of 83 in the case of comprehension, indicating that the test does not discriminate that well among the lowest scorers, particularly in the case of comprehension. This is a *basal effect*, sometimes referred to as a 'floor' effect, and results in a loss of accuracy and precision at the extremes of a test by over-estimating the test taker's skills or abilities. But the situation improves markedly for children aged 6 years 3 months and older on the NARA II in the case of accuracy, and for those aged 6 years 9 months and older in the case of comprehension, as a raw score of 1 in these age-groups yields a standard score of 70, which essentially meets Rathvon's criterion.

A similar phenomenon can be observed at the upper points in the age-range in tests, a *ceiling effect*, in which the scores do not discriminate the top 2 per cent of test takers, that is more than 2 standard deviations above the mean. Following Rathvon (2004), in the case of a test with a mean of 100, and a standard deviation of 15, the highest raw score should be capable of yielding a standard score of 130 or more. However, inspection of the norms for the NARA II confirms that the maximum standard scores which can be obtained by children in the age range 12 years 9 months to 12 years 11 months are 123 for accuracy and 127 for comprehension, indicating a loss of precision which is more marked in the case of accuracy scores.

As a rule of thumb, therefore, test administrators should inspect the norms for any instrument they are considering using and ideally aim to use tests which can discriminate the lowest 2 per cent and the highest 2 per cent of scores, particularly where test information is used to support important decision making. In general, in the case of a test with a mean standard score of 100 and a standard deviation of 15, this would mean using the test only with age-groups for whom the minimum standard score is 70 or less, and the maximum score 130 or more. But the purpose of carrying out the assessment should also be borne in mind. Thus, if a test is being used for screening to identify pupils with difficulties, the presence of a ceiling effect may not be crucial. Provided that the instrument has no basal effects for the age-range in question, it may not be important to differentiate those scoring highly.

Interpretation of the Findings in the Light of Previous Test Results

To interpret test findings adequately, we have to determine what the scores mean. We consider the importance of linking test results with academic performance below, but at this juncture it is important to emphasize that the test administrator should ensure that results obtained are compared with the findings from previous test administrations. Once scoring errors have been eliminated, a discrepancy between administrations of the same or similar tests should be considered in the light of the possibility that it may be due to test error, perhaps as a result of basal or ceiling effects. Test administrators should also be clear about how they report test results where no relevant norms or cut-off tables are available. This may be an issue where a test has been administered to a pupil for whom English is an additional language, or when a test has been administered as a diagnostic tool outside of the age range of the standardization. In both cases, it is important that any written or verbal report contains the appropriate information and that normative results are not provided without comment or explanation for the use of the test or tests in question.

Appropriateness of the Reference Group Used in the Test Standardization

This highlights the importance of the appropriateness of the data from the *reference group* for a test. In its broadest sense, a *reference group* is 'any group of people against which test scores are compared' Urbina (2004, p. 84). The term may be applied to the standardization sample used in the development of the test norms for administration and scoring, but may also be applied to any additional normative sample, used perhaps for the development of local norms or for use with a specific group. A good example of such a reference group would be the sample of children for whom English is an additional language who were used to construct supplementary norms for such children for the BPVS II (see Whetton, 1997). It is important to make use of reference group data and good practice for test authors and developers to provide it.

The manual of a published test will generally provide details of the standardization sample, which may be regarded as the primary reference group. But additional data from more specific groups may also be collected on a test after it is first published. This may itself be published in a research paper or perhaps in a supplementary technical manual, as in the case of the BPVS II. It is good practice for a test user to ensure first, that the standardization sample for a given test is an appropriate one for the test taker, and second, that they are aware of technical supplements or other reports of any additional normative data from relevant reference groups.

Scores, Confidence Intervals and the Standard Error of Measurement

Test scores are not 100 per cent accurate and every test score or measure is subject to error. It is good practice to give an indication of the accuracy and precision of measures from the tests that we use. The current version of the CCET (Level A) bases its approach for estimating such measurement error upon the general model of reliability of 'Classical' Test Theory (CTT) which holds that:

$$X = T + e$$

where X is the observed score on a test, T is the underlying 'true' score, and e is measurement error. This equation can also be expressed in an alternate form as:

$$e = X - T$$

to underline the fact that measurement error is in fact the difference between observed scores and 'true' scores.

CTT assumes that such measurement errors are random and holds that as a consequence 'true' scores are uncorrelated with measurement errors and that measurement errors on different test instruments are also uncorrelated. In CTT, reliability coefficients, such as test-retest, alternate forms, split-half and internal consistency, provide information about sources of measurement error, with reliability (r) defined as the ratio of true score variance to that of observed score variance (i.e., true variance plus error variance).[1]

Each observed score, X, has a single 'true' score, T, and from this a single reliability coefficient can be derived. The SEM is used to indicate for a given obtained score the range of scores within which the 'true' score falls, and hence provides an indication of measurement error. The formula for calculating the SEM is:

$$SEM = SD\sqrt{1 - r_{xx}}$$

Here, the SEM for an obtained score is equal to the standard deviation of test scores provided in the test manual multiplied by the square root of 1 minus the reliability coefficient, which may be either a measure of internal consistency or a measure of test-retest or alternate forms reliability. The smaller the SEM, the more accurate and precise our measurement. The SEM can be calculated using a pocket calculator, but is generally provided in the test manual.

We considered *confidence intervals* in Unit 2 in regard to the Standard Error of the Mean and determining how close the mean of a sample is to the population mean. But we can also calculate confidence intervals around an obtained score from an individual test taker. This is where the SEM comes into its own. The size of these confidence intervals depends upon the probability we select of being wrong. For example, the 68 per cent confidence interval indicates that we are 68 per cent confident that a true score is within the range of plus or minus the SEM of the obtained score. If we wish to be more conservative, we could use the 95 per cent confidence interval, which is obtained by multiplying the SEM by 1.96 and then constructing a range by first adding this value to the obtained score and then subtracting the value from the obtained score. The values of '1' for the 68 per cent confidence interval and '1.96' for the 95 per cent confidence intervals are taken from the z scores associated with these confidence levels (see Salvia and Ysseldyke, 2004, pp. 138–40 for a discussion).

Let us turn to a practical example. The manual of the BPVS II (Dunn *et al.*, 1997, p. 33) reports that the SEM for the test is 5.6 standard score points. If a test taker obtains a standard score of 87, we can be 68 per cent confident that his/her true score lies within the range 87 ± 5.6, which equates to 81.4 to 92.6, or rounding to whole numbers, the range 81–93.

This means that there is a 16 per cent chance that the true score is actually less than 81, and a 16 per cent chance that it is greater than 93. If we are unhappy about being incorrect 32 per cent of the time, we can use the 95 per cent confidence interval. Here, we can be 95 per cent confident that the test taker's true score lies within the range 87 ± (1.96 times 5.6), which in turn equates to a range of 76–98. There is still the chance that the true score lies outside of this range, but the chance that it is less than 76 is only 2.5 per cent, and similarly, there is only a 2.5 per cent chance that it is more than 98. Note that in general the larger the confidence interval, the more certain we are that it will contain the true score.

So far we have considered symmetrical confidence intervals, but some test manuals provide information about *asymmetrical confidence intervals*, which are larger, or skewed in the direction of the mean score (see Nunnally, 1978 for a discussion).

Composite Scores

Many tests yield single scores, but others provide sub-test scores, which can be added together to provide an overall *composite score*. Examples of the latter include the *Wechsler Individual Achievement Test – Second UK Edition* (WIAT II[UK]) (Wechsler, 2005), the *Test of Word Reading Efficiency* (TOWRE) (Torgesen *et al.*, 1999), the *Cognitive Abilities Test: Third Edition* (CAT3) (Lohman *et al.*, 2003) and the *Rogers Personal Adjustment Inventory: Revised* (RPAI-R) (Jeffrey, 1984).

The WIAT II[UK] provides five composite scores: a composite score for reading, which averages performance across tests of word reading, reading comprehension and pseudo-word decoding; one for mathematics, based upon performance on sub-tests of numerical operations and mathematical reasoning; one for written language, based upon tests of spelling and written expression; one for oral language based upon tests of listening comprehension and oral expression; and a composite total score combining the composite scores from the four domains of reading, mathematics, written language and oral language.

The TOWRE provides a composite Total Word Reading Efficiency Standard Score which is based upon the average of scores for Sight Word Efficiency and Phonemic Decoding Efficiency.

The CAT3 yields four composite scores: a verbal battery composite score, based upon performance on sub-tests of verbal classification, sentence completion and verbal analogies; a quantitative battery composite, based upon scores on sub-tests of number analogies, number series and equation building; a non-verbal composite, based on sub-tests of figure classification, figure analogies and figure analysis; and an overall mean

CAT score based upon the composite scores for the verbal, quantitative and non-verbal batteries.

Finally, the RPAI-R yields an overall composite score based upon sub-test scores for personal difficulties, social difficulties, family difficulties and daydreaming.

Composite scores are generally of higher reliability than their constituent sub-test scores (see Murphy and Davidshofer, 1994, pp. 102–3 for a discussion) and the CCET requires assessees to be able to use the information in the test manual to compute them.

Making Connections between Performance on a Test, the Test Taker's Educational Performance and the Original Purpose of the Test

As we have seen, tests are not error-free, and in Unit 1 we considered possible sources of such error, highlighting the importance of gathering additional evidence from school records, portfolios of coursework or direct observation, for example, to corroborate test findings. When interpreting the results from a test, it is important to weigh the findings in relation to information about the test taker's educational performance in the curriculum and also in the light of the purpose of administering the test in the first place. For example, if the purpose of the test is to identify learning difficulties, then the test user should explore whether there is evidence of problems in attainment in core areas of the school curriculum above and beyond the test results. In contrast, if the test was administered to identify areas of particular competence, then the test user should ascertain whether there is confirmatory evidence of high levels of attainment in areas of the curriculum. In the absence of such corroborative evidence, additional information may be necessary to clarify and resolve the situation, including perhaps of the use of an alternative test(s). It goes without saying that any report should also flag up and discuss discrepancies between test findings and other relevant information.

Integrating Test Findings with Other Forms of Information Gathered in the Course of the Assessment to Inform Decision Making and Intervention

Test data represent one source of evidence, and should always be considered with other relevant information. Interpretation of any test results used to inform decision making and intervention in an educational context must always be informed by additional information gathered in the course of the assessment from school records, portfolios of current coursework, direct observation, reports from teachers and parents, and any reports from other professionals. Such information should be integrated with the test findings and may include:

- information about the test taker's background, academic history (including details of learning opportunities and their outcomes) and current educational performance;
- information about the test taker's social relationships and behaviour in his/her school/educational setting;
- information about any concerns expressed by the school/educational setting or caregivers;
- where available, information from experienced professionals in regard to the underlying nature of the test taker's difficulties including the possible impact of factors such as prenatal medical problems, the effects of delays in speech and language development, the effects of hearing or visual development, brain injury, neurological conditions, or difficulties with physical development or motor co-ordination;
- factors which may have affected the test taker's performance during assessment and consequently his/her test score (for example, how the test taker approached the test; adverse environmental conditions in regard to heating, lighting, noise or seating arrangements; test anxiety; any problems the test taker may have experienced in regard to the appropriateness of test materials or in making his/her response due to ethnicity, social class or disability; the effects of the test taker's experience, particularly in regard to the re-administration of instruments; and any problems in establishing rapport, in explaining the instructions, or in maintaining concentration, motivation and interest).

Variation in Test Results and the Effects of Using Different Tests Within a Domain (for example, Reading or Number)

Test scores vary as a function of differences in content and in standardization samples. This is true even when we compare tests within specific domains, such as reading or number. Consider the WIAT II^{UK} (Wechsler, 2005), the Neale Analysis of Reading Ability – Revised (NARA II) (Neale, 1997), and the Salford Sentence Reading Test (Revised) 3rd. Edition (Bookbinder, Revised by Vincent and Crumpler, 2002). All three instruments are measures of reading, but an individual is unlikely to obtain exactly the same score on each of these tests.

The WIAT II^{UK}, for example, measures word reading skills using individual words presented out of context, reading comprehension by means of questions presented following silent reading of passages of text, and pseudo-word decoding using pronounceable non-words. The NARA II, on the other hand, measures accuracy of oral reading of passages and reading comprehension by the presentation of questions after reading aloud. The Salford Sentence Reading Test measures reading sentences aloud. All three tests clearly measure reading, but they do all not measure the same aspects of reading. Further, where they do measure the same sub-skills, for example reading comprehension in the case of the WIAT II^{UK} and the NARA II, they do so in distinctive ways. In addition, although all three tests have norms based upon representative UK standardization samples, these samples are different, which will contribute to systematic between-test variation in the scores obtained.

It is clear that test users should expect the results obtained from different tests to vary to a greater or lesser degree, even where they ostensibly are designed to measure the same skills within a given domain. A standard score or age-equivalent score in reading or in mathematics will not, therefore, be exactly equivalent to that obtained from another test, although we would expect similarities to the extent that the tests measure common skills and the results are correlated.

Providing Appropriate Feedback

The object of test use is to effect some form of change in instruction, educational support or provision, or to inform some other aspect of decision making. This can only be achieved to the extent that test results and assessment findings more generally are not only interpreted correctly, but reported accurately and appropriately to those who have a need and an entitlement to be informed about the outcomes. The feedback that the test administrator provides to the test taker and to other relevant interested parties is thus of great importance. Section 2.8 of The International Test Commission's *International Guidelines for Test Use* (2000, pp. 23–4) (downloadable from www.intestcom.org or from the BPS Psychological Testing Centre www.psychtesting.org.uk, and reproduced in Appendix 8) details considerations of which the test user should be aware.

First, dissemination of test findings should only be with the informed consent and agreement of the test taker, or their caregiver or other legal representative in the case of a young child and, in any event, only to those

who have a legitimate reason for receiving them. It is important, therefore, that the test user be aware of those interested parties who should receive feedback on test results. In general, this will include the referring agent(s), as well as schools and other professional agencies working with the test taker, unless he/she or the legal representative indicate otherwise.

With such a potentially diverse range of recipients, including the test taker himself or herself, it is important that feedback, either verbal or written, is communicated clearly, without jargon, and using language that the recipient can readily understand. This is particularly important in the case of verbal feedback. Verbal communication of results may be difficult, particularly where the outcome of testing is not one that is desired by the test taker, parents or guardian or other legal representative, or indeed other professionals. Written reports can be re-drafted to ensure clarity, but verbal feedback is provided in 'real time' and it is important the test users should rehearse and practise providing such test feedback.

Finally, it is good practice to ensure that test data and other sources of information are integrated when the findings are fed back, together with clear and specific recommendations, which should identify a range of possible options as to how best to proceed.

Completing the Unit 6 Competency Assessments

We shall now see how this fits in with the BPS competences and the assessments that you will be required to undertake. Both short-term and cumulative assessments are required for Unit 6, with short-term assessments discussed in this unit, and cumulative assessment considered in Chapter 8.

How Might Performance on this Unit be Assessed?

As in the case of Unit 5, this Unit requires direct observation by the assessor (or by a delegated assessor) of the actual practice of the assessee. The assessee is required to demonstrate competence in the scoring, interpretation and feedback of results of both individual and group tests. The assessor will base his/her assessment upon observation of test use in an educational workplace setting, or observation of simulated practice, using role play. Observation of a minimum of one individual and one group-administered test will be required. An observation checklist based upon the CCET (Level A) items, as shown below, may be used to indicate whether the assessee has demonstrated competence in regard to each of the elements (i.e. 'Yes', 'No' or non-applicable, 'N/A'). In addition, the assessor may require the assessee to demonstrate their ability to interpret test scores with regard to reliability, validity and the Standard Error of Measurement by asking questions, or by means of worksheets, case studies or simulations. One such worksheet is shown below. Evidence of the ability to integrate test findings and of the ability to provide appropriate feedback (both oral and written) may also be gathered by means of direct observation of test use in a workplace setting, or by simulated role play, as well as by case studies. Note that part of the performance evidence required for appropriate feedback of results requires the assessee to demonstrate their awareness of the fact that the test taker, carer and other legal representative have a right of access to all test data which is kept on file.

As before, note that '6.1' below refers to the assessment for Unit 6 Element 1 and '6.2' to Unit 6 Element 2 and so on. Recall that the competences are shown in full in Appendix 1, and *Guidance for Assessors* may be found in Appendix 2.

Certificate of Competence in Educational Testing (Level A)
Unit 6 Checklist

Assessee's name:
Assessor's name:
Date of observation:

Unit no.	Competence	Outcome	Comments
6.1	Did the assessee select appropriate norm tables from the test manual or supplementary material?	Yes No N/A	
6.2	Did the assessee make appropriate use of information in the test manual with regard to ceiling or basal effects?	Yes No N/A	
6.3	Did the assessee attach suitable cautions to interpretations of the results (including comparisons with previous test performances) and/or make statements as to why certain test results are not quoted where no relevant norms or cut-off tables are available?	Yes No N/A	

cont'd

Unit no.	Competence	Outcome	Comments
6.4	Did the assessee give due consideration to the appropriateness of the reference group used in the test standardization?	Yes No N/A	
6.5	Did the assessee describe the meanings of scale scores in terms which are accurate, which reflect the confidence limits associated with those scores and are intelligible to those who may legitimately have access to them?	Yes No N/A	
6.6	Did the assessee compute composite test battery scores from weightings given in a test manual?	Yes No N/A	
6.7	Did the assessee make appropriate connections between performance on a test, the test taker's educational performance and the original purpose of the test?	Yes No N/A	
6.8	Did the assessee integrate test findings with other forms of information gathered in the course of the assessment to inform decision making and intervention?	Yes No N/A	
6.9	Did the assessee show awareness of the implications of variation in test results and the effects of using different tests within a domain (for example, reading or number)?	Yes No N/A	
6.10	Did the assessee show awareness of the appropriateness or otherwise of providing feedback to test takers of differing ages and/or ability levels?	Yes No N/A	

Concluding Comments

It is worth noting that the checklist deals with 'Classical' Test Theory (CTT) and does not currently cover two important and more recent developments in regard to the relationship between reliability, validity and measurement error, namely Item Response Theory and Generalizability Theory. Rathvon (2004) provides an introduction to both of these in a downloadable format.

Example of How the BPS Competences Might be Assessed and Answered

6.5   Calculate: (a) the Standard Error of Measurement for a test from the data below; and (b) calculate the 95 per cent confidence interval for an obtained score of 88 on this test and explain what it means

$SD = 10$; $r_{xx} = 0.97$

(a)   The formula for calculating the Standard Error of Measurement is:

$$SEM = SD\sqrt{1 - r_{xx}}$$

Inserting the values provided yields a value of 1.73 for the SEM.

(b)   The 95 per cent confidence interval for an obtained score of 88 on this test is 88 ± (1.96 × 1.73), which equals 85–91, rounded to whole numbers. This means that there is a 95 per cent chance that the individual's true score lies within the range 85 to 91, with a 2.5 per cent chance that the true score lies below 85 and a 2.5 per cent chance that the true score lies above 91

Note

1   'Variance' refers to the spread or clustering of scores around the mean and, as we saw in Unit 2, is used to calculate the standard deviation. Formally, it is the average squared distance of the scores from the mean and is calculated by computing the sum of the square of each score, less the mean, divided by the number of scores (N).

7

Unit 7: Maintaining Security and Confidentiality

This final unit deals with the security and confidentiality of test data to ensure that test users comply with the requirements of the UK Data Protection Act (1998) and also with the security and storage of test materials.

Data Protection Legislation

Test results are data that relate to an identified or identifiable person, that is, 'personal data', and accordingly fall within the legislative framework for data privacy and protection. In the UK, this is the Data Protection Act (1998) (DPA), which enacts the European Union Council Data Protection Directive 95/46/EC (1995). Test users should ensure that they are familiar with the implications of this Act for their practice and those who are employees of local authorities or other public bodies should consult their local Data Protection Officer to confirm that they are complying with the requirements of the legislation.

In essence, the DPA gives test takers the right to know:

- what information is held about them;
- what it is being held for;
- who has access to it;
- for how long the information will be held.

These rights apply to all test data, even the results from tests carried out in school. To comply with the legislation, test takers, including those who are pupils in school are entitled to have answers to the four questions above, although it may be more appropriate to inform the parents of very young children of these considerations.

A form of words which covers the requirements may include the following:

- We will keep a record of your results from this test . . .
- The results will be used to help you with your difficulties . . .
- Your parents/caregivers know about this . . .
- The results will be available only to your teachers, parents (or caregivers) or any other person who could help with your problems . . .
- You can see them as well . . .
- We will only keep the results for as long as it would be helpful to you.

The DPA also requires personal data held to be accurate and kept up to date. This has implications for ensuring the accuracy of not only the scoring and recording of results on test forms, but also of any test data included in a report and the conclusions drawn from them. Such information cannot be transferred outside of the European Union unless the country or territory to which is sent has adequate data protection legislation.

Finally, the DPA covers the security of test data and any reports based upon test data. This means that test results and reports based upon them must be stored securely. It is also good practice to store tests and test materials securely to prevent unauthorized access and to ensure that test takers do not have the opportunity to practice or otherwise gain experience of the test.

Completing the Unit 7 Competency Assessments

We shall now see how this fits in with the BPS competences and the assessments that you will be required to undertake. Both short-term and cumulative assessments are required for Unit 7, with short-term assessments discussed in this chapter, and cumulative assessment considered in Chapter 8.

How Might Performance on this Unit be Assessed?

As in the case of Units 5 and 6, this unit requires direct observation by the assessor (or by a delegated assessor) of the actual practice of the assessee. The assessor will base his/her assessment upon observation of practice in regard to security and confidentiality in test use in an educational workplace setting, or observation of simulated practice, using role play. An observation checklist based upon the CCET (Level A) items, as shown below, may be used to indicate whether the assessee has demonstrated competence in regard to each of the elements (i.e. 'Yes', 'No' or non-applicable, 'N/A').

As before, note that '7.1' below refers to the assessment for Unit 7 Element 1 and '7.2' to Unit 7 Element 2 and so on. The competences are shown in full in Appendix 1, and *Guidance for Assessors* may be found in Appendix 2.

Certificate of Competence in Educational Testing (Level A)
Unit 7 Checklist

Assessee's name:
Assessor's name:
Date of observation:

Unit no.	Competence	Outcome	Comments
7.1	Did the assessee ensure that clear descriptions were given to the test taker and/or other relevant parties (for example, other professional/parent/LEA) prior to testing concerning (a) how the results are to be used, (b) who will be given access to them, and (c) for how long they will be retained?	Yes No N/A	
7.2	Did the assessee ensure that all test data are kept in a secure place and that access is not given to unauthorized persons?	Yes No N/A	
7.3	Did the assessee ensure that all test materials are kept in a secure place which is not accessible to people other than authorized test users?	Yes No N/A	
7.4	Did the assessee ensure that all mandatory requirements relating to the test taker's and client's rights and obligations under the Data Protection Act are clearly explained to the parties concerned?	Yes No N/A	

Unit no.	Competence	Outcome	Comments
7.5	Did the assessee ensure that where data is stored, the conditions of the Data Protection Act are abided by?	Yes No N/A	
7.6	Did the assessee ensure that test takers/ potential test takers are not provided with prior access to test materials other than those specifically designed to help test takers prepare for an assessment?	Yes No N/A	

8

Putting it all Together

In the preceding chapters, we considered the short-term evidence required for the CCET (Level A). In this final chapter, we shall consider the requirements for presenting cumulative evidence of competence in test use, which as noted in the Introduction, is designed to ensure that test users in education provide evidence that they can apply the knowledge and skills of the Level A Checklist to everyday practice in the work setting.

But first we will turn to the recommendation in the *Guidance for Assessors* (see Appendix 2) that assessors 'should make use of the links between Units 5, 6 and 7 when gathering information'. In practice, this may mean that some assessors will make use of an observation checklist, which combines the elements from these three units. A version of such a checklist covering test administration, scoring and providing feedback is shown below, with the elements organized into the three phases of 'before the session begins', 'during the session', and 'at the end of the session' for both individual and group tests. As before, the assessor observes actual or simulated practice and uses the checklist to indicate whether the assessee has shown competence in each of the elements. The checklist may also serve as a useful *aide memoire* for assessees and other test users.

Certificate of Competence in Educational Testing (Level A)
Test Administration, Scoring and Feedback Observation Checklist

Assessee's name:
Assessor's name:
Date of observation:

Unit no.	Competence	Outcome	Comments
Before the session begins			
5.1	Did the assessee ensure that any necessary equipment was operating correctly and that sufficient materials were available for the test taker(s)?	Yes No N/A	
5.2	Did the assessee ensure, where re-usable materials were used, that they were carefully checked for marks or notes which may have been made by previous test takers?	Yes No N/A	
5.3	Did the assessee arrange a suitable quiet location for carrying out the testing?	Yes No N/A	
5.4	Did the assessee inform test takers(s) of the time and place well in advance and ensure that they were adequately prepared?	Yes No N/A	
7.1	Did the assessee ensure that clear descriptions were given to the test taker and/or other relevant parties (for example, other professional/parent/LEA) prior to testing concerning: (a) how the results are to be used; (b) who will be given access to them; and (c) for how long they will be retained?	Yes No N/A	
7.4	Did the assessee ensure that all mandatory requirements relating to the test taker's and client's rights and obligations under the Data Protection Act are clearly explained to the parties concerned?	Yes No N/A	

cont'd

Unit no.	Competence	Outcome	Comments
7.6	Did the assessee ensure that test takers/ potential test takers are not provided with prior access to test materials other than those specifically designed to help test takers prepare for an assessment?	Yes No N/A	
In the case of group tests:			
5.21	Did the assessee plan test sessions with due regard to the maximum numbers of test takers who can be assessed in one session and the maximum duration of each session?	Yes No N/A	
In the case of individual tests:			
5.24	Did the assessee establish a satisfactory rapport with the test taker prior to the commencement of testing and maintain this throughout the session?	Yes No N/A	
At the start of the session			
5.5	Did the assessee record the test taker's personal details together with relevant details of the test instruments used, etc?	Yes No N/A	
5.6	Did the assessee use standard test instruction and present them clearly and intelligibly to the test takers?	Yes No N/A	
5.7	Did the assessee provide the test takers with sufficient time to work through any example test items?	Yes No N/A	
5.10	Did the assessee explain any time limits?	Yes No N/A	
In the case of group tests:			
5.22	Did the assessee arrange seating and desk space to maximize comfort and to minimize possibilities for cheating?	Yes No N/A	
During the session			
5.8	Did the assessee make careful checks to ensure proper use of answer sheets and response procedures?	Yes No N/A	

Unit no.	Competence	Outcome	Comments
5.9	Did the assessee deal appropriately with any questions that arose without compromising the purpose of the test?	Yes No N/A	
5.11	Did the assessee adhere strictly to test-specific instructions regarding pacing and timing?	Yes No N/A	
In the case of group tests:			
5.23	Did the assessee ensure that during the test test takers did not distract each other and, where appropriate, maintained silence?	Yes No N/A	
In the case of individual tests:			
5.25	Did the assessee prompt the test taker where appropriate in accordance with the test instructions and without invalidating the test item?	Yes No N/A	
5.26	Did the assessee use appropriately discreet scoring procedures so that the test taker did not become unduly conscious of failure?	Yes No N/A	
5.27	Did the assessee follow discontinuation procedures in line with the guidelines in the test manual while ensuring that the test taker did not become disheartened through obvious failure?	Yes No N/A	
At the end of the session			
5.12	Did the assessee collect all materials when each test was completed?	Yes No N/A	
5.13	Did the assessee carry out a careful check against the inventory of materials to ensure that everything has been returned?	Yes No N/A	
5.14	Did the assessee keep all materials in a secure place with due regard to confidentiality?	Yes No N/A	
5.15	Did the assessee thank test takers for their participation at the conclusion of the test session and explain the next stage in testing (if any) to them?	Yes No N/A	

cont'd

Unit no.	Competence	Outcome	Comments
5.16	Did the assessee make notes on factors that might have affected the test taker's performance (for example, any particular problems that arose during the session; the test taker's motivation, perseverance, or level of anxiety)?	Yes No N/A	
5.17	Did the assessee visually check answer sheets for ambiguous responses which could cause problems in scoring?	Yes No N/A	
7.2	Did the assessee ensure that all test data are kept in a secure place and that access is not given to unauthorized persons?	Yes No N/A	
7.3	Did the assessee ensure that all test materials are kept in a secure place which is not accessible to people other than authorized test users?	Yes No N/A	
7.5	Did the assessee ensure that where data is stored, the conditions of the Data Protection Act are abided by?	Yes No N/A	
5.18	Did the assessee demonstrate the use of a range of different scoring keys and/or 'self-scoring' forms?	Yes No N/A	
5.19	Did the assessee accurately score, compute responses and transfer raw score marks to record sheets?	Yes No N/A	
6.1	Did the assessee select appropriate norm tables from the test manual or supplementary material?	Yes No N/A	
5.20	Did the assessee use norm tables to find relevant percentile and/or standard scores and transfer these to the test takers' record sheets?	Yes No N/A	
6.2	Did the assessee make appropriate use of information in the test manual with regard to ceiling or basal effects?	Yes No N/A	

Unit no.	Competence	Outcome	Comments
6.3	Did the assessee attach suitable cautions to interpretations of the results (including comparisons with previous test performances) and/or make statements as to why certain test results are not quoted where no relevant norms or cut-off tables are available?	Yes No N/A	
6.4	Did the assessee give due consideration to the appropriateness of the reference group used in the test standardization?	Yes No N/A	
6.5	Did the assessee describe the meanings of scale scores in terms that are accurate, reflect the confidence limits associated with those scores and are intelligible to those who may legitimately have access to them?	Yes No N/A	
6.6	Did the assessee compute composite test battery scores from weightings given in a test manual?	Yes No N/A	
6.7	Did the assessee make appropriate connections between performance on a test, the test taker's educational performance and the original purpose of the test?	Yes No N/A	
6.8	Did the assessee integrate test findings with other forms of information gathered in the course of the assessment to inform decision making and intervention?	Yes No N/A	
6.9	Did the assessee show awareness of the implications of variation in test results and the effects of using different tests within a domain (for example, reading or number)?	Yes No N/A	
6.10	Did the assessee show awareness of the appropriateness or otherwise of providing feedback to test takers of differing ages and/or ability levels?	Yes No N/A	

Cumulative Evidence

The cumulative evidence exercise, the final requirement for the CCET (Level A), consists of a commentary on a case study together with case reports based upon the assessee's practice in regard to test use in his/her workplace. One specification for this exercise is as shown below. Assessment here is based upon:

- A detailed case study with commentary, with links to specific elements in Units 4, 5, 6 and 7; and
- Examples of reports of the findings to a lay party (for example, parents or the test taker) and to professionals.

These elements provide evidence of the generalization of the knowledge and skills covered in these units. The assessor will give specific guidance as to the scope, length and detail required in this report. Some assessors may request the use of sub-headings corresponding to the sections in the specification, while others may wish the report to follow the structure and format used by the assessee in their work practice, albeit with the greater level of detail required for this exercise and the examples of the feedback that would be given to the two different stakeholders. An example of a report is provided at the end of this chapter.

Certificate of Competence in Educational Testing (Level A): Cumulative Evidence Exercise

To be able to complete your portfolio of assessments you must be able to use all the information you have gained in your training to select and use tests in your work. This final exercise will expect you write a substantial report on the process and outcome of testing an actual person. Your report should include detailed information on the following:

1 Selection of an individual whom you believe would benefit from testing in an educational context.

2 Justification of your reasons for contemplating the test that you propose to use. *Outline the help you expect that testing will give you. Choose an appropriate test(s). Reflect on the processes which led you to choose this test(s)* [Unit 4: 1–5]. *Comment on any restrictions on areas of use and on whether the test would meet the requirements of Equal Opportunities,*

Race Relations, and Disability Discrimination legislation [Unit 4: 6–7].

3 Description of the way in which you contacted the test taker, other interested parties and explained the need and purpose of testing [Unit 5: 1–4; 21–22]. *Comment also on information given to the test taker and or other relevant parties regarding how the results are to be used, who will have access to them and for how long they will be retained* [Unit 7:1; 4]. *Comment on security and confidentiality issues regarding test data and materials* [Unit 7:2–3].

4 Detailed description of the testing session. *What were the conditions like? How did the test taker react? Did anything unusual happen? What were your observations?* [Unit 5: 5–16; 23–27].

5 Detailed description of the scoring process. *Were there any problems in using the scoring procedures?* [Unit 5: 17–20]

6 Interpretation of the scores. *With reference to other test taker information, comment on the norms used (and any supplementary material) and any criterion-referenced interpretation, issues regarding any ceiling or basal effects, riders to the interpretation of the results, the appropriateness of the reference group used in the test standardization, the meaning of the scores and their associated confidence intervals* [Unit 6: 1–6]. *State what conclusions you draw from the test score(s), taking into account any other information about the test taker's educational performance, the purpose of using the test, and any other forms of information gathered in the course of the assessment. What would be your next course of action?* [Unit 6: 7–9]

7 Feedback. *Prepare two kinds of feedback:*
   - *Written – to the test taker or interested party. Prepare a short written report appropriate to the test taker and lay interested parties;*
   - *Written – to a fellow professional with extensive knowledge and experience in educational testing.*
   Use appropriate statistical concepts in the treatment and interpretation of scores.
   Link to the further action you may recommend [Unit 6:10].

8 Security and confidentiality. *Comment on storage of test data in regard to the conditions of the Data Protection Act* [Unit 7: 6].

Once the short-term and cumulative evidence assignments have been completed and signed off by the assessor using the form provided by the BPS, the assessee will be able to apply for their CCET (Level A) and will be deemed to be a competent test user whose name can be entered on the *Register of Competence in Psychological Testing (Educational)* held by the

BPS. Assessors may also request supporting evidence for the completed competences in the form of a portfolio which may contain some of the following, detailed in Annex A of the BPS *Guidance for Assessors* (2004b):

- reports/worksheets from categorization exercises;
- observation records completed by assessors observing discussions between assessees;
- interview records;
- lists of points/items produced by assessees;
- draft documents (letters of invitation, test logs);
- reports of case studies,
- reviews of tests, case reports;
- reports for feedback to individuals (case study);
- worksheets completed under supervision;
- in-course or end-of-course tests;
- self-assessment tests;
- workplace checklists;
- assessor's report of workplace activity;
- personal report of workplace activity;
- supervisor's or co-worker's report of workplace activity;
- test log(s);
- assessor's report on simulated activity;
- documents in use in assessee's workplace;
- review by assessee of documents in use; and
- an essay.

Concluding Comments

Used or interpreted inappropriately, tests can lead to poor decisions, which may have adverse consequences for test takers. As Cronbach (1984, p. 15) notes:

> In the hands of persons with inadequate training, tests can do harm. Untrained users may administer a test incorrectly. They may place undue reliance on inaccurate measurements, and they may misunderstand what the test measures and reach unsound conclusions. It is, therefore, important to the user to confine herself [sic] to tests that she can handle properly.

As we have seen, an important part of good practice is *knowing when to use a test*. But equally, it is important to know *when not to use a test*. As Urbina (2004, p. 259) notes, a test should not be used when:

1 The purpose of testing is unknown or unclear to the test user.
2 The test user is not completely familiar with all of the necessary test documentation and trained on the procedures related to the test.
3 The test user does not know where the test results will go, or how they will be used, or cannot safeguard their use.
4 The information that is sought from testing is already available, or can be gathered more efficiently, through other sources.
5 The test taker is not willing or able to cooperate with the testing.
6 The test taker is likely to incur some harm due to the testing process itself.
7 The environmental setting and conditions for the testing are inadequate.
8 The test format or materials are inappropriate in light of the test taker's age, sex, cultural or linguistic background, disability status, or any other condition that might invalidate test data.
9 The test norms are outdated, inadequate, or inapplicable for the test taker.
10 The documentation on the reliability and validity of test scores is inadequate.

The aim of the CCET (Level A) is to help promote good practice in the use of tests in educational settings. When well-designed and valid instruments are used competently, educational and psychological testing can make a valuable contribution to decision making about individuals and larger scale programmes and initiatives. We hope that this volume allied to training and the framework of the CCET will help the reader to be competent and confident in his/her use of tests.

Example of a Report Designed to Meet the Requirements of the Cumulative Evidence Exercise for the Award of the CCET (Level A)

Note: The structure of this sample report follows the specification of the cumulative evidence exercise. For our purposes here, the numbered sections from the specification are included to make explicit the links between the text and the requirements. While some assessors may wish you to follow this approach, as noted above, others may wish you to use a format and sub-headings which more closely mirror those of the reports that you are usually asked to provide. In any event, the important thing to ensure is that all the information required for this exercise is included in the report. The report here is based upon the case study used in Unit 4 to illustrate the links between short-term and cumulative assessments.

However, hypothetical data is not appropriate for this assessment: the report must be based upon the assessee's actual test use in their workplace.

1   Selection of an individual whom you believe would benefit from testing in an educational context

Name: John X
Gender: Male
Date of Birth: XX/XX/XX
School: Oakwood Primary School
Class: Year X
Date of Testing: XX/XX/XX
Chronological Age: X years X months

John is aged 10 years 8 months and is a Year 6 pupil in the above primary school, a large school, within an urban socially disadvantaged area. He is the second of three children, all of whom live with their mother, who is separated from the father. John is keeping up with his number work in class, but he is struggling to cope with reading and written language work at a Year 3 level, although he contributes reasonably well to classroom discussion when the topic is of interest to him. John's mother and his teachers have expressed concern about how he is likely to cope with the transition to secondary school in 8 months time.

2   Justification of your reasons for contemplating the test that you propose to use

Outline the help you expect that testing will give you
Use of a test will help answer the following assessment questions which in turn will clarify the nature of John's difficulties in reading and identify areas for further support by the school:

1   How do John's attainments in reading compare with those of pupils of the same age?
2   Does John have difficulties in both reading accuracy and reading comprehension or in only one of these sub-skill areas?
3   How do John's phonemic decoding skills compare with his sight word reading?

Choose an appropriate test(s)
Suitable instruments for addressing the above questions with a pupil of John's age would include the Neale Analysis of Reading Ability (NARA II)

(Second Revised British Edition) (M D Neale, 1997) (further details from http://www.nfer-nelson.co.uk) and the Test of Word Reading Efficiency (TOWRE) (J K Torgesen *et al.*, 1999) (further details from http://www. harcourt-uk.com).

Reflect on the processes which led you to choose this test(s)
[Unit 4: 1–5]
The assessment requirements entail valid and reliable standardized measures of oral reading rate, accuracy and comprehension and also of phonemic decoding efficiency (PDE) and sight word efficiency (SWE). Rate, accuracy and comprehension of reading are measured here by the reading aloud of passages of text and answering standardized questions about them. PDE is measured by the pronunciation of pseudo-words, and SWE by oral reading of individual words which do not have a meaningful context.

The NARA II and the TOWRE were both standardized on large numbers of participants (3,474 and 1,507 respectively). The NARA has a UK standardization, with weighting to ensure that the norms are representative of the population in terms of social disadvantage and in GCSE results. The TOWRE has a US standardization and the sample is highly representative of the US population in regard to gender, race and ethnicity, disability, urban versus rural residence, family income and parents' educational attainment.

The norms for both instruments are based upon adequate numbers of participants at each age-point and are technically appropriate for the purpose of test use here, with the caveat that we do not know the extent to which the derived scores from the TOWRE based upon a US sample are generalizable to test takers in the UK. But note that the assessment question that the TOWRE has been selected to address is concerned with a relative comparison of performance on the SWE and the PDE rather than on the actual standing of the scores in terms of the standardization sample. John's chronological age is well within the age-range for both tests.

In regard to validity, the NARA II and TOWRE both meet the assessment requirements. In the case of content validity, estimates of concurrent validity are provided in the form of correlations between scores on earlier versions of the NARA with scores on the Schonell Graded Word Reading Test (correlations of 0.95, 0.88 and 0.76 for accuracy, comprehension and rate) and with the BAS Word Reading Test (correlations of 0.94 and 0.83 for accuracy and comprehension respectively). In the case of the TOWRE, correlations with the Woodcock Reading Mastery Tests – Revised ranged from 0.92 to 0.94 in the case of Sight Word

Efficiency (SWE) and from 0.89 to 0.91 in the case of Phonemic Decoding Efficiency (PDE).

Turning to predictive validity, scores from the 1988 Australian revision of the NARA for rate, accuracy and comprehension showing significant levels of correlation (0.73, 0.83 and 0.78 respectively) with retest scores after a one-year test-retest interval. The data presented for the TOWRE in regard to predictive validity show the extent to which TOWRE scores are correlated with scores from other reading measures and hence are predictive of them. But it would appear that the scores were all collected at the same time and hence there is no information about how predictive the TOWRE is of performance on these reading measures over a period of time.

Finally, there is evidence of construct-related validity in the form of age differentiation and group differentiation for both the NARA II and the TOWRE and a confirmatory factor analysis which confirms the underlying model of the TOWRE.

The data presented in the test manuals thus confirm that the two instruments are valid measures and fit the assessment requirements. More up-to-date data regarding concurrent validity for the NARA II rather than earlier versions and data on the predictive validity of the TOWRE over an extended time period would have been helpful, however.

With regard to reliability, measures of alternate form reliability for John's age-group on the NARA II range from 0.81 for comprehension to 0.84 for accuracy. In the case of internal consistency reliability, the coefficients range from 0.86 for accuracy to 0.94 for comprehension. Alternate-form reliability coefficients for John's age-group on the TOWRE are somewhat higher (0.95 for SWE, 0.94 for PDE and 0.97 for the composite Total Word Efficiency score (TWE). Test-retest reliability coefficients for Form A are 0.84 for SWE, 0.89 for PDE, and 0.88 for TWE. Inter-scorer reliability is 0.99.

In summary, the above data from the respective test manuals confirm that the norms, reliability and validity of the NARA II and the TOWRE fit the assessment specification.

Comment on any restrictions on areas of use and on whether the test would meet the requirements of Equal Opportunities, Race Relations, and Disability Discrimination legislation [Unit 4: 6–7]
Both the NARA II and the TOWRE have restrictions on use in regard to age. The tests are designed for use within the specified age range covered by the respective norms unless the instrument is being used diagnostically. However, there are no specific limitations cited in either test manual in regard to gender, cultural or ethnic factors, ability range, attainment

level or special educational needs, although it may be assumed that the test taker's ability to access the materials, to understand the instructions, produce a response, and pass the practice items are restrictions to use.

However, there are some cultural assumptions within the NARA II passages which may challenge some pupils from different ethnic or cultural backgrounds, and there is also evidence of ceiling effects between 11 and 12 years due to a lack of items which are sufficiently difficult to differentiate between higher achieving older children. Pupils for whom English is an additional language may also be at a disadvantage for the reasons noted above. Test takers with a visual impairment may also be at a disadvantage in regard to having to read items in a fairly small font and those with a hearing impairment or language disorder may be at a disadvantage in terms of understanding the orally presented instructions and/ or in providing a clear verbal response.

However, John's chronological age is within the age-range for both tests, his first language is English, he does not come from an ethnic background or from a different culture, and he has no known visual or hearing impairments or problems with the fluency or clarity of his speech. Accordingly, there are no issues arising from Equal Opportunities, Race Relations, and Disability Discrimination legislation which would preclude the use of the NARA II or the TOWRE.

3 Description of the way in which you contacted the test taker, other interested parties and explained the need and purpose of testing [Unit 5: 1–4; 21–22]

Following discussion with John's class teacher to clarify her view of the nature of John's difficulties, John's mother was contacted and advised of his teachers' concerns. She confirmed that she was also concerned, and reported a family history of difficulties in reading. She agreed to testing to investigate the nature of John's reading problems with a view to identifying further support by the school. John was also interviewed and agreed to participate. He was advised of the date and approximate time of the testing session.

Comment also on information given to the test taker and or other relevant parties regarding how the results are to be used, who will have access to them and for how long they will be retained
[Unit 7:1; 4]
John and his mother were both advised that two tests would be administered, that the results would be used by John's teachers to help him with his difficulties in reading, and that the results would be available only to his teachers, or any other professional who could help with the problems.

It was also noted that John would also be asked to read from his class reading book. They were further advised that the results would be kept for as long as they would be helpful to John in the course of his school career and that they could also see the results if they wished. John was also informed that his mother knew about the proposal to administer the tests and was in agreement.

Comment on security and confidentiality issues regarding test data and materials [Unit 7: 2–3]
The test materials, manuals and record forms for the NARA II and the TOWRE were collected from a locked filing cabinet where they were stored to ensure that no one could have unauthorized access to them. Completed test forms are also filed in the relevant pupil's progress folder in a locked cabinet to ensure confidentiality of any test data.

4   Detailed description of the testing session

What were the conditions like? How did the test taker react? Did anything unusual happen? What were your observations? [Unit 5: 5–16; 23–27]
Prior to the session, the test materials and a stopwatch were checked and a suitable quiet location, the school resource room, identified and prepared for the individual administration of the test instruments. The room contained a table with two chairs of appropriate height for John and the test administrator and a 'do not disturb' notice was placed on the door.

John was collected from his classroom and taken to the school resource room. He chatted freely on the way to the resource room about the work that he was doing in class and did not seem anxious.

Once in the resource room, John was again advised of the purpose of the testing session, to help provide information about his difficulty in reading and was invited to ask any questions that he might have.

John's personal details and the date were recorded on the test record forms for the NARA II and TOWRE and were also noted on paper to be used for recording his performance from his class reader.

Once the test administrator judged that a satisfactory level of rapport had been established, John was asked to read aloud from his class reading book, which was of a Year 3 level in terms of complexity of material. His responses were recorded using a 'running record' of the words read correctly and incorrectly. He read four pages he had prepared at home with 90 per cent accuracy, and the next four pages (which were unfamiliar) with 80 per cent accuracy, indicating that the book was suitable for independent reading. John talked about the story but reported that, while he prepared the pages set by his teacher at home with his mother, he did not read much on his own for pleasure. He did volunteer that he enjoyed football and that he might be interested in reading stories about sport.

John was advised that the time taken to read the passages on the NARA II would be recorded using a stopwatch and that there was a time limit on the TOWRE.

Form 1 of the NARA II was then administered, followed by Form A of the TOWRE, in both cases following the standardized instructions which included practice items. The Level 1 passage was administered as the starting point on the NARA II, in view of John's known difficulties. He reached the discontinuation point on the NARA II on the Level 3 passage, with 18 errors in reading accuracy.

John had no obvious difficulties in understanding what he was required to do and participated enthusiastically. He did not ask any questions or request any further information, and did not appear to be anxious about the timing of his performance. He persevered even when he was unsure of some of the more difficult words in the Level 3 passage of the NARA II and with some of the harder non-words on the TOWRE. He was offered a short break between the administration of the NARA II and the TOWRE, but elected to carry on. The instructions for recording responses were followed by the test administrator in the case of both tests, together with the discontinuation procedures in the case of the NARA II, and time limits in the case of the TOWRE. The session took 35 minutes in total.

The results from both tests were scored using the test manual appropriate to the instrument. There were no factors evident which may have adversely affected John's performance.

John was provided with preliminary verbal feedback on his performance and thanked for his participation before he returned to his classroom. He was also reminded that the test results would be confidential to those parties already identified and that they would be stored securely. He was invited to ask any questions that he might have, but indicated that he did not have any. The test materials were checked to ensure that they were complete and then returned to the locked cabinet.

5   Detailed description of the scoring process

The records of John's responses were checked for accuracy. There were no ambiguous responses. The test data were scored according to the guidance provided in the test manuals.

Raw scores were summed for the NARA II and the TOWRE together with the derived scores and confidence intervals from the relevant tables in the test manuals, as shown in the tables below:

Test:	Sub-test:	Raw score	SS (68% CIs)	Age equiv. (68% CIs)	Percentiles
NARA II	Rate	41	79 (71–87)	7y 0m (6y 0m – 8y 1m)	8
	Accuracy	32	80 (75–85)	7y 3m (6y 9m – 7y 11m)	9
	Comprehension	16	84 (78–90)	8y 1m (7y 7m – 8y 9m)	14
TOWRE	Sight Word Efficiency	48	83 (80–86)	8y 0m (N/A)	13
	Phonemic Decoding Efficiency	7	71 (67–75)	6y 9m (N/A)	3
	Total Word Reading Efficiency Composite Score	N/A	72 (69–75)	N/A	3

Analysis of Errors on the NARA II			
Mispronunciations	Substitutions	Additions	Omissions
5	8	3	2

Were there any problems in using the scoring procedures?
[Unit 5: 17–20]
No problems or ambiguities were observed in implementing the scoring procedures for either test.

6   Interpretation of the scores

With reference to other test taker information, comment on the norms used (and any supplementary material) and any criterion-referenced interpretation, issues regarding any ceiling or basal effects, riders to the interpretation of the results, the appropriateness of the reference group used in the test standardization, the meaning of the scores and their associated confidence intervals [Unit 6: 1–6]
The norms for the NARA II and the TOWRE are based upon adequate numbers of participants at each age-point and are appropriate for John's chronological age. No ceiling or basal effects are evident. The NARA II standardization is based upon a representative UK sample, which constitutes an appropriate reference group for John. The TOWRE is based upon

a representative US standardization group, but the extent to which the norms are directly generalizable to test takers in the UK is currently unknown. Interpretation of the results from the TOWRE requires a rider to this effect. Additional criterion-referenced information is available in the form of the analysis of errors on the NARA II, using the categories provided in the manual.

The results indicate that John's scores on both the NARA II and the TOWRE are below average for his age. In the case of the NARA II, he achieved standard scores of 79 for rate of reading, 80 for accuracy of reading, and 84 for reading comprehension, all below the average score of 100 which might be expected of a pupil of his age. However, these scores are not statistically different, indicating that John's comprehension is not stronger than his accuracy or rate of reading.

The 68 per cent confidence intervals for these observed standard scores reveal only a a 16 per cent chance that John's true score is above 87 or below 71 in the case of rate, above 85 or below 75 in the case of accuracy, and above 90 or below 78 in the case of comprehension.

John's reading age equivalent scores for rate, accuracy and comprehension were 7y 0m, 7y 3m and 8y 1m respectively. The 68 per cent confidence intervals for these observed reading ages reveal only a 16 per cent chance that John's true score is above 8y 1m or below 6y 0m in the case of rate, above 7y 11m or below 6y 9m in the case of accuracy, and above 8y 9m or below 7y 7m in the case of comprehension.

Finally, percentile ranks for John's scores indicate that only 8 per cent of pupils in the standardization sample of the NARA II achieved a score at the same level or below that of John's for rate, 9 per cent in the case of accuracy, and 14 per cent in the case of comprehension.

Qualitative analysis of John's reading errors reveals that most of his errors were substitutions of words with the same initial letter as the word in the text read incorrectly (8 out of 18 errors) and mispronunciations (5 out of 18 errors), where he was unable to produce a recognizable word. The substitutions also fitted into the context of the story. In addition, John both added words (3 out of 18 errors) and omitted words (2 out of 18 errors) while reading the three passages aloud.

In the case of the TOWRE, John achieved standard scores of 83 for SWE, 71 for PDE and 72 for Total Word Reading Efficiency (TWRE), an equally weighted composite of SWE and PDE. These scores are again below the average of 100 which would be expected of a pupil of John's age, indicating that John has difficulties in both sight word reading and in phonemic decoding. The difference in the standard scores for SWE and PDE, 12 score points, exceeds the value of 11 score points tabled in the manual for a statistically significant difference at the 5 per cent level. This means that John's score on the PDE was significantly poorer than his score on the SWE, and that there is only one chance in twenty that a difference of this magnitude could be due to chance error.

The 68 per cent confidence intervals for these observed standard scores reveal only a a 16 per cent chance that John's true score is above 86 or below 80 in the case of SWE, above 75 or below 67 in the case of PDE, and above 75 or below 69 in the case of TWRE.

John's age equivalent scores for SWE and PDE were 8 y 0 m and 6 y 9 m respectively. No confidence intervals are provided for age equivalent scores in the manual.

The percentile ranks for John's scores indicate that 13 per cent of pupils in the standardization sample of the TOWRE achieved a score at the same level or below that of John's for SWE, 3 per cent in the case of PDE, and 3 per cent in the case of TWRE.

It should be noted, however, that the TOWRE was normed on a representative US standardization sample, and that how the above normative results map on to a UK population is presently unknown in the absence of a validation study to calibrate the scores. However, the relative comparison between SWE and PDE is unlikely to be affected by this.

State what conclusions you draw from the test score(s), taking into account any other information about the test taker's educational performance, the purpose of using the test, and any other forms of information gathered in the course of the assessment. What would be your next course of action? [Unit 6: 7–9]
The above scores support the conclusion that John has problems in the accuracy of his reading which adversely affect both the rate at which he reads and his understanding of the material. These problems are associated with particularly marked difficulties in phonemic decoding. John requires reading material at around a Year 3/Year 4 level, and his current reading books are appropriate at present in terms of level of difficulty. The relatively high number of substitutions that John makes while reading text and the fact that the majority of these make sense in the context of the passage are indicative of the fact that he makes use of contextual cues as well as initial letter cues to 'guess' words he does not know. Further supporting evidence for this comes from fact that he both adds and leaves out words while reading (additions and omissions).

In terms of action required, intervention to address the difficulties in decoding unknown words is a priority for John and the introduction of a suitable programme should be discussed with his teachers. In view of the fact that he copes with mathematics and oral language work, it may be that John has a specific learning difficulty and this should be further investigated.

He would also benefit from reading material which taps into areas of interest, such as sport. In addition, it would also be helpful to discuss with John and his mother how best to provide support for his reading at home. Here, it would be important to ensure that he is reading regularly, for an appropriate time period on each occasion, and that John's mother has clear strategies both for helping John with unknown words and for asking him questions about the material he is reading.

7 Feedback

Prepare two kinds of feedback: Written – to the test taker or interested party. Prepare a short written report appropriate to the test taker and lay interested parties. Use appropriate statistical concepts in the treatment and interpretation of scores. Link to the further action you may recommend [Unit 6: 10]

Name: John X
Gender: Male
Date of Birth: XX/XX/XX
School: Oakwood Primary School
Class: Year 6
Date of Testing: XX/XX/XX
Chronological Age: X years X months

John was seen in school for an assessment of his reading skills on XX/XX/XX because of concerns by his teachers and his mother. John is the second of three children and no difficulties in hearing or vision are reported. He attends school regularly, and his teachers indicate that while he is keeping up with number work in class, he finds reading and written language work hard, and is currently working at a Year 3 level, although he takes part in classroom discussions when he finds the topic of interest.

John's reading was assessed using his current class reading book and also the Neale Analysis of Reading Ability II (NARA II) and the Test of Word Reading Efficiency (TOWRE). The NARA II test consists of short stories, which John read aloud, and also questions about the stories. The TOWRE consists of a list of words and a list of non-words, which can be pronounced, which John read. This is a summary report, and a copy of the full report sent to the school is enclosed.

John did not appear to be anxious during assessment and was very cooperative. The scores are thus likely to be an accurate reflection of his reading ability.

John's scores on both the NARA II and the TOWRE show that he has difficulty with reading and that he is reading at around a Year 3/Year 4 level. Less than 10 per cent of pupils of John's age would read at John's level in terms of speed and accuracy of reading, and less than 15 per cent in terms of understanding what is read.

John has problems in the accuracy of his reading which mean that he reads slowly and this in turn also makes it difficult for him to understand what he reads. These problems seem to be due to the fact that he finds it difficult to accurately sound out unknown or unfamiliar words. As a result, when John comes across an unknown word while reading, he uses the first letter of the word and his understanding of the story to 'guess' what the word is. John needs to develop his skills in 'decoding', or sounding out words.

Recommendations

A suitable programme to help John with his decoding skills would be helpful, and this will be discussed with his teachers.

John requires reading material at around a Year 3/Year 4 level, and his current class reading books are appropriate at the present time. However, he would benefit from supplementary reading material which taps into areas of interest to him, for example, sport. This will also be discussed with John and his teachers.

In addition, it would also be helpful to discuss how best to help John with his reading at home, to make sure that he is reading regularly (for example, a minimum of three times a week) and for a suitable period of time (for example, no less than 15 minutes) on each occasion. Advice on ways of helping John cope with unknown words and on how best to ask him questions about what he is reading will be provided.

Finally, as John is coping in mathematics and oral work, it may be that he has a specific learning difficulty. That is, that he has learning difficulties in some, but not all areas of his school curriculum. This will be further investigated to ensure that he can receive any additional support to which he may be eligible.

If there are any aspects of this report which you would like to discuss, please do not hesitate to contact me at the telephone number below.

Prepare two kinds of feedback: Written – to a fellow professional with extensive knowledge and experience in educational testing. Use appropriate statistical concepts in the treatment and interpretation of scores. Link to the further action you may recommend. [Unit 6: 10]

Report To:
Date:
Name: John X
Gender: Male
Date of Birth: XX/XX/XX
School: Oakwood Primary School
Class: Year 6
Date of Testing: XX/XX/XX
Chronological Age: X years X months

John is a Year 6 Pupil at Oakwood Primary School and an assessment of his reading skills was carried out in school on XX/XX/XX in the light of concerns expressed by his teachers and his mother about secondary transfer in 8 months time. John is the second of three children and no difficulties in hearing or vision are reported. He attends school regularly, and his teachers indicate that while he is keeping up with number work in class, he is struggling to cope with reading and written language, and is currently working at a Year 3 level, although he contributes reasonably well to classroom discussion when the topic is of interest to him.

John's reading was assessed using his current class reading book and also the Neale Analysis of Reading Ability II (NARA II) and the Test of Word Reading Efficiency (TOWRE). John did not appear to be anxious during this session and cooperated throughout. The scores are thus likely to be an accurate reflection of his reading ability.

His scores on both the NARA II and the TOWRE were below average for his age. In the case of the NARA II, he achieved standard scores of 79 for rate of reading, 80 for accuracy of reading, and 84 for reading comprehension, all below the average score of 100 which might be expected of a pupil of his age. However, these scores are not statistically different, indicating that John's comprehension is not stronger than his accuracy or rate of reading.

The 68 per cent confidence intervals for these observed standard scores reveal only a 16 per cent chance that John's true score is above 87 or below 71 in the case of rate, above 85 or below 75 in the case of accuracy, and above 90 or below 78 in the case of comprehension.

John's reading age equivalent scores for rate, accuracy and comprehension were 7y 0m, 7y 3m and 8y 1m respectively. The 68 per cent confidence intervals for these observed reading ages reveal only a 16 per cent chance that John's true score is above 8y 1m or below 6y 0m in the case of rate, above 7y 11m or below 6y 9m in the case of accuracy, and above 8y 9m or below 7y 7m in the case of comprehension.

Finally, percentile ranks for John's scores indicate that only 8 per cent of pupils in the standardization sample of the NARA II achieved a score at the same level or below that of John's for rate, 9 per cent in the case of accuracy, and 14 per cent in the case of comprehension.

Qualitative analysis of John's reading errors reveals that most of his errors were substitutions of words with the same initial letter as the word in the text read incorrectly (8 out of 18 errors) and mispronunciations (5 out of 18 errors), where he was unable to produce a recognizable word. The substitutions also fitted into the context of the story. In addition, while reading the three passages aloud, John both added words (3 out of 18 errors) and omitted words (2 out of 18 errors).

In the case of the TOWRE, John achieved standard scores of 83 for SWE, 71 for PDE and 72 for Total Word Reading Efficiency (TWRE), an equally weighted composite of SWE and PDE. These scores are again below the average of 100 which would be expected of a pupil of John's age, indicating that John has difficulties in both sight word reading and in phonemic decoding. The difference in the standard scores for SWE and PDE, 12 score points, exceeds the value of 11 score points tabled in the manual for a statistically significant difference at the 5 per cent level. This means that John's score on the PDE was significantly poorer than this score on the SWE, and that there is only one chance in 20 that a difference of this magnitude could be due to chance error.

The 68 per cent confidence intervals for these observed standard scores reveal only a a 16 per cent chance that John's true score is above 86 or below 80 in the case of SWE, above 75 or below 67 in the case of PDE, and above 75 or below 69 in the case of TWRE.

John's age equivalent scores for SWE and PDE were 8 y 0 m and 6 y 9 m respectively. (No confidence intervals are provided for age equivalent scores in the manual.)

The percentile ranks for John's scores indicate that 13 per cent of pupils in the standardization sample of the TOWRE achieved a score at the same level or below that of John's for SWE, 3 per cent in the case of PDE, and 3 per cent in the case of TWRE.

It should be noted, however, that the TOWRE was normed on a representative US standardization sample, and that how the above normative results map on to a UK population is presently unknown in the absence of a suitable validation study to calibrate the scores. However, the relative comparison between SWE and PDE is unlikely to be affected by this.

Conclusion

The above scores support the conclusion that John has problems in the accuracy of his reading which adversely affects both the rate at which he reads and his understanding of the material. These problems are associated with marked difficulties in phonemic decoding. The relatively high number of substitutions that John makes while reading text and the fact that the majority of these make sense in the context of the passage are indicative of the fact that he makes use of contextual cues as well as initial letter cues to 'guess' words he does not know. Further supporting evidence for this comes from fact that he both adds and leaves out words while reading (additions and omissions). In view of his reported strengths in mathematics and oral work, there is a possibility that John may have a specific learning difficulty.

Recommendations
Intervention to address the difficulties in decoding unknown words is a priority for John and the introduction of a suitable programme will be discussed with his teachers.

John requires reading material at around a Year 3/Year 4 level, and his current reading books are appropriate at present in terms of level of difficulty. However, he would benefit from supplementary reading material which taps into areas of interest, such as sport.

In addition, it would also be helpful to discuss with John and his mother how best to provide support for his reading at home. Here, it would be important to ensure that he is reading regularly, for an appropriate time period on each occasion, and that John's mother has clear strategies for both helping John with unknown words and for asking him questions about the material he is reading.

Finally, the possibility that John may have a specific learning difficulty should be further explored to ensure that he receives the benefits of any additional support to which he may be eligible.

8   Security and confidentiality

Comment on storage of test data in regard to the conditions of the Data Protection Act [Unit 7: 6]
Test materials and the completed test record form are both stored securely in the school. The tests are kept in a locked test cupboard in the school to which only designated members of staff have access, and the record form is stored in John's file which is kept in a locked filing cabinet in the school office. Only John's teachers, parents, the LEA and other professionals working with him have access to the information contained in the test form. John also has the right to see the form.

References

American Educational Research Association, American Psychological Association and National Council on Measurement in Education (1999) *Standards for Educational and Psychological Testing*. Washington, DC: American Psychological Association.

ASE (2000) Testing people with disabilities. Retrieved 22 August 2005 from http://www.ase-solutions.co.uk/support.asp?id=46

Australian Psychological Society (1997) *Supplement to Guidelines for the Use of Psychological Tests*. Canberra: Australian Psychological Society.

Black, P. and William, D. (1998) *Inside the Black Box: Raising Standards through Classroom Assessment*. Windsor: nferNelson.

Bookbinder, G.E., Vincent, D. and Crumpler, M. (2002) *Salford Sentence Reading Test (Revised), 3rd Edition*. London: Hodder and Stoughton.

British Psychological Society (1995) *Level A Competences in Occupational Psychology*. Leicester: The British Psychological Society.

British Psychological Society (1998) *Certificate and Register of Competence in Occupational Testing: General Information Pack (Level A)*. Leicester: The British Psychological Society.

British Psychological Society (2003) *Psychological Testing: A Test Taker's Guide*. Leicester: The British Psychological Society.

British Psychological Society (2004a) *General Information Pack: Certificate of Competence in Educational Testing (Level A)*. Leicester: The British Psychological Society.

British Psychological Society (2004b) *Guidance for Assessors: Certificate of Competence in Educational Testing (Level A)*. Leicester: The British Psychological Society.

British Psychological Society (2004c) *Assessor's Information Pack Educational Testing (Level A)*. Leicester: The British Psychological Society.

British Psychological Society (2004d) *Code of Good Practice for Educational Testing (Level A)*. Leicester: The British Psychological Society.

Canadian Psychological Association (1987) *Guidelines for Educational and Psychological Testing.* Ottawa: Canadian Psychological Association.

Cronbach, L.J. (1984) *Essentials of Psychological Testing. (Fourth Edition).* New York: Harper and Row.

Data Protection Act (1998) Retrieved 26 October 2005 from http://www.opsi.gov.uk/acts/acts1998/19980029.htm

Disability Rights Commission (2002) *Code of Practice for Schools.* London: The Stationery Office. Retrieved 19 August 2005 from http://www.drc-gb.org/publicationsandreports/publicationdetails.asp?id=220&section=ed

Dunn, L.M., Dunn, L.M., Whetton, C. and Burley, J. (1997) *The British Picture Vocabulary Test (Second Edition).* Windsor: nferNelson.

Elliott, C.D. (1997) The *British Ability Scales Second Edition (BAS-II).* Windsor: nferNelson.

Elliott, C.D., Murray, D.J. and Pearson, L.S. (1979) *British Ability Scales.* Windsor: nferNelson.

European Union Council Directive 95/46/EC (1995) Retrieved 26 October 2005 from europa.eu.int/eur-lex/pri/en/oj/dat/2002/l_201/l_20120020731en00370047.pdf

Eysenck, H.J. and Eysenck, M.W. (1975) *Manual of the Eysenck Personality Questionnaire.* San Diego, CA: Educational and Industrial Testing Service.

Flynn, J.R. (1987) Massive IQ Gains in 14 Nations: What IQ Tests Really Measure. *Psychological Bulletin,* 101, 171–91.

Frederickson, N., Frith, U. and Reason, R. (1997) *Phonological Assessment Battery (PhAB).* Windsor: nferNelson.

Gordon, E.E. (1979) *Primary Measures of Music Audiation Grade K–3.* Chicago, IL: GIA Publications Inc.

Gordon, E.E. (1982) *Intermediate Measures of Music Audiation Grades 1–6.* Chicago, IL: GIA Publications Inc.

Gregory, H.M. and Gregory, A.H. (1994) A Comparison of the Neale and BAS Reading Tests. *Educational Psychology in Practice,* 10(1), 15–18.

Hoff, E. (2001) *Language Development. Second Edition.* Belmont, CA: Wadsworth.

International Test Commission (2000) *International Guidelines for Test Use: Version 2000.* Retrieved 22 August 2005 from http://www.intestcom.org

Jeffrey, P. (1984) *Rogers Personal Adjustment Inventory (Revised Edition).* Windsor: nferNelson.

Lidz, C.S. (1991) *Practitioner's Guide to Dynamic Assessment.* New York: The Guilford Press.

Lohman, D.F., Hagen, E.P. and Thorndike, R.L. (2003) *Cognitive Abilities Test: Third Edition (CAT3).* Windsor: nferNelson.

Murphy, K.R. and Davidshofer, C.O. (1994) *Psychological Testing: Principles and Applications. Third Edition.* London: Prentice-Hall.

Myers, I.B. and McCauley, M.H. (1985) *Manual: A Guide to the Development and Use of the Myers-Briggs Type Indicator.* Palo Alto, CA: Consulting Psychologists Press.

Naglieri, J. (1999) *Essentials of CAS Assessment*. New York: Wiley.

Neale, M.D. (1997) *Neale Analysis of Reading Ability (NARA II) (Second Revised British Edition)*. Windsor: nferNelson.

Neale, M.D. and McKay, M.F. (1985) A Three Year Longitudinal Study of Academic Performance Related to Pre-school Developmental Characteristics on the Neale Scales of Early Child Development. Unpublished paper, Monash University, Australia.

Neale, M.D., Chrisophers, U. and Whetton, C. (1989) *Neale Analysis of Reading Ability – Revised British Edition*. Windsor: nferNelson.

New Zealand Psychological Society (2002) *Code of Ethics for Psychologists Working in Aotearoa/New Zealand*. Auckland: New Zealand Psychological Society.

Nunnally, J. (1978) *Psychometric Theory (Second Edition)*. New York: McGraw Hill.

Oakland, T. (2004) Use of Educational and Psychological Tests Internationally. *Applied Psychology: An International Review*, 53(2), 157–72.

Oakland, T. and Hu, S. (1993) International Perspectives on Tests Used with Children and Youths. *Journal of School Psychology*, 31(4), 501–17.

Rathvon, N. (2004) *Early Reading Assessment: A Practitioner's Handbook*. New York: The Guilford Press. Retrieved 20 October 2005 from http://www.guilford.com/excerpts/rathvon2.pdf

Rudner, L.M. (1994) Questions to Ask When Evaluating Tests. *Practical Assessment, Research & Evaluation*, 4(2). Retrieved 8 August 2005 from http://PAREonline.net/getvn.asp?v=4&n=2

Rust, J. and Golombok, S. (2000) *Modern Psychometrics: The Science of Psychological Assessment. Second Edition*. London: Routledge.

Salvia, J. and Ysseldyke, J.E. (2004) *Assessment in Special and Inclusive Education. Ninth Edition*. Boston: Houghton Mifflin Company.

Schonell, F.J. and Goodacre, E. (1974) *The Psychology and Teaching of Reading*. London: Oliver & Boyd.

SHL (2000) *Testing of People with Disabilities*. Retrieved 22 August 2005 from http://www.shl.com/SHL/en-int/Thought_Leadership/Best_Practices_Guides/

Simons, R., Goddard, R. and Patton, W. (2002) Hand-scoring Rates in Psychological Testing. *Assessment*, 9(3), 292–300.

SPSS, Inc (2003) *SPSS for Windows Version 12*. Chicago: SPSS, Inc.

Torgesen, J.K., Wagner, R.K. and Rashotte, C.A. (1999) *TOWRE: Test of Word Reading Efficiency*. Austin, TX: pro-ed.

Tzuriel, D. (1990) *Cognitive Modifiability Battery (CMB)*. Ramat-Gan, Israel; Bar-Ilan University.

Tzuriel, D. (2000) The Cognitive Modifiability Battery (CMB): Assessment and Intervention. In C.S. Lidz and J.G. Elliott (eds), *Dynamic Assessment: Prevailing Models and Applications* (pp. 375–406). Amsterdam: JAI/Elsevier Science.

Urbina, S. (2004) *Essentials in Psychological Testing*. Hoboken, NJ: John Wiley.

Wechsler, D. (1974) *Manual for Wechsler Intelligence Scale for Children – Revised (WISC-R)*. London: The Psychological Corporation.

Wechsler, D. (1993) *Wechsler Objective Reading Dimensions (WORD)*. London: Harcourt Assessment/The Psychological Corporation.

Wechsler, D. (1996) *Wechsler Objective Numerical Dimensions (WOND)*. London: Harcourt Assessment/The Psychological Corporation.

Wechsler, D. (2004) *Wechsler Intelligence Scale for Children Fourth UK Edition (WISC-IV^{UK})*. London: Harcourt Assessment/The Psychological Corporation.

Wechsler, D. (2005) *Wechsler Individual Achievement Test – Second UK Edition (WIAT-II^{UK})*. London: Harcourt Assessment/The Psychological Corporation.

Whetton, C. (1997) *BPVS II Technical Supplement: Supplementary Data and Norms for Pupils with English as an Additional Language*. Windsor: nferNelson.

William, D. (2000) Integrating Formative and Summative Functions of Assessment. Paper presented to Working Group 10 of the International Congress on Mathematics Education, Makuhari, Tokyo, August 2000. Retrieved 8 August 2005 from http://www.kcl.ac.uk/depsta/education/publications/ICME9%3DWGA10.pdf

Woodcock, R.W. (1987) *Woodcock Reading Mastery Tests – Revised*. Circle Pines, MN: American Guidance Service.

Appendix 1

General Information Pack: Certificate of Competence in Educational Testing (Level A)

The
British
Psychological
Society

Certificate of Competence in Educational Testing (Level A)

General Information Pack

Psychological Testing Centre
www.psychtesting.org.uk

GIP LA–ED

The Society has established a Psychological Testing Centre to consolidate its activities in the areas of psychological testing. As part of the services offered by the Centre the Society has a website devoted to provide information, guidance and links to test takers, test users and test publishers alike. The website can be found at http://www.psychtesting.org.uk

Other relevant FREE publications are available on our website or by contacting the Society:
- Psychological Testing: A User's Guide
- Psychological Testing: A Taker's Guide

Contents

General Information

Training

To obtain a Certificate of Competence in Educational Testing (Level A) you must first undertake training and then have your competence affirmed by an Assessor (that is, a Chartered Psychologist whose assessment methods have been verified by the Society). In many cases Trainers are also Assessors, but not necessarily so.

A list of Assessors is obtainable on the website: www.psychtesting.org.uk. Before starting any training, you should check with the Trainer that the course will lead to eligibility for the issue of a Certificate, and that the Assessor holds a current Assessor's Certificate.

Although there are many points of similarities between the Certificate of Competence in Educational Testing (Level A) and the Certificate of Competence in Occupational Testing (Level A) there are also sufficient differences regarding contexts of test use to require that competence is demonstrated in each Certificate whether or not the applicant has completed the equivalent level certificate in educational or occupational testing. However, certain core competencies may be accredited as prior learning.

The benefits of the scheme

The main benefits of the scheme for local authorities, schools, professionals, carers, students, pupils and learners are that it:

■ provides the potential test user with a clear specification of what he/she needs to know and be able to do, to use tests properly;
■ provides a set of minimum standards for training in the use of educational testing procedures;
■ provides the students on training courses with a set of specific objectives which they can match against the content of their training course;
■ provides evidence of qualification which should be 'transferable' between various providers of training in testing and between the various publishers and other suppliers of test materials;
■ provides a nationally recognised transferable qualification in test use in education which is not dependent on specific tests, publishers or trainers.

The adoption of the scheme has positive benefits for teaching of psychology in that it encourages the inclusion of relevant teaching and training at both postgraduate and undergraduate levels. The scheme also places the responsibility for judging competence squarely on the shoulders of Chartered Psychologists – who are accountable should they act outside their areas of competence.

The Level A Certificate will not qualify people in the use of certain tests (such as the Wechsler Ability Scales, BAS-II, Stanford-Binet, McCarthy Scales etc.) used in the formal assessment of cognitive abilities, which require a more detailed knowledge of test construction and interpretation. Practitioner Level Competences, which are broader and more rigorous in their coverage of underlying theory, will be required for the use of tests of this kind.

The Level A Certificate can be used as evidence of competence for people wishing to use or purchase test materials. As such, evidence that one has attained the required standard for all the essential elements of competence is deemed by the Society as being a necessary (but not sufficient) condition for access to test materials.

While publishers and suppliers of test materials cannot be bound by the Society, the Society encourages them to accept the Certificate as a basis for their registration of test users. Suppliers of tests may, of course, require evidence of additional areas of competence as being required for particular tests or may require users to have additional specialist training in the use of particular instruments. Any person who has the minimum competence defined by the standards should of necessity be in a position to appreciate the need for additional training where it is required.

To apply for the Certificate of Competence

You will need to have the Affirmation of Competence (on the back of the application form) completed by one or more suitably qualified people who should be Chartered Psychologists who hold either a Statement or Certificate of Competence in Educational Testing and have had their assessment methods verified and hold a current valid assessors certificate. The completed Affirmation should then be returned to the Society.

If you are a Chartered Psychologist with a current Practising Certificate, there will be no charge for the Certificate of Competence. If you are not a Chartered Psychologist holding a current Practising Certificate, please enclose payment of £65 with your application.

To be entered on the Register of Competence in Psychological Testing (Educational), please enclose £20 for the first year's subscription, together with your payment for a certificate.

To apply for a Statement of Competence (grandparent route)

The Statement of Competence in Educational Testing (Level A) is provided as a qualification for those who are Chartered Educational Psychologists with the Society and/or members of the Association of Educational Psychologists (AEP). This is an interim measure until the establishment of the Certificate of Competence in Educational Testing. This route will stop being available from 31 December 2007. (From January 2008 all applicants will need to complete the Affirmation of Competence and apply for a Certificate of Competence in the normal way).

The Statement of Competence is regarded by the Society as recognition of a level of competence equivalent to that recognised by the Certificate of Competence in Educational Testing. Please see the application form for the Statement of Competence (centrefold). There is no charge for the Statement of Competence in Educational Testing (Level A) for Chartered Educational Psychologists who hold a current Practising Certificate. Members of the AEP and Chartered Educational Psychologists who do not hold a current Practising Certificate applying for the Statement of Competence will need to pay an application fee of £65.

Holders of the Statement of Competence in Educational Testing (Level A) will be required to join the Register of Competence in Psychological Testing (Educational) for payment of £20 a year. All holders of the Statement or Certificate of Competence in Educational Testing will be expected to maintain their membership of this Register.

Special cases route

A special case route is also available. Please contact the Psychological Testing Centre for more details: direct line 0116 252 9530; e-mail enquiry@psychtesting.org.uk

Certification Scheme – background and explanation

The most widely used tests in the UK are educational tests of ability, attainment and aptitude. Teachers and others in the United States have long had access to standards for educational and psychological testing published jointly by the American Psychological Society, the America Educational Research Association and the National Council on Measurement in Education, but nothing comparable has been available in the United Kingdom.

There is a resurgence of interest in the use of tests for monitoring standards of attainment in literacy and numeracy and assessing the progress of individual students/pupils/learners. The Qualifications and Curriculum Authority (QCA), for example, is currently developing new standardised attainment tests for use in all local authority schools in England and Wales. In addition, the proposal to re-introduce selection will have implications for standardised test use in schools.

However, there is a danger that this pressure may result in the inappropriate use of tests rather than the wider range of assessment techniques of which testing is only one. While many teachers have practical experience of administering such tests not all will have confidence in their ability to score, interpret, and justify their findings. Training in the use of tests in education also varies considerably, with educational psychologists and speech and language therapists in general fairing better than teachers. The British Psychological Society, through the Steering Committee for Test Standards (SCTS), has been instrumental in developing standards for responsible test use in occupational settings (the Level A and Level B standards). The Society, assisted by three major UK test publishers, is now developing a system of certification for psychologists, teachers, speech and language therapists, careers officers, occupational therapists and the like, who wish an objective means of demonstrating their competence in the use of published tests in education.

Increasingly, teachers and other professionals in education are required to substantiate their professional opinions. In England and Wales, for example, 3,048 appeals against special needs provision for individual pupils were heard by the Special Educational Needs Tribunal in one year alone. The appropriate use of tests can provide an evidence-base that permits comparison between a student/pupil/learner's performance and that of her age-peers, which may be a key element in making the correct decisions in such cases and defending them against appeal. The interpretation of test findings may also be an important consideration with regard to an apparent fall in standards in a particular school, a dispute between carers and an authority relating to the placement of a student/pupil/learner, or parental concern about progress. Appropriate test use may even help to offset appeals to tribunals.

Examples of test misuse such as allegations of test coaching, deliberate leaking of answers and the allowance of extra time in the administration of the Key Stage 2 SATs (England and Wales) have received publicity. Test publishers also report instances of bad practice:

- schools using the manual and norms from one test to administer and score different tests;
- schools using actual test material as practice papers;
- schools using tests with no access to the interpretative data;
- the use of experimental tests with no supporting data to identify specific learning difficulties/dyslexia.

Such poor practice increases the risks of making inappropriate decisions affecting the future lives of students/pupils/learners, resulting in adverse publicity for the schools and LEAs concerned and the possibility of court cases with potentially damaging financial penalties.

However, the proposed educational testing standards will provide teachers and others with a means of supplying evidence to employers and carers of a high level of competence in the selection, administration, scoring and interpretation of results from tests of ability, attainment and aptitude.

General Outline of the Certification Scheme

The standards have been designed to fulfil two functions:

- the provision of criteria which may be used in the assessment of an individual's competence to use tests;
- guidance for those who may wish to use tests, or who may be approached by users or purveyors of such procedures.

Detailed specifications of standards of competence derived from earlier work on the Level A occupational testing standards, cover the following areas:

- **Relevant underpinning knowledge** – in the learner's development, in the nature and theories of ability and techniques of assessment including psychometrics and the theory of testing;
- **Task skills** – relating to test administration and providing feedback appropriate to the age and ability of the student/pupil/learner;
- **Task management skills** – required to achieve overall functional competence: organising test procedures, control and security of materials, etc.;
- **Contingency management skills** – to deal with problems, difficulties, breakdowns in routine, dealing with questions during test administration etc.;
- **Contextual skills** – defining assessment needs, knowing when to use tests and when to use alternative approaches such as curriculum-based assessment, criterion-referenced assessment or dynamic assessment, and knowing how to integrate the outcomes of these different forms of assessment;
- **Instrumental skills** – relating to specific test procedures or instruments;
- **Interpretation of results** – relating to the appropriate explanation of the meaning and significance of test findings.

Outline of the Procedures

A checklist of Competences in Educational testing is attached and defines the minimum levels required for any user. An individual who has met the standards required for ALL the items on the Checklist will be eligible to apply to the Society for a **British Psychological Society Certificate of Competence in Educational Testing (Level A)**. The Level A Certificate can be used as evidence of competence for people wishing to use or purchase test materials. The Society encourages publishers and suppliers of test materials to accept the Certificate as a basis for their registration of test users, although suppliers of tests may require additional specialist training in the use of particular instruments.

It is hoped that the Level A qualification may be of interest to psychologists, teachers and other professionals working in education and by providing an explicit common set of criteria for judging competence may lead to greater uniformity and higher standards in test use.

Who will be responsible for assessing an individual's competence?

Assessment of the competence of an individual seeking certification will be the responsibility of suitably qualified Assessors.

To whom does this scheme apply?

Any person wishing to make use of tests in education. The certification arrangement will dispense with the distinction between psychologist and non-psychologist in this context. Instead it will enable two groups to be identified:

- People who can provide evidence of their competence;
- People who cannot provide evidence of their competence.

It must be stressed that the proposed qualification is not a qualification in educational psychology, but a qualification in the theoretical background and practical aspects of educational testing.

How will standards be maintained?

Standards will be maintained in two ways. Firstly, the Assessor, who completes and signs the Checklist, is accountable to the Society (although this accountability is for their own actions: actual responsibility for misuse or abuse of tests must lie with the test user). Secondly, the Society maintains a Register of Competence in Psychological Testing (Education) (RCPT) of those who have a Statement or Level A Certificate.

Verification of Assessment Methods

A system to verify the assessment methods used by Assessors to affirm applicants for the Certificate of Competence has been developed.

The verification process has been set up to aid the development of nationwide standards for assessment and considers only the assessment methods used by the Assessors. It DOES NOT consider the methods of training or the qualities of the Assessor.

When the verification has been completed Assessors will be issued with an Assessor's Certificate which confirms that their assessment methods have been verified by The British Psychological Society. These Certificates should be displayed where applicants can see them.

The Society in collaboration with the test publishers and training course organisers will put in place procedures to monitor the success of the scheme. Because of its voluntary nature, the scheme can work only with the good will and support of others outside the Society, in particular the test publishers.

The Society reserves its position to make changes and introduce additional procedures for monitoring and maintaining standards if necessary.

How Does The Certification Procedure Operate?

Any person who can provide 'proof of general competence' will be eligible to receive a Certificate and to have their names placed on a Register of Competence in Psychological Testing (Educational) on payment of the relevant fees.

Proof of general competence is provided by production to the Society of the Affirmation of Competence form on which a signature from a 'qualified person' has been obtained against each of the units on the list. This checking-off procedure is known as an 'Affirmation of Competence'. Assessors who are intending to sign an 'Affirmation' should obtain an Assessors Information Pack – Educational Level A, from the Society.

A 'qualified person' for this purpose is someone who holds an Assessor's Certificate (Level A) in Educational Testing.

Test Use
The Society encourages test publishers and distributors to supply relevant tests for use in educational settings only to people who hold a Certificate of Competence in Educational Testing. The Society is also publicising the standards so that non-psychologists will be aware of the importance of ensuring that tests are used only under the supervision of people who hold a Certificate of Competence.

Training Courses
Assessors who direct training courses in Educational Testing need to have obtained a Statement or Certificate of Competence in Educational Testing Level A and have had their assessment methods verified by the Society. Assessors who direct training courses in Educational Testing which cover ALL the competences in the Checklist may advertise those courses as:
- 'Providing training leading to fulfilment of requirements for the British Psychological Society Certificate of Competence in Educational Testing (Level A).'

Assessors who direct training courses in Educational Testing which cover SOME but not all of the competences in the checklist may advertise those courses as:
- 'Providing training leading to partial fulfilment of the requirements for the British Psychological Society Certificate of Competence in Educational Testing (Level A).'

Charges
The Society charges a once only fee of £65 for the award of each Certificate. However, the fee is waived for Chartered Psychologists who hold annual Practising Certificates qualifying for a Certificate of Competence in Educational Testing (such people having already paid registration fees to the Society to have their qualifications recognised).

Register of Competence in Psychological Testing (Educational)

The Society makes positive efforts to encourage employers only to use competent test users, and the Register is their basic source guide to check the credentials of the individuals they intend to consult or employ. The Register is the best way for competent test users to keep in touch with developments in the field.

For an additional annual fee of £20, holders of Statements or Certificates of Competence in Educational Testing will be added to the Register of Competence in Psychological Testing (Educational).

When awarded a Statement or Certificate, applicants will be required to be entered on the Register of Competence in Psychological Testing (Educational) and will be expected by the Society to remain on the Register while they are continuing to use testing in their work.

Registrants' details are held on the Society's database. Details are available to enquirers who mention a person by name, but not available as part of a more general listing.

If you wish to check if a person is or is not on the Register, please contact the Psychological Testing Centre on direct line: 0116 2529530.

Introduction to the Checklist

The Checklist

This Checklist defines those things which the Society considers you should know and should be able to do in order to use tests fairly, properly and in a professional manner. It does not cover everything you should know – it covers the minimum requirements for using most standardised group and individual tests of literacy, numeracy and curriculum subjects, together with group tests of reasoning ability. As a general introduction to psychological testing you should also read Psychological Testing – A User's Guide (available from the Society and on our website www.psychtesting.org.uk) and A Framework for Psychological Assessment and Intervention (Division of Educational and Child Psychology Newsletter (1998), Volume 84, pp 5–8).

Reading through Psychological Testing – A User's Guide, A Framework for Psychological Assessment and Intervention and through the Checklist of Competences should help to make you aware of what you do and do not know or understand about testing. The Checklist also provides you with a means of evaluating the content and coverage of any training course you might attend.

While self-assessment using the Checklist may give you some insights into your own degree of competence and training needs, formal assessment of your competence must be carried out by an Assessor who holds a Statement or Certificate of Competence in Educational Testing (Level A).

When you have obtained signatures for all seven units on the Checklist of Competences, you will be eligible to apply for your own Certificate of Competence in Educational Testing (Level A). To submit your application for your Certificate you should complete the personal details on the application form and send it, together with the appropriate registration fee, to the Society.

Satisfying the requirements set out in the Checklist does not give you the right to obtain and use whatever materials you wish, nor can it be counted as a formal qualification in psychology. The Certificate can be used as evidence of competence when you apply to publishers to register as a qualified test user. However, each publisher may quite properly require additional information or evidence or require you to attend special training courses for certain instruments. As a test-user, you are responsible for ensuring that you do not act outside your own areas of competence; you are responsible for the way you use tests and for what happens to information obtained with them.

General descriptions of the Units of Competence

The Checklist covers seven UNITS of Competence. A UNIT is a coherent group of specific competences. Anyone who meets the requirements of all seven UNITS will be eligible for the award of Certificate of Competence in Educational Testing (Level A).

LA UNIT 1. Defining the assessment needs
This UNIT deals with the purpose of testing in the context of assessment needs and different types of testing (e.g. ability and attainment, norm-referenced, criterion-referenced and curriculum-based assessment).The next two UNITS concern the relevant underpinning knowledge and understanding required to make proper use of psychological tests.

The next two UNITS concern the relevant underpinning knowledge and understanding required to make proper use of psychological tests.

LA UNIT 2. The basic principles of scaling and standardisation
This deals with the fundamental statistical concepts required to use educational tests.

LA UNIT 3. The importance of reliability and validity
Considerable stress is based on understanding a number of essential concepts in psychometrics.

The remaining Units focus on practical issues relating to test administration, relationships with clients and candidates, use of test information and so on. Each is seen as a necessary precursor to the next.

LA UNIT 4. Deciding when psychological tests should or should not be used as part of an assessment process
This covers the selection of tests and their appropriateness within specific assessment situations.

LA UNIT 5. Administering tests to one or more students/pupils/learners and dealing with scoring procedures
This is very much a skill-based unit with the stress on the test user's competence to follow good professional practices in test administration, ensuring the maintenance of standard conditions and fairness.

LA UNIT 6. Making appropriate use of test results
Stress is placed on competence in the interpersonal skills required to provide face-to-face feedback of test results as well as the oral and written communication skills required to score and interpret the results.

LA UNIT 7. Maintaining security and confidentiality
This deals with issues of security and confidentiality which are of central importance in the professional relationship between test user, candidate and client.

Notes
In the following Checklist:
■ 'Assessee' refers to the person whose competence is being assessed;
■ 'Client' is used to refer to the 'commissioning agent' – the person or organisation for whom the test is carried out.

Checklist of Competences in Educational Testing (Level A)

LA UNIT 1. Defining the assessment needs
Can the Assessee:

1. Demonstrate an understanding of the purpose of testing within the overall context of assessment.

2. Identify and justify those assessment needs which can best be addressed by the use of a test procedure and those for which an alternative assessment approach is more appropriate.

3. Justify carrying out a particular kind of test using knowledge of both the learner's development and the skill(s) being assessed to support reasons for choice.

4. Describe how measures of ability and attainment of students/pupils/learners are influenced by environmental factors, giving specific examples.

5. Give examples of the kinds of information which may be used to corroborate the information elicited by a test or other assessment technique.

6. Distinguish between tests of attainment, tests of ability and tests of aptitude.

7. Explain the difference between formative and summative uses of tests, giving examples of each type.

8. Demonstrate an understanding of the differences between norm-referenced, criterion-referenced and curriculum-based measures.

LA UNIT 2. The basic principles of scaling and standardisation
Can the Assessee:

1. Depict graphically how a sample of test scores accumulate at different points throughout the range of ability covered by the test.

2. Undertake calculations to convey how much variation there is amongst a set of test scores.

3. Describe how the alternative ways of expressing the average of a set of test scores (mean, median or mode) are affected by their distribution throughout the range of the scores.

4. Describe the relationship between the Standard Error of the mean of a sample of scores and the size of the sample.

5. Explain how the variation amongst a standardisation sample of test scores and their mean can be used to determine the level of confidence that we can have in people's scores on that test.

6. Demonstrate an understanding of the properties of the Normal Distribution and their relevance to measurement in general.

7. Use a set of statistical tables to establish the percentage of cases likely to fall below a particular test score.

8. Demonstrate how raw test scores can be converted into any of the scales frequently used to measure test performance (e.g. percentile scores, z-scores, T-scores, etc.).

LA UNIT 3. The importance of reliability and validity
Can the Assessee:
1. Explain the notion of correlation as a measure of the degree of relationship between two measures.

2. Define the conditions under which correlation is maximised (both positively and negatively) and minimised.

3. Provide reasonable rough estimates of the correlation coefficients represented by examples of various bivariate scattergrams.

4. Explain in outline the methods of estimating reliability (interrater reliability, internal consistency, test-retest, same or alternate form) and describe their relative pros and cons.

5. Describe and illustrate the distinctions between face, content, construct domain and criterion-related validity.

LA UNIT 4. Deciding when psychological tests should or should not be used as part of an assessment process
Can the Assessee:
1. Use test publishers' catalogues, specimen sets or other reference materials to identify one or more instruments potentially suitable for a particular function.

2. Identify, for each test, information in the test manual which relates to the test's rationale, development, reliability, validity, its norms and any specific restrictions or limitations on its areas of use.

3. Identify relevant practical considerations (ease of administration, time required, special equipment needed etc.).

4. Compare information presented about the test's validity with relevant aspects of the requirements of the assessment and make an appropriate judgement about their fit.

5. Examine the norms and make a suitable judgement about their appropriateness in terms of representativeness and sample size.

6. Examine any restrictions on areas of use (e.g. age, gender, cultural or ethnic limitations; ability range; attainment level; special educational needs; the influence of possible practice effects upon the frequency of use of a test etc.) and make an appropriate judgement as to whether a test should be used.

7. Identify whether use of the test would meet the requirements of Equal Opportunities, Race Relations,
Sex Discrimination and Disability Discrimination legislation.

LA UNIT 5. Administering tests to one or more students/pupils/learners and dealing with scoring procedures
Does the Assessee:
1. Ensure that any necessary equipment is operating correctly and that sufficient test materials are available for the test taker(s).

2. Ensure, where re-usable materials are being used, that they are carefully checked for marks or notes which may have been made by previous test takers.

3. Arrange a suitable quiet location for carrying out the testing.
4. Inform test taker(s) of the time and place well in advance and ensure that they are adequately prepared.

5. Record the test taker's personal details together with relevant details of the test instruments used, etc.

6. Use standard test instructions and present them clearly and intelligibly to the test takers.

7. Provide the test takers with sufficient time to work through any example test items.

8. Make careful checks to ensure proper use of answer sheets and response procedures.

9. Deal appropriately with any questions which arise without compromising the purpose of the test.

10. Explain any time limits.

11. Adhere strictly to test-specific instructions regarding pacing and timing.

12. Collect all materials when each test is completed.

13. Carry out a careful check against the inventory of materials to ensure that everything has been returned.

14. Keep all materials in a secure place with due regard to confidentiality.

15. Thank test takers for their participation at the conclusion of the test session and explain the next stage in testing (if any) to them.

16. Make notes on factors which might have affected the test taker's performance (e.g. any particular problems which arose during the session; the test taker's motivation, perseverance, or level of anxiety etc.).

17. Visually check answer sheets for ambiguous responses which could cause problems in scoring.

18. Demonstrate use of a range of different scoring keys and/or 'self-scoring' forms

19. Accurately score, compute responses and transfer raw score marks to record sheets.

20. Use norm tables to find relevant percentile and/or standard scores and transfer these to the test takers' record sheets.

In the case of group tests:

21. Plan test sessions with due regard to the maximum numbers of test takers who can be assessed in one session and the maximum duration of each session.

22. Arrange seating and desk space to maximise comfort and to minimise possibilities for cheating.

23. Ensure that during the test test-takers do not distract each other and, where appropriate, maintain silence.

In the case of individual testing:

24. Establish a satisfactory rapport with the test taker prior to the commencement of testing and maintain this through the session.

25. Prompt the test taker where appropriate in accordance with the test instructions and without invalidating the test item.

26. Use appropriately discreet scoring procedures so that the test taker does not become unduly conscious of failure.

27. Follow discontinuation procedures in line with the guidelines in the test manual while ensuring that the test taker does not become disheartened through obvious failure.

LA UNIT 6. Making appropriate use of test results and providing accurate written and oral feedback to clients and candidates

Can the Assessee:

1. Select appropriate norm tables from the test manual or supplementary material.

2. Make appropriate use of information in the test manual with regard to ceiling or basal effects.

3. Attach suitable cautions to interpretations of the results (including comparisons with previous test performances) and/or make statements as to why certain test results are not quoted where no relevant norms or cut-off tables are available.

4. Give due consideration to the appropriateness of the reference group used in the test standardisation.

5. Describe the meanings of scale scores in terms which are accurate, which reflect the confidence limits associated with those scores and are intelligible to those who may legitimately have access to them.

6. Compute composite test battery scores from weightings given in a test manual.

7. Make appropriate connections between performance on a test, the test taker's educational performance and the original purpose of the test.

8. Integrate test findings with other forms of information gathered in the course of the assessment to inform decision-making and intervention.

Does the Assessee:

9. Show awareness of the implications of variation in test results and the effects of using different tests within a domain (e.g. reading or number).

10. Show awareness of the appropriateness or otherwise of providing feedback to test takers of differing ages and/or ability levels.

LA UNIT 7. Maintaining security and confidentiality

Does the Assessee ensure that:

1. Clear descriptions are given to the test taker and/or other relevant parties (e.g. other professional/parent / LEA) prior to testing concerning:
   - how the results are to be used;
   - who will be given access to them;
   - for how long they will be retained.

2. All test data are kept in a secure place and that access is not given to unauthorised persons.

3. All test materials are kept in a secure place which is not accessible to people other than authorised test users.

4. All mandatory requirements relating to the test taker's and client's rights and obligations under the Data Protection Act are clearly explained to the parties concerned.

5. Where data is stored, the conditions of the Data Protection Act are abided by.

6. Potential test takers are not provided with prior access to test materials other than those specifically designed to help test takers prepare for an assessment.

NOTES FOR ASSESSORS

- No formal assessment procedures have been defined, but the Society has developed *Guidance for Assessors*, updates of which will be circulated;
- No formal training requirements have been defined.

Assessments of competence must be carried out by an Assessor who holds a Statement or Certificate of Competence in Educational Testing (Level A) and who should base his or her judgements of competence on direct experience of the person's performance in realistic situations and the solution of real-life, rather than 'academic', problems. Assessors must have their assessment methods verified by the Society.

The assessor must initial each item on the Checklist. Where all the items on the checklist for a UNIT have been initialled, the Affirmation of Competence in that UNIT should be signed and dated.

Code of Good Practice for Educational Testing

People who use psychological tests in educational settings are expected by The British Psychological Society to:

- Take steps to ensure that they are able to meet all the standards of competence defined by the Society for the relevant Certificate(s) of Competence in Educational Testing, and to endeavour, where possible, to develop and enhance their competence as test users.

- Monitor the limits of their competence in psychometric testing and not to offer services which lie outside their competence nor encourage or cause others to do so.

- Use tests only in conjunction with other assessment methods and only when their use can be supported by the available technical information.

- Administer, score and interpret tests in accordance with the instructions provided by the test distributor and to the standards defined by the Society.

- Store test materials securely and to ensure that no unqualified person has access to them.

- Keep test results securely, in a form suitable for developing norms, validation, and monitoring for bias.

- Obtain the informed consent of potential test takers and parents/carers, making sure that they understand why the tests will be used, what will be done with their results and who will be provided with access to them.

- Ensure that all test takers are well informed and well prepared for the test session, and that all have had access to practice or familiarisation materials where appropriate.

- Give due consideration to factors such as gender, ethnicity, age, disability and special needs, educational background and level of ability in using and interpreting the results of tests.

- Provide the test taker, parents/carers and other authorised persons with feedback about the results in a form which makes clear the implications of the results, is clear and in a style appropriate to their level of understanding.

- Ensure test results are stored securely, are not accessible to unauthorised or unqualified persons and are not used for any purposes other than those agreed with the test taker.

The British Psychological Society was founded in 1901 and incorporated by Royal Charter in 1965. Its principle object is to promote the advancement and diffusion of a knowledge of psychology pure and applied and especially to promote the efficiency and usefulness of Members of the Society by setting up a high standard of professional education and knowledge.

The Society has more than 42,000 members and:

- has branches in England, Northern Ireland, Scotland and Wales;
- accredits nearly 800 undergraduate degrees;
- accredits nearly 150 postgraduate professional training courses;
- confers Fellowships for distinguished achievements;
- confers Chartered Status for professionally qualified psychologists;
- awards grants to support research and scholarship;
- publishes 10 scientific journals and also jointly publishes *Evidence Based Mental Health* with the British Medical Association and the Royal College of Psychiatrists;
- publishes books in partnership with Blackwells;
- publishes *The Psychologist* each month;
- supports the recruitment of psychologists through the *Appointments Memorandum* and *www.appmemo.co.uk*;
- provides a free 'Research Digest' by e-mail;
- publishes newsletters for its constituent groups;
- maintains a website *(www.bps.org.uk)*;
- has international links with psychological societies and associations throughout the world;
- provides a service for the news media and the public;
- has an Ethics Committee and provides service to the Professional Conduct Board;
- maintains a Register of more than 12,000 Chartered Psychologists;
- prepares policy statements and responses to government consultations;
- holds conferences, workshops, continuing professional development and training events;
- recognises distinguished contributions to psychological science and practice through individual awards and honours;
- maintains a Register of Psychologists Specialising in Psychotherapy.

The Society continues to work to enhance:

- recruitment – the target is 50,000 members by 2006;
- services – the Society has offices in England, Northern Ireland, Scotland and Wales;
- public understanding of psychology – addressed by regular media activity and outreach events;
- influence on public policy – through the work of its Boards and Parliamentary Officer;
- membership activities – to fully utilise the strengths and diversity of the Society membership.

The British Psychological Society
St Andrews House, 48 Princess Road East, Leicester LE1 7DR, UK
Tel: 0116 252 9568   Fax: 0116 247 0787   E-mail: mail@bps.org.uk   Website: www.bps.org.uk

Incorporated by Royal Charter Registered Charity No 229642   RCPTED01/10.05

Psychological Testing Centre
www.psychtesting.org.uk

The
British
Psychological
Society

Statement of Competence in Educational Testing Level A

Application Form – Available until 31 December 2007

These notes should be read in conjunction with the General Information Pack Educational Testing (Level A).

Before completing this form please refer to notes overleaf to see if you qualify for a Statement.

PLEASE COMPLETE THIS FORM IN BLOCK CAPITALS

Surname .... Title ....

Forenames (in full) .... Date of Birth ....

Address ....

....

.... Postcode..

Tel No.   Work .... Home ....

E-mail   Work... Home ....

BPS Membership no. (if applicable) ....

Are you a member of The Association of Educational Psychologists (AEP)? YES/NO
AEP Membership no. (if applicable) ....

Declaration
I hereby apply for a Level A Statement and agree to adhere to the Code of Good Practice in Educational Testing.

Signature: .... Date:...

> The completed application form must bear original signature of the applicant.

Do you qualify for a Statement?

To qualify for a Statement of Competence you must fulfil one of the following criteria:
Either
1 You are a Chartered Educational Psychologist and can affirm that your knowledge and skills meet the standards defined in the Checklist of Competencies in the General Information Pack.
Note: Statements of Competence will be issued to Chartered Educational Psychologists who are either current or past members of the Division of Educational and Child Psychology or the Scottish Division of Educational Psychologists, that is, anyone who has established eligibility of either of the two Divisions.

Or
2 You are a member of the Association of Educational Psychologists and have the necessary qualifications to practise as an educational psychologist in the United Kingdom, and you can confirm your current membership with the Association.
If you fulfil the requirements for either point 1 or 2, then you may apply for the Statement of Competence. If you do not, then proceed to point 3.

3 You will need to apply for a Certificate of Competence in Educational Testing (Level A) for which you must first undertake training and then have your competences affirmed by an Assessor (that is, a Chartered Psychologist whose assessment methods have been verified by the Society). In many cases Trainers are also Assessors. A list of Assessors is obtainable on the website: www.psychtesting.org.uk

Special case route

A special case route is also available. Please contact the Psychological Testing Centre for more details (direct line 0116 252 9530; e-mail enquiry@psychtesting.org.uk).

How to apply

Complete the attached form and send it to the Society. If you are a full member of the Association of Educational Psychologists, please give your membership number.

Fees

If you are a Chartered Educational Psychologist holding a current Practising Certificate, there will be no charge for the Statement of Competence. Holders of the Statement of Competence in Educational Testing (Level A) are expected join the Register of Competence in Psychological Testing (Educational) for an annual fee of £20. All holders of the Statement or Certificate of Competence in Educational Testing are expected to maintain their membership of this Register.

If you intend applying for the Certificate of Competence, please refer to the General Information Pack and complete the relevant application form.

FEES *(please tick appropriate boxes)*		Amount (£)
Certificate of Competence (Level A)		
☐ Chartered Psychologist with Practising Certificate	Nil	
☐ All others	£65	
Entry on Register of Competence in Psychological Testing		
☐ All applicants (first year's fee)	£20	
NB: It is not possible to have an entry on the Register without applying for a Certificate		
	Total Due £	

Method of Payment

I wish to pay for: ☐ £65 for Statement of Competence (Level A);
☐ £20 for entry on the Register of Competence in Psychological Testing.

Credit/debit card payment slip
☐ Please charge my Credit/Debit Card (complete the details below)

Total Amount £: .... Name of Cardholder: ....
Please write in amount

Card Number: ....
Card Issuer: ☐ Visa   ☐ Amex   ☐ Mastercard   ☐ Delta   ☐ Switch

Valid From: .... Expiry Date:...Issue No: .... *(switch only)*

Signature: .... Date:......................................

Payment by cheque/sterling bank draft

☐ I enclose a cheque for £ .... *(made payable to The British Psychological Society)*

NB. If you do not have a Sterling bank account, and do not wish to pay by credit/debit card, please make payment by Sterling money order drawn on a UK bank. If you use this method, please allow an additional 10% to cover the cost of currency conversion.

Request for invoice
☐ Please send invoice to: ....

....

.... Purchase Order No: ....

Psychological Testing Centre
www.psychtesting.org.uk

The
British
Psychological
Society

Certificate of Competence in Educational Testing Level A
Application Form

PLEASE COMPLETE THIS FORM IN BLOCK CAPITALS

Surname .... Title ....

Forenames (in full) .... Date of Birth ....

Address ....

....

.... Postcode...

Tel No.　Work .... Home ....

E-mail　Work.. Home ....

BPS Membership no. (if applicable) ....

Declaration

I hereby apply for a Level A Certificate and agree to adhere to the Code of Good Practice in Educational Testing.

Signature: .... Date:...

> The completed application form must bear original signatures both of the applicant and the Assessor(s).

APPLICANT'S FULL NAME ....

Affirmation of Competence in Educational Testing (Level A)

Note to Assessors: Assessors should not normally be close relatives of applicants, or members of their immediate household, or their business partners. In other words, they should not have close personal connections with the applicant. Where such connections do exist, they must be disclosed. Assessors must have had either provisional or full verification of their assessment methods.

LA UNIT 1. Defining the assessment needs
Assessor's name .... Date...

Signature .... Statement/Certificate no ....

LA UNIT 2. The basic principles of scaling and standardisation
Assessor's name .... Date...

Signature .... Statement/Certificate no ....

LA UNIT 3. The importance of reliability and validity
Assessor's name .... Date...

Signature .... Statement/Certificate no ....

LA UNIT 4. Deciding when psychological tests should or should not be used as part of an assessment process
Assessor's name .... Date...

Signature .... Statement/Certificate no ....

LA UNIT 5. Administering tests to one or more students/pupils/learners and dealing with scoring procedures
Assessor's name .... Date...

Signature .... Statement/Certificate no ....

LA UNIT 6. Making appropriate use of test results and providing accurate written and oral feedback to clients and candidates
Assessor's name .... Date...

Signature .... Statement/Certificate no ....

LA UNIT 7. Maintaining security and confidentiality
Assessor's name .... Date...

Signature .... Statement/Certificate no ....

I affirm successful completion of all seven units.

Assessor's name .... Date...

Signature .... Statement/Certificate no ....

FEES *(please tick appropriate boxes)*		Amount (£)
Certificate of Competence (Level A)		
☐ Chartered Psychologist with Practising Certificate	Nil	
☐ All others	£65	
Entry on Register of Competence in Psychological Testing		
☐ All applicants (first year's fee)	£20	
NB: It is not possible to have an entry on the Register without applying for a Certificate		
	Total Due £	

By providing the personal information in the application form you are agreeing to the Society processing and holding it only for the purposes stated in our Data Protection Act registration. For further information about these purposes and the Act itself please visit the privacy\DPA policy hyperlink at the foot of the Society's website home page at *www.bps.org.uk.*

Method of Payment

I wish to pay for: ☐   £65 for Certificate of Competence (Level A);
                ☐   £20 for entry on the Register of Competence.

Credit/debit card payment slip
☐ Please charge my Credit/Debit Card (complete the details below)

Total Amount £: .... Name of Cardholder: ....
Please write in amount

Card Number: ....
Card Issuer: ☐ Visa   ☐ Amex   ☐ Mastercard   ☐ Delta   ☐ Switch

Valid From: .... Expiry Date:...................................Issue No: .... *(switch only)*

Signature: .... Date:....................................

Payment by cheque/sterling bank draft

☐ I enclose a cheque for £ .... *(made payable to The British Psychological Society)*

NB. If you do not have a Sterling bank account, and do not wish to pay by credit/debit card, please make payment by Sterling money order drawn on a UK bank. If you use this method, please allow an additional 10% to cover the cost of currency conversion.

Request for invoice
☐ Please send invoice to: ....

....

.... Purchase Order No: ....

Appendix 2

Guidance for Assessors: Certificate of Competence in Educational Testing (Level A)

The
British
Psychological
Society

Certificate of Competence in Educational Testing
(Level A)

Guidance for Assessors

Psychological Testing Centre
www.psychtesting.org.uk

GFA–EDA

Contents

Introduction

These notes have been developed by the Steering Committee on Test Standards (SCTS) to provide Assessors with guidance regarding the levels of competence required to fulfil the requirements of the Certificate of Competence in Educational Testing (Level A). They were drawn up by a working group of educational psychologists at a residential workshop and are based upon materials developed by the Division of Occupational Psychology.

The notes are designed:

■   To help trainers develop suitable course materials and activities;
■   To help Assessors set their level of assessment appropriately and to help them devise appropriate forms of assessment activity;
■   To assist in the evolution of a uniform standard of competence in educational testing.

The notes deal with issues such as:

■   What methods are suitable for assessing each element (written or verbal questioning, observation of performance etc.)?
■   What depth of knowledge or level of skill is required?
■   What range of knowledge is required?
■   What constitutes sufficient evidence of competence?
■   What help can be provided to ensure uniformity of assessment standards across different Assessors?

Note that the adequacy of assessments must be affirmed by a Verifier appointed by The British Psychological Society. A number of members have contributed to the development of standards in Educational Testing and the Society's thanks must go to them for their time and commitment to this project.

Guiding Principles

This scheme consists of 71 core competences which must all be demonstrated to achieve the Certificate of Competence in Educational Testing (Level A). Evidence collected should relate clearly to the core competences. These notes provide guidelines for trainers to determine whether competences have been adequately demonstrated.

The Society is publicising the standards so that non-psychologists will be aware of the importance of ensuring that tests are used only under the supervision of people who hold a Certificate of Competence in Educational Testing.

Characterising the Test User

Any person wishing to make use of tests in education is eligible to take the Certificate. The Certificate of Competence is awarded to people who are judged to be competent test users. A 'test user' is defined as someone who is:

■ Competent to make informed choices between the merits of alternative tests on the basis of information provided in manuals and other sources and with due regard for the context within which the test will be used;

■ Able to administer tests;

■ Able to judge the suitability of tests for various purposes;

■ Able to interpret test findings.

The Certificate of Competence in Educational Testing (Level A) indicates basic competence in the administration and use of tests: it does not imply that the holder can use any or all types of assessment, such as some individual tests of cognitive abilities (e.g. the Wechsler Ability Scales, the BAS-II, the Stanford-Binet and McCarthy Scales) and personality tests (e.g. the 16PF and the HSPQ) which require a more detailed knowledge of test construction, underlying theory and interpretation.

This Certificate is designed primarily for people who are responsible for test use. It is not a qualification in educational psychology, but a qualification in the theoretical background and practical aspects of educational testing. Neither is it intended for those who simply administer tests or have been trained only in the use of one specific instrument.

Differences in assessment requirements between the UNITS

The Units of competence can be classified into three broad sets:

1. Underpinning knowledge – the basic foundations: Units 1, 2 and 3;
2. Practical task skills – Units 5, 6 and 7;
3. Practical application of this knowledge – Unit 4.

Assessors need to ask whether the person whose competence is being assessed (i.e. the Assessee) is capable of administering tests and able to integrate and apply their relevant knowledge in practical situations. Unit 4 is thus the 'key' unit, and assessment of this unit is best based around project work – either real or simulated case studies. Such activities are also likely to provide evidence of competence relating to Units 1, 2 and 3.

The prime mode of assessing the practical task skills should be through direct observation of the Assessee's performance in realistic test administrations, with questioning providing supplementary evidence. For Units 1, 2 and 3, however, the prime mode of assessment will tend to be through forms of questioning, with evidence from other types of performance having been used as supplementary or corroborative.

General guidance on the assessment procedure

In assessment, three main issues need to be addressed:

■ How can evidence of competence be generated?

■ How can it be collected?

■ How should it be judged?

In addition, consideration has to be given to the question of verification procedures (i.e. Quality Assurance) and the problem of monitoring standards of assessment.

Generation of Evidence

Evidence can be generated from four main sources:

Historical evidence – in the present context this will be confined to already affirmed Units of Competence in educational testing.

Questioning (written/computer-based/oral etc.) – is the most direct approach to assessing relevant knowledge and understanding. However one must be careful to tailor the questioning process to ensure that one is assessing knowledge at a practical and applied level. The following detailed guidance attempts to show how the various elements of competence (particularly those in Units 2 and 3) can be assessed in an appropriate context.

Performance on specially set tasks – simulations, case studies, projects etc, are the most practical methods of obtaining evidence about what someone can or cannot do under controlled conditions.

Performance at work (reports, test session logs, observation, witness testimony and personal reporting) – is particularly 'relevant' evidence, but often the most difficult to arrange and assess. Such evidence will have to be obtained indirectly and be used to supplement evidence from performance on specially set tasks.

Guidance for the assessment of competence in educational testing

Collecting Evidence. The problems relating to the collection of evidence concern the following questions:

- *How much evidence is needed* – what constitutes sufficient evidence of competence?
- *When and where should it be collected* – during training, at the end of training, from follow-up assessment; in the work-place or in special assessment settings?
- *Who should collect it* – trainers, special Assessors, colleagues?

Judgement of Evidence. The person who is going to sign the Affirmation of Competence will be regarded as being responsible for having judged the applicant's competence. The person who collects the evidence and the one who judges it need not be the same person – though they may often be. The person who signs the affirmation of competence must:

- be a Chartered Psychologist holding a current Practising Certificate;
- hold a Statement or Certificate of Competence in Educational Testing (Level A);
- have had their assessment methods verified and hold a current valid Assessors Certificate.

Assessors and Trainers should note that completion of a training course in Educational Testing will not lead immediately to a full affirmation of competence. A further period of cumulative assessment (project work, case studies, portfolios, etc.) will be necessary for some units/elements.

It is important to recognise that a conventional short course is only one of many possible models for developing competence in testing. Assessors of competence should focus their attention on what the Assessee knows and what the Assessee can do – not how or when they acquired their knowledge and skill.

Training Courses

Assessors who direct training courses in Educational Testing need to have obtained a Statement or Certificate of Competence in Educational Testing Level A and have had their assessment methods verified by the Society. Assessors who direct training courses in Educational Testing which cover ALL the competences in the Checklist may advertise those courses as:

- 'Providing training leading to fulfilment of requirements for the British Psychological Society Certificate of Competence in Educational Testing (Level A).'

Assessors who direct training courses in Educational Testing which cover SOME but not all of the competences in the checklist may advertise those courses as:

- 'Providing training leading to partial fulfilment of the requirements for the British Psychological Society Certificate of Competence in Educational Testing (Level A).'

Section One – Assessment Methods

1. More than one method may need to be used to attain adequate evidence of competence: for example, a statistics worksheet completed without supervision could be supplemented by an interview to ensure comprehension of the concepts involved.

2. It is not necessary to deploy every method listed to obtain sufficient evidence: Section Two clarifies alternative/ complementary methods available.

3. Evidence of performance in actual assessment situations will form an essential component of assessment as it is highly unlikely that sufficient competence will be demonstrated within a single short course.

4. A portfolio of evidence of competence containing Assessors' observation records, test logs, draft documents, worksheets etc. forms a record of the evidence of the assessment of one Assessee. Portfolios are an essential basis for verification (see Annex A).

5. The order of Units does not determine the order of assessment (e.g. people with a formal training in statistics may be able to demonstrate competence before learning test administration; others may start off as test administrators).

6. Records of Assessors' findings/observations should be maintained to support affirmations of competence e.g. records of interviews (1.3 below) or observed simulations (1.11). (Note: these need not be retained by Assessors – see Annex A.)

7. Assessment should include checks on the Assessee's capacity to integrate underpinning knowledge into workplace practice in the medium term using cumulative evidence in addition to testing short-term retention of facts, as in an end-of-course test.

8. Assessment outside the workplace will usually be 'open-book', since it is unrealistic to expect retention of a substantial amount of detail on what may be a single component of a complex job. Adequate support documentation and thorough familiarity with this will enable speedy access to the correct information. Competent Assessees should have the necessary knowledge to perform the task in hand in situations where looking up information is inappropriate.

Methods of assessment
The following paragraphs provide brief comments and examples for each assessment method covered. A one-page summary of these comments forms the key to the grid in Annex B. The methods included are:

1.1 Exercises using catalogues/manuals/specimen sets (oral or written responses);
1.2 Observation by Assessor of discussion between Assessees;
1.3 Interview by Assessor of single Assessee (formal or informal);
1.4 Listing by Assessee of examples/ features with oral or written response;
1.5 Drafting of documentation for potential use;
1.6 Case studies, project work, for supervised or unsupervised response;
1.7 Worksheets or tests, with open-ended or multi-choice format, for supervised completion;
1.8 Self-assessment tests;
1.9 Observation of Assessee's workplace activity;
1.10 Personal/supervisor's report of workplace activity;
1.11 Observation of simulated activity e.g. during training;
1.12 Presentation by Assessee of documents actually in use;
1.13 Essays.

1.1 Exercises based on catalogue manuals or specimen sets
The output of these exercises may be an essay, a discussion, a report or may form part of a case study e.g. on the choice of tests for a specified situation (see 1.6). It may occur both during learning and in actual assessment situations. A range of catalogues etc. from different publishers should be available to ensure adequate breadth.

1.1.1 From a range of catalogues (or from a library or selection of tests) classify and categorise tests according to whether they are attainment, aptitude or ability tests; norm-referenced, content-referenced or curriculum-based test. (See UNIT 1, ELEMENTS 6, 7, 8; UNIT 4, ELEMENTS 1, 2.)

1.1.2 Interpret correctly information presented in test manual, in relation to reliability, validity (face, content, construct and criterion-related). Likely effect of range restriction and unreliable criterion measures on validity coefficients. Ask appropriate questions about the relevance of the test to a specified situation; the degree to which it may be reasonable to generalise from information in the manual. (See UNIT 4, ELEMENTS 2, 4, 5, 6.)

1.2 Observation by Assessor of discussion between Assessees

Some evidence which is obtained through interviews of single Assessees by an Assessor (1.3) could be obtained by extremely careful observation of simulated/structured discussion between two Assessees. In using this, or any other method requiring observation of Assessees, Assessors are required to develop and use a marking frame or checklist to record the evidence obtained.

1.2.1 While preparing to conduct a test session, Assessees discuss with each other the factors they will need to take into account in their preparation. (See UNIT 5, ELEMENTS 1–4.) Note that this exercise is a supplement to the demonstration of practical skill and is of itself insufficient evidence of competence in these elements.

1.3 Interviews by Assessor of a single Assessee

Interviews will most often be used to clarify the outcome of another method, e.g. to evaluate an Assessee's understanding of the application of a statistic calculated in a worksheet or to check that a decision process was not the automatic application of a rule of thumb. Interviews will generally be structured, enabling relatively easy record-keeping. Several of the topics lend themselves to inclusion in case studies (1.6) or to worksheets (e.g. for short answer or paragraph length response, see 1.7).

1.3.1 The purpose of testing within the overall context of assessment. (See UNIT 1, ELEMENT 1.)
1.3.2 Situations where particular types of test may be more appropriate. (See UNIT1, ELEMENT 2.)
1.3.3 How the standard error of the mean is related to the distribution of sample means from a population; the significance of a 95% confidence limit; the proportion of cases falling within +/- 1 or 2 SD of the mean. (See UNIT 2, ELEMENT 4.)
1.3.4 Conditions under which a correlation is minimised; maximised. (See UNIT 3, ELEMENT 2.)
1.3.5 Validity: definition; nature of; types of; quantifiability; usefulness. (See UNIT 3, ELEMENT 5.)
1.3.6 Understanding of the law relating to equal opportunities. (See UNIT 4, ELEMENT 7.)
1.3.7 Good test administration and why it is important. (See UNIT 5, ELEMENTS 5–13.) Note that this is a supplement to the demonstration of practical skill and is of itself insufficient evidence of competence in these elements.
1.3.8 Security of materials and why it is important; appropriate security procedures. (See UNIT 5, ELEMENT 15.) Note that this is a supplement to the demonstration of practical skill and is of itself insufficient evidence of competence in these elements.

1.4 Listing by Assessee of examples/features with oral/written response

Lists may be drawn up orally or in writing, during learning or in the workplace. If the lists are generated orally, they should be recorded and evaluated against a checklist.

1.4.1 List the principal environmental factors which may impinge on ability, with an appreciation of the significance of each. (See UNIT 1, ELEMENT 4.)
1.4.2 List the conditions in which a correlation is minimised and maximised. (See UNIT 3, ELEMENT 2.)
1.4.3 Define reliability; identify its relationship to error; and list the procedures for obtaining different measures of reliability. (See UNIT 3, ELEMENT 4.)
1.4.4 Prepare a check-list of the ideal conditions for a testing session. (See UNIT 5, ELEMENTS 1, 2, 3, 4.) Note that this exercise is a supplement to the demonstration of practical skill and is of itself insufficient evidence of competence in these elements.

1.5 Drafting of documentation for potential use

These exercises require the Assessee to actually draft documents, e.g. a good practice guideline for the learning establishment. The purpose of such an exercise is to provide evidence of the Assessee's understanding and competence. The documentation drafted can be included in a portfolio.

1.5.1 Draft an example of the introduction/explanation which be given to candidates at the beginning of a test session. (See UNIT 5, ELEMENT 4.) Note that Exercise 1.5.1 supplements the demonstration of practical skill and is insufficient evidence of competence in these elements.

1.6 Case studies or project work

These may be assessments of comprehension in the short term, preparatory to the conduct of practical activities in actual assessment situations or medium-term projects to be conducted in the workplace. Where possible, data, if not actually real, should be as realistic as possible, a close simulation of the anticipated work place tasks. Key features of a case study include:

■ the integrated assessment of a number of elements, possibly from different Units and
■ decision-making based on sound underpinning knowledge, rather than the listing/definition required in 1.4 above.

1.6.1 Review a specimen test set using a checklist of points to comment on features relating to reliability, validity and other characteristics of the test. (See UNIT 1, ELEMENT 3; UNIT 3, ELEMENTS 4, 5.) Note that while this case study contains some features apparently relevant to Unit 4, it requires detailed consideration of particular tests and their adequacy rather than consideration of those features relative to those of other tests in a situation of choice.

1.6.2 Comment critically in writing on a previously prepared scenario or case study reporting on the use of or selection of tests, which contain errors, examples of bad practice etc. using a structured format which highlights understanding of all relevant elements. (See UNIT 1, ELEMENT 3; UNIT 3, ELEMENTS 4, 5.) Note the comments for 1.6.1.

1.6.3 Given appropriate data, use the SEdiff to compare, for example, test and re-test scores for the same person; relative abilities for the same individual on different tests; and relative abilities of different people on the same test. Select appropriate norms from a manual or similar; evaluate the use of cut-off score provided; compute composite scores. Make notes preparatory to reporting on the findings. (See UNIT 3, ELEMENT 4; UNIT 6, ELEMENTS 1,2,3 4 5,6,7,8,9.)

1.7 Worksheets or tests for supervised completion

If they are to provide evidence of the competence of an individual, these exercises must be completed in a situation where collusion with another is not possible. Where they require the computation of statistics they would generally be carried out in an 'open-book' situation allowing access to familiar material (e.g. course notes). Answers may be multiple-choice or short-answer or paragraph length. Some topics covered in 1.3 (Interview) may also be suitable for short-answer or paragraph length response to worksheet questions.

1.7.1 Construct a frequency distribution of 15–20 scores presented on the worksheet. (NB the exercise should be repeated to cover both normal and non-normal distributions). Calculate means and SDs for these scores. Mark the positions of the mean and SD on the distributions and locate the median and mode. (See UNIT 2, ELEMENTS 1, 2, 3, 4.)

1.7.2 Convert sets of raw scores into percentiles and z-scores. Use tables (not graphs) to convert percentiles to z-scores and vice versa. Convert raw data to non-normalised z-scores, T-scores, stens and stanines and vice versa. Use norm tables to find percentile equivalents of raw scores, then obtain z-scores and T-scores from normal distribution tables.
(See UNIT 2, ELEMENT 8.) Note that this exercise foreshadows the practical requirements for Unit 5 Element 7 and Unit 6 Elements 1–5. It may form a sequence with 1.7.1.

1.7.3 Recognise data which could be correlated and distinguish it from data which cannot be correlated. Rank order a set of correlations by strength, independent of direction. Estimate Y from X from a scattergram, giving due weight to the margin of error. Test the significance of r using appropriate tables. Transfer data to a scattergram. Identify positive, negative and 0 correlations; match a range of scattergrams to values given and identify which are stronger/weaker. (See UNIT 3, ELEMENTS 1, 3.)

1.8 Self-assessment tests

By definition these tests, often used as progress checks, cannot stand alone as evidence of competence. They may be optional, offered to enable Assessors to seek information and guidance on areas of weakness. Self-assessment tests can provide additional evidence and/or evidence of the Assessor's approach to assessment (e.g. for verifiers). They could thus be included in portfolios. (See UNITS 1, 2, 3; UNIT 4, ELEMENTS 1, 5.)

1.9 Direct observation of Assessee's workplace activity

This is most likely to occur where the Assessor works on the same site in a supervisory or consultant capacity. Assessment within this context should focus upon specific competences, recorded perhaps using a checklist.

1.9.1 Observe the process of choice of instruments in relation to an actual assessment, noting use of information in manuals regarding rationale, reliability, validity, practical considerations etc., to the point of final selection of tests. (See UNIT 4, ELEMENTS 2, 3, 4, 5, 6, 7.)

1.9.2 Observe the preparation, starting, conduct and ending of a session of testing. (See UNIT 5, ELEMENTS 1–15, 21–27.)

1.9.3 Observe the scoring of a variety of tests, including preparation for scoring and application of norms. (See UNIT 5, ELEMENTS 17, 18, 19, 20.)

1.10 Personal/supervisor's report of workplace activity

Personal reports may be oral or written, oral reports being recorded by the assessor e.g. against a checklist. A supervisor (or colleague) presenting a report would usually be expected to be a holder of the Certificate of Competence in Educational Testing (Level A).

1.10.1 Provide a detailed personal report on the process of choice of instruments in relation to an actual assessment, noting use of information in manuals regarding rationale, reliability, validity, practical considerations etc., to the point of final selection of tests. (See UNIT 1, ELEMENT 2, 3; UNIT 4, ELEMENTS 2–7.)

1.11 Observation of simulated activity

Simulations, like case reports, enable a more controlled collection of adequate evidence by providing opportunities which may not arise in other ways. Assessors' observations should be recorded.

1.11.1 Given an actual situation, work from catalogues, specimen sets and/or reference materials to arrive at a final choice of tests to use and provide oral or written justification of that choice by reference to reliability, validity, norms, practical and legal issues. (See UNIT 1, ELEMENTS 1, 2, 3; UNIT 4, ELEMENTS 1–6.)

1.11.2 Conduct a session of testing, alone or with an assistant, to cover advance preparation, introduction, examples, start, conduct, ending and post-session activities, either with one candidate or with several. Use the test session log. Repeat the exercise with a different test. (See UNIT 5, ELEMENTS 1–16, 21–27.)

1.11.3 Score a set of completed answer sheets which require the use of a range of hand-scoring keys/self scoring forms and use norm tables to find percentile and/or standard scores. (See UNIT 5, ELEMENTS 17–20.)

1.11.4 Provide feedback to an individual in a realistic situation on the basis of test results; to be followed by advice to the Assessor from both parties. (See UNIT 6, ELEMENT 10.)

1.12 Presentation of documents actually in use

1.12.1 Use of advance material describing testing procedures and content. (See UNIT 5, ELEMENT 4.) Note that where these are not documents designed/drafted by the Assessee evidence can be obtained either from a brief oral or written review of the suitability of documents currently in use or from drafting exercises (see 1.5).

1.13 Essays

Where essays are written unsupervised, they would be followed up by interview or observed discussion and marked against a checklist. The same would follow for 'long' end-of-course test questions.

Section Two – Elements of Competence

In the guidance notes which follow:
Performance Evidence describes the content of the competences relevant to the Units
Assessment describes possible assessment methods
- *Short-term* refers to assessments which typically can be conducted during a course and at discrete intervals,e.g. multiple-choice tests)
- *Cumulative* refers to assessments which are the result of longer-term exercises, e.g. projects or case studies carried out in the workplace, in the case of Units 4–7.

UNIT 1, ELEMENTS 1, 2, 3, 4, 5:

Testing in Context

Performance Evidence
Assessees should be able to demonstrate (giving specific examples) that testing is a subset of the overall process of assessment and that testing may not always be the most appropriate means of carrying relevant data. Assessees should also be able to demonstrate why a specific test has been chosen with reference to knowledge of the learner's development and the skills being assessed. The effects of environmental factors such as ethnicity, gender, social class and disability should be described together with more direct factors affecting the test situation such as heat, noise, test anxiety and assessor variables. Assessees should also be able to provide examples of the kind of information which may be used to cross-validate the information elicited by a test or other form of assessment.

Assessment
Short-Term
- Short notes
- Commentary on case studies and scenarios provided by Assessor
- Worksheet/multiple choice questions.

Repeat until mastery has been achieved, with a minimum of two pieces of evidence per element.

UNIT 1, ELEMENTS 6, 7, 8:
Types of Assessment

Performance Evidence
Assesses should be able to distinguish between:
- tests of attainment (which measure relative levels of performance in specific domains, such as reading, spelling, number etc.), tests of aptitude (which measure aptitude for practical tasks) and tests of ability (which measure cognitive functions (e.g. verbal ability, numerical ability)
- tests of general ability (which measure the potential for performance in a wide range of intellectual/cognitive tasks) and tests of specific ability (which focus on a narrower range of tasks)
- formative assessment (which deals with process) and summative assessment (which deals with outcome)
- norm-referenced assessment (where scores are judged relative to those obtained by some specific population of other people), criterion-referenced assessment (where scores are interpreted in terms of an empirical, statistical relationship between test scores and some external measure) and curriculum-based assessment (where scores are interpreted in terms of specific aspects of the pupil's curriculum)

Assessment
Short-Term
Multiple choice questions
- Simulation exercises using catalogues.

Repeat to mastery level, with a minimum of two pieces of evidence per element.

UNIT 2: ELEMENTS 1, 2, 3, 4:

Descriptive Statistics

Performance Evidence

Assessees should be able to construct a frequency distribution of normal and non-normal scores; calculate means and standard deviations by whatever means (e.g. calculator, computer program etc.); and mark positions of means, standard deviation, median and mode on normal, negatively skewed and positively skewed distributions. Repeat until mastery is achieved.

Assessment

Short-Term

■   Worksheet/test involving calculation

■   Short answer question.

UNIT 2: ELEMENTS 5, 6, 7:
Sample Statistics

Performance Evidence

Assessees should be able to demonstrate that the Standard Error of the Mean decreases as sample size increases and to describe what confidence limits are. They should also be able to calculate by whatever means (e.g. calculator, computer program etc.) the Standard Error of the Mean and confidence limits for sample means, given the mean, standard deviation and sample size; and the 68% and 95% confidence limits. Repeat until mastery is achieved.

Assessment

Short-Term

■   Worksheet/test involving calculation

■   Short answer question

■   Multiple choice questions.

UNIT 2: ELEMENT 8:
Transformations

Performance Evidence

Assessees should be able to demonstrate an understanding of the relationship between percentile scores, z-scores and T-scores. Assessees should be able to convert different raw scores provided by the assessor into percentiles and z-scores. Assessees should also be able to use tables familiar to them to convert percentiles to z-scores and vice versa. They should also be able to derive standardised scores and percentile scores from raw data and to convert raw data to non-normalised z-scores, stens and stanines and vice versa. They should be able to use norm tables to find percentile equivalents of raw scores and then to obtain z-scores and T-scores from normal distributions. Repeat until mastery in both calculation and use of tables is achieved.

Assessment

Short-Term

■   Open book exercises covering simulated or actual sets of scores and a minimum of one exercise for each formula and table. This should be to mastery standard.

UNIT 3: ELEMENTS 1, 2, 3:
Correlations

Performance Evidence

Assessees should be able to demonstrate an understanding that the correlation is maximised when two variables increase in proportion. They should also be able to recognise data which can be correlated and distinguish it from data which cannot be correlated. They should be able to estimate correlation coefficients from scattergrams. They should be able to use r as the notation for a correlation and to use tables to test its significance. They should also be able to demonstrate an understanding of the fact that the correlation coefficient is the basis of measurement of reliability and validity.

Assessment Evidence

Short-Term

■   Worksheets and calculations to test these elements
■   Identification of these points from assessments relating to reliability and validity
■   Estimates of correlations from data from a range of scattergrams
■   Exercises in using tables of significance for the correlation coefficient, r
■   Awareness that correlation is not causation.

Repeat until mastery is achieved.

UNIT 3: ELEMENT 4:

Reliability

Performance Evidence

Assessees should be able to list and describe the following measures of reliability and to identify the strengths and weakness of each: inter-rater, internal consistency, test-retest, parallel or alternate forms.

Assessment

Short-Term

Worksheets and calculations to test these elements. Short answers. Open book calculation. Multiple choice questions. Commentary on case studies and scenarious provided by the Assessor.

UNIT 3: ELEMENT 5:

Validity

Performance Evidence

Assessees should be able to list and describe the following measures of validity and describe the strengths and weaknesses of each: face, content, construct and criterion-related.

Assessment

Short-Term

■   Short answers
■   Multiple choice questions.

UNIT 4: ELEMENTS 1, 2, 3, 4, 5:

Test Selection

Performance Evidence

Assessees should be able to demonstrate the appropriate use of testing to gather relevant assessment data and to select appropriate test or tests from a selection of specimen sets or reference materials. A minimum of three attainment tests, one ability test and one test of personal/social development is required to demonstrate mastery.

Assessment
Short-Term
■   Catalogue exercises
■   Commentary on case studies and scenarios provided by the Assessor.
■   Simulations.

UNIT 4: ELEMENTS 6, 7

Equal Opportunities

Performance Evidence
Assessees should be able to demonstrate the ability to decide on the appropriateness of the use of a specific test in the light of consideration of:
■   age, gender, cultural or ethnic limitations
■   ability range
■   attainment level
■   special educational needs
■   any possible practice effects resulting from the frequency of use of the test, etc.
■   the requirements of Equal Opportunities, Race Relations, Sex Discrimination and Disability Discrimination legislation.

Assessment
Short-Term
■   Commentary on case studies and scenarios provided by the Assessor.
■   Simulations
■   Short notes.
Cumulative
■   Case study and case reports from Assessees' workplaces.

UNIT 5: ELEMENTS 1, 2, 3, 4, 21, 22: (Assessors may wish to take advantage of the links between Units 5, 6 and 7 when gathering evidence.)

Pre-Testing Arrangements

Performance Evidence
Performance evidence in this Unit is obtained in the context of the use of group and individual tests in actual educational settings. Assessees should be able to demonstrate the ability to prepare the test taker; organise the test setting and materials; check and take account of any special considerations that might affect the test taker's performance (e.g. sensory impairment, English as an additional language, cultural and religious factors, learning or mobility difficulties).

Assessment
Short-Term
■   Direct observation by the Assessor of administration arrangements for one group and one individually administered test preferably in an actual educational workplace setting, but including role-play, with the results of observation recorded on a checklist.
      Repeat until mastery is achieved.
Cumulative
■   Commentary on case study and case reports from Assessees' workplaces.

UNIT 5: ELEMENTS 5, 6, 7, 8, 9, 10, 11, 12, 13, 14, 15, 16, 23, 24, 25, 26, 27:

Conducting the Test

Performance Evidence
Performance evidence in this Unit is obtained in the context of the use of group and individual tests in actual educational settings. Assessees should be able to demonstrate the ability to administer the test according to the instructions laid down in the manual or record sheet.

Assessment
Short-Term
- Direct observation by the Assessor of the administration of one group and one individually administered test preferably in an educational workplace setting, but including role-play, with the results of observation recorded on a checklist.
  Repeat until mastery is achieved.
Cumulative
- Commentary on case study and case reports from Assessees' workplaces.

UNIT 5: ELEMENTS 17, 18, 19, 20

Scoring the Test

Performance Evidence
Performance evidence in this Unit is obtained in the context of use of group and individual tests in actual educational settings. Assessees should be able to score test responses, transfer the raw scores to record sheets and compute any standard or age-equivalent scores according to the instructions in the test manual. Assessees should also be able to demonstrate the ability to use the guidance in the test manual to score ambiguous responses.

Assessment
Short-Term
- Direct observation by the Assessor of the scoring of one group and one individually administered test preferably in an educational workplace setting, but including role-play, with the results of observation recorded on a checklist.
  Repeat until mastery is achieved.
Cumulative
- Case study and case reports from Assessees' workplaces.
  Repeat to mastery, with a minimum of one individual and one group test.

UNIT 6: ELEMENTS 1, 2, 3, 4, 5, 6: (Assessors may wish to take advantage of the links between Units 5, 6 and 7 when gathering evidence.)

Interpreting Test Results

Performance Evidence
Performance evidence in this Unit is obtained in the context of the use of group and individual tests in actual educational settings. Assessees should be able to demonstrate their ability to interpret individual test scores in the light of information regarding reliability, validity and the Standard Error of Measurement.

Assessment
Short-Term
- Direct observation by the Assessor of the interpretation of test results from one group and one individually administered test preferably from an educational workplace setting, with the results of observation recorded on a checklist provided by the Assessor
- Commentary on case studies and scenarios provided by the Assessor.
- Worksheets for the calculation of Standard Error of Measurement and composite scores.
Cumulative
- Case study and case reports from Assessees' workplaces

■   Written reports to colleagues or carers.
     Repeat to mastery, with a minimum of one individual and one group test.

UNIT 6: ELEMENTS 7, 8, 9:

Integration of Findings

Performance Evidence
Performance evidence in this Unit is obtained in the context of the use of group and individual tests in actual educational settings. Assessees should be able to demonstrate their ability to draw upon information such as performance in the educational setting, other test and assessment results and learning behaviour in different educational settings in the interpretation of test results.

Assessment
Short-Term
■   Direct observation by the Assessor of the integration of test results from one group and one individually-administered test preferably from an educational workplace setting with other assessment findings (the results of observation should be recorded on a checklist provided by the Assessor)
■   Commentary on case studies and scenarios provided by the Assessor.
     Repeat until mastery is achieved.
Cumulative
■   Case study and written case reports from Assessees' workplaces
■   Written reports to colleagues or carers.
     Repeat to mastery, with a minimum of one individual and one group test.

UNIT 6: ELEMENT 10:

Feedback

Performance Evidence
Performance evidence in this Unit is obtained in the context of the use of group and individual tests in actual educational settings. Assessees should be able to demonstrate their ability to provide sensitive and appropriate feedback (both oral and in writing) which is mindful of the needs of the test taker and will be understood by the recipient. In general, this will include feedback of both quantitative and qualitative data. Assessees should also be able to demonstrate an understanding of test takers' and carers' rights of access to all data (including test data) kept on file.

Assessment
Short-Term
■   Direct observation by the Assessor of feedback of results from one group and one individually administered test preferably from an educational workplace setting (the results of such observation should be recorded on a checklist provided by the Assessor)
■   Short notes
■   Commentary on case studies and scenarios provided by the Assessor.
     Repeat until mastery is achieved.
Cumulative
■   Case study and case reports from Assessees' workplaces
■   Written reports to colleagues or carers.
     Repeat to mastery, with a minimum of one individual and one group test.

UNIT 7: ELEMENTS 1, 2, 3, 4, 5, 6 (Assessors may wish to take advantage of the links between Units 5, 6 and 7 when gathering evidence.)

Security and Confidentiality

Performance Evidence

Performance evidence in this Unit is obtained in the context of the use of group and individual tests in actual educational settings. Assessees should be able to demonstrate their ability to provide test takers and carers with a clear indication of how test results will be used. Assessees should also be able demonstrate:

■ their awareness of the rights of test takers and carers to be informed if test results are stored on computer

■ that they have stored test materials and records in a secure place where only authorised persons have access to them

■ their awareness of the need to ensure that test takers and their carers do not have prior access to test materials prior to testing.

Assessment

Short-Term

■ Direct observation by the Assessor recorded on a checklist provided by the Assessor. Repeat until mastery is achieved.

Cumulative

■ Commentary on case study and case reports from Assessees' workplaces.

Section Three – Good Practice

Basis for affirmation

The Certificate of Competence in Educational Testing (Level A) is awarded on the basis of demonstrable evidence of competence. There is no automatic grant of the Certificate solely on the basis of course attendance.

Affirmation of competence must be carried out by a Chartered Psychologist who is a verified Assessor for the Certificate. All Verified Assessors should display a current Assessor's Certificate, awarded by The British Psychological Society which is valid for five years.

Duration of assessment

Cumulative evidence should be gathered over time. In addition, competence in certain elements cannot reasonably be assessed without information on the Assessee's workplace practice.

Recovery assessment

Assessors should build into their programme the opportunity for recovery assessment (i.e. Assessees should be given further opportunities to demonstrate their competence if they have been unsuccessful).

Breadth of competence

Holders of the Certificate are expected to have broad competence and a wide understanding of current practice in educational testing. Assessors should therefore provide opportunities for them to demonstrate competence in the use of tests and materials from a range of sources and publishers. Materials should be representative of those currently available and in general use.

Limits of competence

The Certificate of Competence in Educational Testing (Level A) qualifies the holder to use psychological and educational tests in a range of appropriate situations. Assessors should ensure that aspiring Certificate-holders comprehend that additional skills are generally required to perform these functions effectively. Aspiring holders of the Certificate must be made aware that their own competence in test use is limited to the normal range of educational assessment functions.

Tests in context

In developing competence in the use of tests, Assessees should consider tests to be one of a number of possible methods which may be deployed in assessment. Tests should not be presented in isolation but should be integrated with, and compared to, a wide range of methods (e.g. observation-, criterion- and curriculum-based assessment).

Delegation of assessment functions to observers/workplace supervisors

As long as some of the evidence of competence is collected by the Verified Assessor in direct contact with the Assessee (e.g. recording observations, marking worksheets), some delegation to observers may be possible, provided that the person collecting the evidence, if not themselves a Verified Assessor is:

■   a holder of the Certificate/Statement at the relevant level and
■   monitored by the Verified Assessor at frequent intervals.

The Verified Assessor remains personally responsible to the Society for maintaining the standard of the Certificate and for affirming competence. Workplace supervisors may act as observers on behalf of the Assessor if they fulfil the conditions set out above.

Maintenance of standards

Standards will be maintained in two ways. Firstly, the Assessor, who completes and signs the Checklist, is accountable to the Society (although this accountability is for their own actions: actual responsibility for misuse or abuse of tests must lie with the test user). Secondly, the Society will maintain a Register of Competence in Psychological Testing (Educational) of those who have a Statement or Level A Certificate.

Annex A: Portfolios of Evidence of Competence for the Certificate of Competence in Educational Testing (Level A)

The following documents would be appropriate for Assessees to include in a portfolio of evidence for submission to an Assessor. Portfolios may prove useful even if the main medium of short-term assessment is a formal training course. Some elements require that affirmation of competence be based jointly on acquired knowledge and on evidence of subsequent practical skill e.g. demonstrated in the workplace.

Portfolios of evidence also provide a valuable tool for verification, and their constituent documents may be rendered anonymous if the Assessor or Assessee wishes to retain confidentiality. The following list is by no means exclusive. The numbers in parentheses refer to the items in Section One.

- Reports/worksheets from categorisation exercises (1.1).
- Observation records completed by Assessors observing discussions between Assessees (1.2).
- Interview records (1.3).
- Lists of points/items produced by Assessees (1.4).
- Draft documents (letters of invitation, test logs) (1.5).
- Reports of case studies (1.6).
- Reviews of tests, case reports (1.6).
- Reports for feedback to individuals (case study) (1.6).
- Worksheets completed under supervision (1.7).
- In-course or end-of-course tests (1.7).
- Self-assessment tests (see note to 1.8).
- Workplace checklists (see note to 1.9).
- Assessor's report of workplace activity (1.9).
- Personal report of workplace activity (1.10).
- Supervisor's or co-worker's report of workplace activity (1.10).
- Test log(s) (1.10, 1.11).
- Assessor's report on simulated activity (1.11).
- Documents in use in Assessee's workplace (1.12).
- Review by Assessee of documents in use (1.12).
- Essay (1.13).

It is good practice for Assessors or Trainers to retain the original assessment materials or portfolios. Where this is not possible (e.g. where the Assessee needs to have access to that portfolio) then there should be a note referring the Assessor to the location of the originals. Assessors should be prepared to have access to at least two portfolios for re-verification.

Annex B: Assessment Method Grid – Short-Term Assessments

ELEMENT BY ASSESSMENT METHOD GRID Type of assessment method (key follows on page 20)														
Unit/Elements	CAT	DIS	INT	LIS	DRF	CAS	TES	WRK	SELF	REP	SIM	DOC	ESS	OTHER
1: 1-5 tests; purpose														
1: 6-8 tests; types														
2: 1-4 descrip stats														
2: 5-7 sample stats														
2: 8 transform														
3: 1-3 correl														
3: 4 reliability														
3: 5 validity														
4: 1-5 test selection														
4: 6-7 equal opps														
5: 1-4; 21-22 pre-test														
5: 5-16; 23-27 conducting test session														
5: 17-20 scoring tests														
6: 1-6 interpreting findings														
6: 7-9 integrating findings														
6: 10 feedback														
7: 1-6 security/ confidentiality														

Annex B: Assessment Method Grid – Cumulative

ELEMENT BY ASSESSMENT METHOD GRID Type of assessment method (key follows on next page)													
Unit/Elements	CAT	DIS	INT	LIS	DRF	CAS	TES	WRK	SELF	REP	SIM	DOC	ESS	OTHER
4: 1-5 test selection														
4: 6-7 equal opps														
5: 1-4; 21-22 pre-test														
5: 5-16; 23-27 conducting test session														
5: 17-20 scoring tests														
6: 1-6 interpreting findings														
6: 7-9 integrating findings														
6: 10 feedback														
7: 1-6 security/ confidentiality														

Assessments

Key to assessment method grid

N.B. The assessment methods listed are those so far encountered by verifiers. Inclusion in the list does not necessarily indicate suitability, and vice versa. Where oral responses provide evidence, a record would usually be kept by the assessor (e.g. a checklist)

CATALOGUE/MANUAL/SPECIMEN SET: based around a selection of current materials from a range of publishers; have oral or written response e.g. essay, discussion, report; may form part of a case study e.g. on the choice of tests for a specified situation; may take place during learning and/or actual assessment situations.

OBSERVED DISCUSSIONS: simulated/structured discussion between pairs of Assessees, requiring extremely careful observation and unlikely to stand alone.

INTERVIEWS BY THE ASSESSOR: generally structured; most likely to be used to clarify the outcome of another method.

LIST OF EXAMPLES OR FEATURES: drawn up orally or in writing, during learning or in the workplace; assessor might record using checklist.

DRAFT DOCUMENTATION: actual drafting by the assessee to provide evidence of competence and understanding especially where the necessary documentation is already in existence at the workplace.

CASE STUDIES OR PROJECT WORK: based on realistic data; providing a means of integrated assessment of a number of elements and/or of decision-making based on underpinning knowledge. Used both for assessment in the short-term and for workplace projects.

WORKSHEETS OR TESTS (FOR SUPERVISED COMPLETION): not always supervised by assessor (e.g. a trainer or supervisor). Multiple-choice or short-answer or paragraph-length responses. Open-book computation of statistics using familiar material.

SELF-ASSESSMENT TESTS: a useful and valid means of checking on the development of competence in an assessee, but cannot stand alone as evidence of competence. They could provide supplementary evidence in a portfolio e.g. of an Assessor's approach to assessment.

WORKPLACE OBSERVATION: e.g. where the assessor works on the same site in a supervisory or consultant capacity. Can be intrusive (e.g. of one-to-one feedback).

REPORTS OF WORKPLACE ACTIVITY: made by the assessee or by a supervisor or colleague e.g. someone already holding the Statement or Certificate.

OBSERVED SIMULATIONS: provide opportunities which may not arise in actual assessment situations. Records of the Assessor's observations form part of the evidence.

PRESENTATION OF DOCUMENTS IN USE: (whether drafted by the Assessee or not): Assessees may discuss/make a critique of existing documents, orally or in writing.

ESSAYS: probably in conjunction with an interview if written unsupervised; marked against an objective checklist.

N.B. The above list is neither exhaustive nor prescriptive; space is available for Assessors to insert their own additional methods, or they may insert their own descriptions.

More than one method will often be appropriate to obtain full evidence of competence; some methods (e.g. interviews, discussions, self-assessment tests) are unlikely to stand alone. Some Assessors will prefer to use only a few methods.

Similar methods can often be used for both short-term and cumulative assessment.

Annex C: Verification of Assessment Materials and Activities

1. A system to verify the assessment methods used by Assessors to affirm applicants for the Certificate of Competence has been developed.
2. The verification process has been set up to aid the development of nationwide standards for assessment and considers only the assessment methods used by the Assessors. It DOES NOT consider the methods of training or the qualities of the Assessor.
3. Educational Psychologists who wish to become Assessors for the Certificate must be practising Chartered Psychologists with a current Certificate or Statement of Competence in Educational Testing and will be responsible for assessing individuals who apply for the Certificate of Competence in Educational Testing (Level A).
4. Those who wish to be Verifiers must be Educational Testing Assessors who are practising Chartered Educational Psychologists with a current Certificate or Statement of Competence in Educational Testing. Verifiers will be responsible for verifying Assessors' assessment methods.
5. When the verification has been successfully completed, Assessors will be issued with an Assessor's Certificate which confirms that their assessment methods have been verified by The British Psychological Society.
6. Assessors who direct training courses in Educational Testing which cover ALL the competences in the Checklist may advertise those courses as: 'Providing training leading to fulfilment of requirements for the British Psychological Society Certificate of Competence in Educational Testing (Level A).'

Annex D – Affirmation of Competence

1. Any person who can provide 'proof of general competence' is eligible to receive a Certificate of Competence in Educational Testing (Level A) and to have their name placed on a Register of Competence in Psychological Testing (Educational) on payment of the relevant fees.
2. Proof of general competence is provided by production to the Society of the Affirmation of Competence form on which a signature from a 'qualified person' has been obtained against each of the units on the list. This checking-off procedure is known as an 'Affirmation of Competence'. A 'qualified person' for this purpose is someone who holds a valid Assessor's Certificate for Educational Testing (Level A).
3. The Society, in collaboration with the test publishers and training course organisers, will put in place procedures to monitor the success of the scheme. Because of its voluntary nature, the scheme can work only with the good will and support of others outside the Society, in particular the test publishers.
4. The Society reserves its position to make changes and introduce additional procedures for monitoring and maintaining standards if necessary.

Annex E – Units and Elements

Checklist of Competences in Educational Testing (Level A)

The Checklist covers seven UNITS of Competence. A UNIT is a coherent group of specific competences. Anyone who meets the requirements of all seven UNITS, will be eligible for the award of Certificate of Competence in Educational Testing (Level A).

In the following Checklist:

- 'Assessee' refers to the person whose competence is being assessed.
- 'Client' refers to the 'commissioning agent' – the person or organisation for whom the test is carried out

Unit 1: Defining the assessment needs

Can the Assessee:

1. Demonstrate an understanding of the purpose of testing within the overall context of assessment.
2. Identify and justify those assessment needs which can best be addressed by the use of a test procedure and those for which an alternative assessment approach is more appropriate.
3. Justify carrying out a particular kind of test using knowledge of both the learner's development and the skill(s) being assessed to support reasons for choice.
4. Describe how measures of ability and attainment are influenced by environmental factors, giving specific examples.
5. Give examples of the kinds of information which may be used to corroborate the information elicited by a test or other assessment technique.
6. Distinguish between tests of attainment, tests of ability and tests of aptitude.
7. Explain the difference between formative and summative uses of tests, giving examples of each type.
8. Demonstrate an understanding of the differences between norm-referenced, criterion-referenced and curriculum-based measures.

Unit 2: The basic principles of scaling and standardisation

Can the Assessee:

1. Depict graphically how a sample of test scores accumulate at different points throughout the range of ability covered by the test.
2. Undertake calculations to convey how much variation there is amongst a set of test scores.
3. Describe how the alternative ways of expressing the average of a set of test scores (mean, median or mode) are affected by their distribution throughout the range of the scores.
4. Describe the relationship between the Standard Error of the mean of a sample of scores and the size of the sample.
5. Explain how the variation amongst a standardisation sample of test scores and their mean can be used to determine the level of confidence that we can have in people's scores on that test.
6. Demonstrate an understanding of the properties of the Normal Distribution and their relevance to measurement in general.
7. Use a set of statistical tables to establish percentage of cases likely to fall below a particular test score.
8. Demonstrate how raw test scores can be converted into any of the scales frequently used to measure test performance (e.g. percentile scores, z-scores, T-scores etc.).

Unit 3: The importance of reliability and validity

Can the Assessee:

1. Explain the notion of correlation as a measure of the degree of relationship between two measures.
2. Define the conditions under which correlation is maximised (both positively and negatively) and minimised.
3. Provide reasonable rough estimates of the correlation coefficients represented by examples of various bivariate scattergrams.
4. Explain in outline the methods of estimating reliability (interrater reliability, internal consistency, test-retest, same or alternate form) and describe their relative pros and cons.
5. Describe and illustrate the distinctions between face, content, construct domain and criterion-related validity.

Unit 4: Deciding whether a particular test should or should not be used as part of an assessment process

Can the Assessee:

1. Use test publishers' catalogues, specimen sets or other reference materials to identify one or more instruments potentially suitable for a particular function.
2. Identify, for each test, information in the test manual which relates to the test's rationale, development, reliability, validity, its norms and any specific restrictions or limitations on its areas of use.
3. Identify relevant practical considerations (ease of administration, time required, special equipment needed etc.).
4. Compare information presented about the test's validity with relevant aspects of the requirements of the assessment and make an appropriate judgement about their fit.
5. Examine the norms and make a suitable judgement about their appropriateness in terms of representativeness and sample size.
6. Examine any restrictions on areas of use (e.g. age, gender, cultural or ethnic limitations; ability range; attainment level; special educational needs; the influence of possible practice effects upon the frequency of use of a test etc.) and make an appropriate judgement as to whether a test should be used.
7. Identify whether use of the test would meet the requirements of Equal Opportunities, Race Relations, Sex Discrimination and Disability Discrimination legislation.

Unit 5: Administering tests to one or more students/pupils/learners and dealing with scoring procedures

Does the Assessee:

In the case of both individual and group tests:

1. Ensure that any necessary equipment is operating correctly and that sufficient test materials are available for the test taker(s).
2. Ensure, where re-usable materials are being used, that they are carefully checked for marks or notes which may have been made by previous test takers.
3. Arrange a suitable quiet location for carrying out the testing.
4. Inform the test taker(s) of the time and place well in advance and ensure that they are adequately prepared.
5. Record the test taker's personal details together with relevant details of the test instruments used, etc.
6. Use standard test instructions and present them clearly and intelligibly to the test taker(s).
7. Provide the test taker(s) with sufficient time to work through any example test items.
8. Make careful checks to ensure proper use of answer sheets and response procedures.
9. Deal appropriately with any questions which arise without compromising the purpose of the test.
10. Explain any time limits.
11. Adhere strictly to test-specific instructions regarding pacing and timing.
12. Collect all materials when each test is completed.
13. Carry out a careful check against the inventory of materials to ensure that everything has been returned.
14. Keep all materials in a secure place with due regard to confidentiality.
15. Thank the test taker(s) for their participation at the conclusion of the test session and explain the next stage in testing (if any) to them.
16. Make notes on factors which might have affected the test taker's performance (e.g. any particular problems which arose during the session; the test taker's motivation, perseverence, or level of anxiety etc.).
17. Visually check answer sheets for ambiguous responses which could cause problems in scoring.
18. Demonstrate use of a range of different scoring keys and/or 'self-scoring' forms
19. Accurately score, compute responses and transfer raw score marks to record sheets.
20. Use norm tables to find relevant percentile and/or standard scores and transfer these to the test takers' record sheets.

In the case of group tests:

21. Plan test sessions with due regard to the maximum numbers of test takers who can be assessed in one session and the maximum duration of each session.
22. Arrange seating and desk space to maximise comfort and to minimise possibilities for cheating.
23. Ensure that during the test, test takers do not distract each other and, where appropriate, maintain silence.

In the case of individual testing:

24. Establish a satisfactory rapport with the test taker prior to the commencement of testing and maintain this throughout the session.
25. Prompt the test taker where appropriate in accordance with the test instructions and without invalidating the test item.
26. Use appropriately discreet scoring procedures so that the test taker does not become unduly conscious of failure.
27. Follow discontinuation procedures in line with the guidelines in the test manual while ensuring that the test taker does not become disheartened through obvious failure.

Unit 6: Making appropriate use of test results

Can the Assessee:

1. Select appropriate norm tables from the test manual or supplementary material.
2. Make appropriate use of information in the test manual with regard to ceiling or basal effects.
3. Attach suitable cautions to interpretations of the results (including comparisons with previous test performances) and/or make statements as to why certain test results are not quoted where no relevant norms or cut-off tables are available.
4. Give due consideration to the appropriateness of the reference group used in the test standardisation.
5. Describe the meanings of scale scores in terms which are accurate, which reflect the confidence limits associated with those scores and are intelligible to those who may legitimately have access to them.
6. Compute composite test battery scores from weightings given in a test manual.
7. Make appropriate connections between performance on a test, the test taker's educational performance and the original purpose of the test.
8. Integrate test findings with other forms of information gathered in the course of the assessment to inform decision-making and intervention.

Does the Assessee:

9. Show awareness of the implications of variation in test results and the effects of using different tests within a domain (e.g. reading or number).
10. Show awareness of the appropriateness or otherwise of providing feedback to test takers of differing ages and/or ability levels.

Unit 7: Maintaining security and confidentiality.

Does the Assessee ensure that:

1. Clear descriptions are given to the test taker and/or other relevant parties (e.g. other professional/parent / LEA) prior to testing concerning:
■ how the results are to be used
■ who will be given access to them;
■ for how long they will be retained.

2. All test data are kept in a secure place and that access is not given to unauthorised persons.
3. All test materials are kept in a secure place which is not accessible to people other than authorised test users.
4. All mandatory requirements relating to the test taker's and client's rights and obligations under the Data Protection Act are clearly explained to the parties concerned.
5. Where data is stored, the conditions of the Data Protection Act are abided by.
6. Potential test takers are not provided with prior access to test materials other than those specifically designed to help test takers prepare for an assessment.

The British Psychological Society was founded in 1901 and incorporated by Royal Charter in 1965. Its principle object is to promote the advancement and diffusion of a knowledge of psychology pure and applied and especially to promote the efficiency and usefulness of Members of the Society by setting up a high standard of professional education and knowledge.

The Society has more than 42,000 members and:

- has branches in England, Northern Ireland, Scotland and Wales;
- accredits nearly 800 undergraduate degrees;
- accredits nearly 150 postgraduate professional training courses;
- confers Fellowships for distinguished achievements;
- confers Chartered Status for professionally qualified psychologists;
- awards grants to support research and scholarship;
- publishes 10 scientific journals and also jointly publishes *Evidence Based Mental Health* with the British Medical Association and the Royal College of Psychiatrists;
- publishes books in partnership with Blackwells;
- publishes *The Psychologist* each month;
- supports the recruitment of psychologists through the *Appointments Memorandum* and *www.appmemo.co.uk*;
- provides a free 'Research Digest' by e-mail;
- publishes newsletters for its constituent groups;
- maintains a website *(www.bps.org.uk)*;
- has international links with psychological societies and associations throughout the world;
- provides a service for the news media and the public;
- has an Ethics Committee and provides service to the Professional Conduct Board;
- maintains a Register of more than 12,000 Chartered Psychologists;
- prepares policy statements and responses to government consultations;
- holds conferences, workshops, continuing professional development and training events;
- recognises distinguished contributions to psychological science and practice through individual awards and honours;
- maintains a Register of Psychologists Specialising in Psychotherapy.

The Society continues to work to enhance:

- recruitment – the target is 50,000 members by 2006;
- services – the Society has offices in England, Northern Ireland, Scotland and Wales;
- public understanding of psychology – addressed by regular media activity and outreach events;
- influence on public policy – through the work of its Boards and Parliamentary Officer;
- membership activities – to fully utilise the strengths and diversity of the Society membership.

The British Psychological Society
St. Andrews House, 48 Princess Road East, Leicester LE1 7DR, UK
Tel: 0116 252 9568 Fax: 0116 247 0787 E-mail: mail@bps.org.uk Website: www.bps.org.uk

Incorporated by Royal Charter Registered Charity No 229642   RCPTED02/08.05

Appendix 3

The British Psychological Society Psychological Testing Centre

The British Psychological Society
Psychological Testing Centre
St Andrews House
48 Princess Road East
Leicester
LE1 7DR

The British Psychological Society has established a Psychological Testing Centre to consolidate its activities in the areas of psychological testing. The Centre has a website at http://www.psychtesting.org.uk which provides information, guidance and links of interest to test users.

Other relevant publications are available on the website or by contacting the Testing Centre:

- British Psychological Society (2004) *General Information Pack: Certificate of Competence in Educational Testing (Level A)*. Leicester: The British Psychological Society (see Appendix 1)
- British Psychological Society (2004) *Guidance for Assessors: Certificate of Competence in Educational Testing (Level A)*. Leicester: The British Psychological Society (see Appendix 2)
- *Psychological Testing: A User's Guide*
- *Psychological Testing: A Taker's Guide*
- Non-evaluative list of UK test publishers
- *Code of Good Practice for Educational Testing* (see Appendix 1)

Appendix 4

Websites of Educational Test Publishers in the UK

http://www.harcourt-uk.com
http://www.hoddertests.co.uk
http://www.ldalearning.com
http://www.luckyduck.co.uk
http://www.mhs.com/uk
http://www.nfer-nelson.co.uk

Appendix 5

Examples of Educational Tests Available in the UK

The individually administered and group tests listed here are examples of those available for use by teachers in the UK, and are grouped by publisher and by the following domains: cognitive abilities, dynamic assessment, reading, diagnostic tests of reading, spelling, language, number, motor skills, self-esteem/coping/emotional literacy, Attention Deficit Hyperactivity Disorder (ADHD), and Autism/Asperger's Syndrome. Some of the instruments cover more than one domain. For each test addresses are provided for publishers' websites for further information from the publisher.

Please note:

1 Additional training/qualifications in Special Needs are required for those with a single asterisk, '*'. The test publishers should be contacted for more information.
2 Tests indicated by a double asterisk, '**', are normally restricted to Educational or Clinical Psychologists, but teachers can use them provided that the psychologist is satisfied about the teacher's competence to administer the test, that the test is used under the supervision of the psychologist, is ordered by the psychologist and that its use is tied to the work of the psychologist in the teacher's school.

Cognitive Abilities Tests

Additional training/qualifications in Special Needs are required for those tests with a single asterisk, '*'. The test publishers should be contacted for more information.

Further details from http://www.harcourt-uk.com

Gifted Rating Scales (GRS) (S. Pfeiffer and T. Jarosewich, 2003)*
Naglieri Nonverbal Ability Test – Individual Administration (NNAT)
(J.A. Naglieri, 2002)*
Naglieri Nonverbal Ability Test – Multilevel Form (NNAT) (J.A. Naglieri, 1997)*
Wide Range Achievement Test – Expanded Edition (WRAT-Expanded) (G.J. Robertson, 2000)
Working Memory Test Battery for Children (WMTB-C) (S. Pickering and S. Gathercole, 2001)*

Further details from http://www.hoddertests.co.uk

Edinburgh Picture Test (University of Edinburgh, 1985)
Non-Reading Intelligence Tests 1, 2 and 3 (D. Vincent, 1989)
Nonverbal Abilities Test 6–10 (D. Vincent and M. Crumpler, 2002)
Nonverbal Abilities Test 8–13 (D. Vincent and M. Crumpler, 2002)
Reasoning Progress Tests Nonverbal Tests 1–6 (D. Vincent and M. Crumpler, 2002)
Secondary Screening Profiles (Reasoning) (Forms A and B) (University of Edinburgh, 1995)
Verbal Abilities Tests 6–10 (D. Vincent and M. Crumpler, 2002)
Verbal Abilities Tests 8–13 (D. Vincent and M. Crumpler, 2002)

Further details from http://www.nfer-nelson.co.uk

AH Tests 1–4 (A.W. Heim, K.P. Watts and V. Simmonds, undated)
Cognitive Abilities Test: Third Edition (CAT3) (D.F. Lohman, E.P. Hagen and R.L. Thorndike, 2003)
Non-Verbal Reasoning (P. Smith and N. Hagues, undated)
Raven's Progressive Matrices and Vocabulary Scales (J.C. Raven, undated)
Schedule of Growing Skills in Practice (SGS-II) (M. Bellman, S. Lingam and A. Aukett, 1996)
Spatial Reasoning (P. Smith and T.R. Lord, undated)
Verbal Reasoning (N. Hughes and D. Courtenay, undated)

Dynamic Assessment Tests

Further details from http://faculty.biu.ac.il/~tzuried/

Children's Analogical Thinking Modifiability Test (CATM) (D. Tzuriel and P.S. Klein, 1990)
Children's Conceptual and Perceptual Analogical Modifiability Test (CCPAM) (D. Tzuriel and E. Galinka, 2000)

Children's Inferential Thinking Modifiability Test (CITM) (D. Tzuriel, 1989)
Children's Seriational Thinking Modifiability Test (CSTM) (D. Tzuriel, 1995)
Cognitive Modifiability Battery (CMB) (D. Tzuriel, 1995)
Seria-Think Instrument (D. Tzuriel, 1998)

Further details from http://www.icelp.org

The Dynamic Assessment of Cognitive Modifiability: The Learning Propensity
Assessment Device: Theory, Instruments, and Techniques (R. Feuerstein, R.S.
Feuerstein, L.H. Falik and Y. Rand, 2003)

Further details from Newcastle Educational Psychology Service, Eastview Clinic, Newcastle

The Bunny Bag: A dynamic approach to the assessment of preschool children (J.
Waters and P. Stringer, 1997)

Further details from http://www.proedinc.com

Swanson Cognitive Processing Test (S-CPT) (H.L. Swanson, 1996)

Reading Tests

Additional training/qualifications in Special Needs are required for those tests
with a single asterisk, '*'. The test publishers should be contacted for more
information.

Tests with a double asterisk, '**', are normally restricted to Educational or
Clinical Psychologists, but teachers can use this instrument provided that the
psychologist is satisfied about the teacher's competence to administer the test,
that the test is used under the supervision of the psychologist, is ordered by the
psychologist and that its use is tied to the work of the psychologist in the teacher's
school.

Further details from http://www.harcourt-uk.com

Adult Reading Test (ART) (P. Brooks, J. Everatt and R. Fidler, 2004)
Gray Oral Reading Tests (GORT-4) – Fourth Edition (J.L. Wiederholt and B.R.
Bryant, 2001)
Gray Silent Reading Tests (GSRT) (J.L. Wiederholt and G. Blalock, 2000)
Test of Silent Word Reading Fluency (TOSWRF) (N. Mather, D.D. Hammill, E.
A. Allen and R. Roberts, 2004)*
Wechsler Individual Achievement Test – Second UK Edition (WIAT-II^{UK}) (D.
Wechsler, 2005)**
Wide Range Achievement Test – Expanded Edition (WRAT-Expanded) (G.J.
Robertson, 2000)
Wide Range Achievement Test 3 (WRAT3) (G.S. Wilkinson, 1993)

Further details from http://www.hoddertests.co.uk

Cloze Reading Tests 1–3 (D. Young, 2002)
Early Literacy Test (B. Gillham, 2000)
Edinburgh Reading Tests 1–4 (University of Edinburgh, 2002)
Group Literacy Assessment (F. Spooncer, 1999)
Group Reading Test (D. Young, 1999)
Group Reading Test/SPAR Tests (D. Young, 1974)
Hodder Group Reading Tests 1–3 (D. Vincent and M Crumpler, 2002)
Nonword Reading Test (M. Crumpler and C. McCarty, 2004)
Reading Progress Tests 1–6 (D. Vincent and M. Crumpler, 1997; 2002)
Salford Sentence Reading Test (Revised) 3rd Edition (G.E. Bookbinder, Revised
    by D. Vincent and M. Crumpler, 2002)
Shortened Edinburgh Reading Test (University of Edinburgh, 1994)
SPAR (Spelling and Reading) Tests A and B (D. Vincent, 1992)

Further details from http://www.nfer-nelson.co.uk

Graded Word Reading Test (The Macmillan Test Unit, undated)
Group Reading Test 6–14 – Second Edition (The Macmillan Test Unit with Neil
    Hagues and Juliet Burley (NFER), undated)
Individual Reading Analysis (D. Vincent, M. De La Mare, Consultant – Helen
    Arnold, undated)
London Reading Test (Centre for Educational Research, LSE and Neil Hagues
    (NFER), undated)
Neale Analysis of Reading Ability (NARA II) (Second Revised British Edition)
    (M.D. Neale, 1997)
New Reading Analysis (D. Vincent, M. De La Mare, Consultant – Helen Arnold,
    undated)
Primary Reading Test (Levels 1 and 2) (N. France, undated)
Progress in English 5–14 test series (A. Kispall, N. Hagues and G. Ruddock
    (NFER), undated)
Reading Ability Series (A. Kispall, S. Gorman and C. Whetton (NFER),
    undated)
Reading Now (J. Morris (NFER), 2004)
Richmond Tests of Basic Skills: Second Edition (A.N. Hieronymous, E.F. Lindquist
    and N. France, undated)
Suffolk Reading Scale: Second Edition (Fred Hagley, undated)

Diagnostic Reading Tests

Additional training/qualifications in Special Needs are required for those tests
with a single asterisk, '*'. The test publishers should be contacted for more
information.

Further details from http://www.harcourt-uk.com

Comprehensive Test of Phonological Processing (CTOPP) (R. Wagner, J. Torgesen and C. Rashotte, 1999)*
Dyslexia Adult Screening Test (DAST) (A. Fawcett and R. Nicolson, 1998)
Dyslexia Early Screening Test – Second Edition (DEST-2) (R. Nicolson and A. Fawcett, 2004)
Dyslexia Screening Test – Junior (DST-J) (A. Fawcett and R. Nicholson, 2004)
Dyslexia Screening Test – Secondary (DST-S) (A. Fawcett and R. Nicolson, 2004)
Graded Nonword Reading Test (M. Snowling, S. Stothard and J. McLean, 1996)*
Phonological Abilities Test (PAT) (V. Muter, C. Hulme and M. Snowling, 1997)
Preschool and Primary Inventory of Phonological Awareness (PIPA) (B. Dodd, S. Crosbie, B. McIntosh, T. Teitzel and A. Ozanne, 2000)
Pre-School Screening Test (PREST) (A. Fawcett, R. Nicholson and R. Lee, 2001)
Test of Phonological Awareness – Second Edition: PLUS (TOPA-2+) (J. K. Torgesen and B.R. Bryant, 2004)
Test of Word Reading Efficiency (TOWRE) (J. K. Torgesen, R. Wagner and C. Rashotte, 1999)*
Wechsler Individual Achievement Test – Second UK Edition (WIAT-II) (D. Wechsler, 2005)**

Further details from http://www.hoddertests.co.uk

Diagnostic Reading Analysis (M. Crumpler and C. McCarty, 2004)
Listening and Literacy Index (C. Weedon and G. Reid, 2001)
Literacy Probe 7–9 Tests 1–2 (Forms A and B) (D. Bentley and D. Reid, 1999)
Secondary Screening Profiles (Reading) (Forms A and B) (University of Edinburgh, 1995)
Steps in Phonic Assessment (D. Oldham, 2000)
Word Recognition and Phonic Skills (WraPS) (Forms A and B) (2nd Edition) (D. Moseley, 2003)

Further details from www.ldalearning.com

Active Literacy Kit (Dyslexia Institute, undated)
Aston Portfolio (M. Newton, M. Thomson, undated)
Bangor Dyslexia Test (T. Miles, undated)

Further details from http://www.nfer-nelson.co.uk

Children's Test of Nonword Repetition (CN-REP) (S. Gathercole and A. Baddeley, 1996)*
Dyslexia Screener (M. Turner and P. Smith, 2003)

LARR Test of Emergent Literacy (J. Downing, B. Schaefer and J.D. Ayres, undated)
Listening Comprehension Test Series (N. Hagues, R. Siddiqui and P. Merwood, undated)
Literacy Impact (NFER, undated)
Phonological Assessment Battery (PhAB) (N. Frederickson, U. Frith and R. Reason, 1997)

Spelling Tests

Tests with a double asterisk, '**', are normally restricted to Educational or Clinical Psychologists, but teachers can use this instrument provided that the psychologist is satisfied about the teacher's competence to administer the test, that the test is used under the supervision of the psychologist, is ordered by the psychologist and that its use is tied to the work of the psychologist in the teacher's school.

Further details from http://www.harcourt-uk.com

Wechsler Individual Achievement Test – Second UK Edition (WIAT-II) (D. Wechsler, 2005)**
Wide Range Achievement Test 3 (WRAT3) (G.S. Wilkinson, 1993)

Further details from http://www.hoddertests.co.uk

Graded Word Spelling Test (P.E. Vernon, 1998)
Parallel Spelling Tests (2nd Edition) (D. Young, 1998)
SPAR (Spelling and Reading Tests) (Forms A and B) (D. Young, 1992)

Further details from http://www.nfer-nelson.co.uk

British Spelling Test Series (D. Vincent and M. Crumpler, undated)
Single Word Spelling Test (L. Sacre and J. Masterson, undated)

Language Tests

Additional training/qualifications in Special Needs are required for those tests with a single asterisk, '*'. The test publishers should be contacted for more information.

Tests with a double asterisk, '**', are normally restricted to Educational or Clinical Psychologists, but teachers can use this instrument provided that the psychologist is satisfied about the teacher's competence to administer the test, that the test is used under the supervision of the psychologist, is ordered by the psychologist and that its use is tied to the work of the psychologist in the teacher's school.

Further details from http://www.harcourt-uk.com

Boehm Test of Basic Concepts – Third Edition (Boehm-3) (A.E. Boehm, 2000)
Boehm-3 Preschool (A.E. Boehm, 2001)
Bracken Basic Concept Scale – Revised (BBCS–R) (B.A. Bracken, 1998)*
Bracken School Readiness Assessment (BSRA) (B. A. Bracken, 2002)*
Listening Skills Test (LIST) (P. Lloyd, I. Peers and C. Foster, 2001)*
Wechsler Individual Achievement Test – Second UK Edition (WIAT-II) (D. Wechsler, 2005)**
Wilson Syntax Screening Test (M.S. Wilson, 2000)

Further details from http://www.nfer-nelson.co.uk

British Picture Vocabulary Scale (BPVS II) (L.M. Dunn, L.M. Dunn, C. Whetton and J. Burley, 1997)
Living Language (A. Locke, undated)
Peabody Picture Vocabulary Test: Third Edition (L. M. Dunn and L. M. Dunn, undated)
Richmond Tests of Basic Skills: Second Edition (A.N. Hieronymous, E.F. Lindquist and N. France, undated)

Number Tests

Tests with a double asterisk, '**', are normally restricted to Educational or Clinical Psychologists, but teachers can use this instrument provided that the psychologist is satisfied about the teacher's competence to administer the test, that the test is used under the supervision of the psychologist, is ordered by the psychologist and that its use is tied to the work of the psychologist in the teacher's school.

Further details from http://www.harcourt-uk.com

Wechsler Individual Achievement Test – Second UK Edition (WIAT-II) (D. Wechsler, 2005)**
Wide Range Achievement Test – Expanded Edition (WRAT-Expanded) (G.J. Robertson, 2000)
Wide Range Achievement Test 3 (WRAT3) (G.S. Wilkinson, 1993)

Further details from http://www.hoddertests.co.uk

Basic Number Diagnostic Test (B. Gillham, 2001)
Basic Number Screening Test (B. Gillham and K. Hesse, 2001)
Graded Arithmetic-Mathematics Test (P.E. Vernon and K.M. Miller, 1998)
Graded Mathematics Test (D. Young, 1996)
Mathematics Competency Test (P.E. Vernon, K.M. Miller and J. Izard, 1995)

Numeracy Progress Tests Numeracy Baseline/Tests 1–6 (D. Vincent and M. Crumpler, 2002)

Prawf Sgrinio Rhif Sylfaenol (Basic Number Screening Test–Welsh Edition) (B. Gillham and K. Hesse, 2002)

Secondary Screening Profiles (Mathematics) (Forms A and B) (University of Edinburgh, 1995)

Further details from http://www.nfer-nelson.co.uk

Dyscalculia Screener (Brian Butterworth, 2003)

Early Mathematics (J. Ashby, G. Ruddock and S. Sizmur (NFER), undated)

Early Mathematics Diagnostic Kit (D. Lumb and M. Lumb, 1987)

Mathemateg 5–11 (Y Mudiad Cenedlaethol ar gyfer Ymchwilio Addysgol (MCYA/NFER) with Peter Patilla, undated)

Mathematical Minds: A Guide to Assessing Attainment Target One (NFER, 2003)

Mathematics 5–14 test series (NFER, with Peter Patilla, undated)

Mental Mathematics 6–14 (NFER, undated)

Numeracy Impact Tests (NFER, undated)

Profile of Mathematical Skills (Levels 1 and 2) (N. France, undated)

Richmond Tests of Basic Skills: Second Edition (A.N. Hieronymous, E.F. Lindquist and N. France, undated)

The Staffordshire Mathematics Test (C. Barcham, R. Bushell, K. Lawson and C. McDonnell, undated)

Tests of Motor Skills

Further details from http://www.harcourt-uk.com

Minnesota Handwriting Assessment (J. Reisman, 1999)

Movement Assessment Battery for Children Checklist (Movement ABC) (S.E. Henderson and D.A. Sugden, 1992)

Tests of Self-esteem/Coping/Emotional Literacy

Additional training/qualifications in Special Needs are required for those tests with a single asterisk, '*'. The test publishers should be contacted for more information.

Further details from http://www.harcourt-uk.com

Beck Youth Inventories of Emotional and Social Impairment (J.S. Beck, A.T. Beck and J. Jolly, 2001)*

Bully-Victimization Distress Scale (BVDS) (W. Reynolds, 2003)*
Bully-Victimization Scale (BVS) (W. Reynolds, 2003)*
Reynolds Bully-Victimization Scales for Schools (W. Reynolds, 2003)
School Function Assessment (SFA) (W. Coster, T. Deeney, J. Haltiwanger and S. Haley, 1998)*
School Violence Anxiety Scale (SVAS) (W. Reynolds, 2003)*
Self Image Profile for Adults (SIP-Adult) (R.J. Butler and S.L. Gasson, 2004)*
Self Image Profiles (SIP) (R.J. Butler, 2001)*

Further details from http://www.luckyduck.co.uk

B/G-Esteem (B. Maines and G. Robinson, 1998)

Further details from http://www.mhs.com/uk

Children's Depression Inventory (CDI) (M. Kovacs, no date)
Conners' Rating Scales – Revised CERS-R (C.K. Conners, no date)*
Emotional Quotient Inventory: Youth Version (EQ-i: YV™) (R. Bar-On, no date)*
Feelings, Attitudes and Behaviour Scale for Children (FAB-C) (J. Beitchman, no date)*
Jesness Inventory – Revised JI-R (C.F. Jessness, no date)

Further details from http://www.nfer-nelson.co.uk

Adolescent Coping Scale (E. Frydenberg and R. Lewis, undated)
Emotional Literacy – Assessment and Intervention (Southampton Psychology Service. Editor: Adrian Faupel, undated)
Myself as a Learner Scale (R. Burden, undated)
Rogers Personal Adjustment Inventory: Revised (P. Jeffrey, 1984)

Tests of Attention Deficit Hyperactivity Disorder

Further details from http://www.harcourt-uk.com

Brown Attention-Deficit Disorder Scales (Brown ADD Scales) (T.E. Brown, 2001, 1996)*
Conners' Rating Scales – Revised (CRS-R) (C.K. Conners, 1996)*

Tests of Autism/Asperger's Syndrome

Additional training/qualifications in Special Needs are required for those tests with a single asterisk, '*'. The test publishers should be contacted for more information.

Further details from http://www.harcourt-uk.com

Asperger Syndrome Diagnostic Scale (ASDS) (B. Myles, S. Jones-Bock and R.L. Simpson, 2000)

Childhood Autism Rating Scale (CARS) (E. Schopler, R.L. Reichler and B. Rochen Renner, 1988)

Gilliam Asperger's Disorder Scale (GADS) (J.E. Gilliam, 2000)

Gilliam Autism Rating Scale (GARS) (J.E. Gilliam, 1995)

Pervasive Developmental Disorders Screening Test-II (PDDST-II) (B. Siegel, 2004)*

Examples of Tests of Aptitude

Further details from http://www.giamusic.com

Primary Measures of Music Audiation (K–Grade 3) (E.E. Gordon, 1979)

Intermediate Measures of Music Audiation (Grade 1–6) (E.E. Gordon, 1982)

Music Aptitude Profile (Grades 5–12) (E.E. Gordon, 1995)

Further details from http://www.2lti.com/mlate.htm

Modern Language Aptitude Test – Elementary (J. Carroll and S. Sapon, 1967)

Appendix 6

Answers to Multiple Choice Items

1.1 Which of the following assessment needs would you consider a test to be 'highly appropriate' in addressing?

Assessment need	Indicate 'Yes' or 'No'
To compare the learner's knowledge base with the norm for his/her age	Yes
To assess the content of a learner's knowledge base within a specific domain	Yes
To generate hypotheses about how the test taker learns	Yes
To investigate how responsive the learner is to attempts to intervene	Yes
To assess what may be interfering with the learner's ability to benefit from existing levels of instruction	Yes
To determine the amount of time a learner spends 'off-task' in class	No

Comments
A norm-referenced test is a highly appropriate means of comparing a test taker's performance with that of others of a similar age. A criterion-referenced test would be a highly appropriate means of assessing the content of a learner's knowledge base. However, while a norm-referenced or criterion-referenced test, particularly a diagnostic test, may yield some information which might be helpful in generating hypotheses and investigating responsivity to instruction, a dynamic assessment approach, which might include the use of a specialized test such as the CMB

(Tzuriel, 1990; 2000), would be highly appropriate in addressing these assessment needs. Lastly, a test would not be an appropriate means of measuring 'off-task' behaviour: structured observation over a period of time would be preferable.

1.2   Complete the following table to match assessment approach to assessment need. Indicate which assessment needs would best be addressed by the use of a test procedure and those which might be more appropriately addressed by means of an alternative approach

	Assessment need		
Assessment approach	Entitlement/ Eligibility	Accountability	Instruction
Norm-referenced	√√	√√	√
Criterion-referenced	√	√	√√
Curriculum-based	√	√	√√
Dynamic assessment	X	X	√√

√√ denotes highly appropriate, √ appropriate and X not particularly appropriate

Comments
Norm-referenced tests are particularly informative in addressing assessment needs related to entitlement/eligibility and accountability issues. Criterion-referenced, curriculum-based or dynamic assessment approaches would be more appropriate in regard to addressing assessment needs relating to instruction.

1.6   Consult the publishers' catalogues and indicate which of
the following are tests of attainment, which tests of ability
and which tests of aptitude

Test	Test of attainment	Test of ability	Test of aptitude
Naglieri Nonverbal Ability Test – Individual Administration (NNAT) (http://www.harcourt-uk.com)		√	
Wechsler Individual Achievement Test – Second UK Edition (WIAT-II) (http://www.harcourt-uk.com)	√		
SPAR (Spelling and Reading) Tests A and B (http://www.hoddertests.co.uk)	√		
Verbal Abilities Tests 6–10 (http://www.hoddertests.co.uk)		√	
Music Aptitude Profile (Grades 5–12) (http://www.giamusic.com)			√
Raven's Progressive Matrices and Vocabulary Scales (http://www.nfer-nelson.co.uk)		√	
Primary Reading Test (Levels 1 and 2) (http://www.nfer-nelson.co.uk)	√		
Modern Language Aptitude Test – Elementary (http://www.2lti.com/mlate.htm)			√

Appendix 7

Some Useful Websites

http://PAREonline.net/
Free access to the online journal *Practical Assessment Research & Evaluation*.

www.qca.org.uk/ca/5–14/afl/
The Assessment Reform Group's (2002) '*Assessment for Learning*' framework

www.childreninscotland.org.uk/enquire.htm
The National Advice Service for Special Educational Needs Children in Scotland.

http://www.drc-gb.org/library/publications/education.aspx
Disability Rights Commission homepage website, providing information and advice to disabled people on their rights and also to service providers on their duties under the Disability Discrimination Act 1995 and the Special Educational Needs and Disability Act 2001.

www.disability.gov.uk
Website with information about public services for disabled people.

www.accac.org.uk
Qualifications, Curriculum and Assessment Authority for Wales.

www.nc.uk.net
Qualifications and Curriculum Authority.

www.dfes.gov.uk
The DfES website.

http://www.deni.gov.uk/index.htm
The Northern Ireland Executive Department of Education website.

http://www.scotland.gov.uk/Topics/Education
Scottish Executive Education Department website

http://www.learning.wales.gov.uk/
Welsh Assembly Government's Training and Education website.

Appendix 8

Extracts from the International Test Commission Guidelines on Test Use[1]

2.3 Give Due Consideration to Issues of Fairness in Testing

When tests are to be used with individuals from different groups (for example, groups differing in terms of gender, cultural background, education, ethnic origin, or age), competent test users will make all reasonable efforts to ensure that:

2.3.1   The tests are unbiased and appropriate for the various groups that will be tested.

2.3.2   The constructs being assessed are meaningful in each of the groups represented.

2.3.3   Evidence is available on possible group differences in performance on the test.

2.3.4   Evidence relating to differential item functioning (DIF) is available, where relevant.

2.3.5   There is validity evidence to support the intended use of the test in the various groups.

2.3.6   Effects of group differences not relevant to the main purpose (for example, differences in motivation to answer, or reading ability) are minimized.

2.3.7   In all cases, Guidelines relating to the fair use of tests are interpreted in the context of local policy and legislation.[2]

When testing in more than one language (within or across countries),[3] competent test users will make all reasonable efforts to ensure that:

2.3.8   Each language or dialect version has been developed using a rigorous methodology meeting the requirements of best practice.

2.3.9   The developers have been sensitive to issues of content, culture and language.

2.3.10   The test administrators can communicate clearly in the language in which the test is to be administered.

2.3.11   The test taker's level of proficiency in the language in which the test will be administered is determined systematically and the appropriate language version is administered or bilingual assessment is performed, if appropriate.

When tests are to be used with people with disabilities, competent test users will make all reasonable efforts to ensure that:

2.3.12   Advice is sought from relevant experts on the potential effects of the various disabilities on test performance.

2.3.13   Potential test takers are consulted and their needs and wishes are given proper consideration.

2.3.14   Adequate arrangements are made when test takers include people with hearing, visual or motor impairments, or other disabilities (for example, learning impairments, dyslexia).

2.3.15   Use of alternative assessment procedures, rather than modifications to tests, is considered (for example, other more suitable tests, or alternative structured forms of assessment).

2.3.16   Relevant professional advice is sought if the degree of modification required for use by those with disabilities is beyond the experience of the test user.

2.3.17   Modifications, when necessary, are tailored to the nature of the disability and are designed to minimize impact on score validity.

2.3.18   Information regarding the nature of any modifications made to a test or testing procedure is provided to those who interpret or act upon the test scores whenever the withholding of such information might otherwise result in biased interpretation or an unfair decision.

2.8   Communicate the Results Clearly and Accurately to Relevant Others

Competent test users will:

2.8.1   Identify appropriate parties who may legitimately receive test results.

2.8.2   With the informed consent of the test takers, or their legal representatives, produce written or oral reports for relevant interested parties.

2.8.3   Ensure that the technical and linguistic levels of any reports are appropriate for the level of understanding of the recipients.

2.8.4   Make clear that the test data represent just one source of information and should always be considered in conjunction with other information.

2.8.5   Explain how the importance of the test results should be weighted in relation to other information about the people being assessed.

2.8.6   Use a form and structure for a report that is appropriate to the context of the assessment.

2.8.7   When appropriate, provide decision makers with information on how results may be used to inform their decisions.

2.8.8   Explain and support the use of test results used to classify people into categories (for example, for diagnostic purposes or for job selection).

2.8.9   Include within written reports a clear summary, and when relevant, specific recommendations.

2.8.10   Present oral feedback to test takers in a constructive and supportive manner.

Notes

1   International Test Commission (2000, pp. 19–20 and 23–4).

2   The Guidelines in this section focus on what is 'best practice'. However, in many countries, issues relating to the fair use of tests must also take account of national laws (for example, the Disabilities Act, 1990, in the USA, or the Race Relations Act, 1976, in the UK).

3   These Guidelines relate not only to different national languages and dialects, but also to special forms of communication, such as sign language, used to overcome the effects of forms of disability.

Appendix 9

Test Evaluation Proforma

Title

Author

Publisher

Date of publication

Administration time

Description of test, items, scoring and design

Rationale for item selection

Adequacy of directions/training required to administer

Norms (type of scale, selection of sample)

Reliability (e.g. inter-rater; internal consistency; split-half; test-retest; alternate, equivalent or parallel form)

Validity (e.g. face; content; criterion-related; construct)

Comments regarding fairness (including any specific restrictions/limitations on areas of use)

General comments

Index

Lightning Source UK Ltd.
Milton Keynes UK
UKOW05f0448130214

226362UK00001B/92/P